CliffsNotes®

CIVIL SERVICE EXAM

CRAM PLAN™

CliffsNotes®

CIVIL SERVICE EXAM
CRAM PLAN™

Northeast Editing, Inc.

WILEY

Wiley Publishing, Inc.

Editorial	*Composition*
Acquisition Editor: Greg Tubach	**Proofreader:** Cynthia Fields
Project Editor: Elizabeth Kuball	Wiley Publishing, Inc., Composition Services
Copy Editor: Elizabeth Kuball	
Technical Editors: Jane Burstein, Karl Huehne, Loren Luedemann, Michael McAsey, and Mary Jane Sterling	

CliffsNotes® Civil Service Exam Cram Plan™

Published by:
Wiley Publishing, Inc.
111 River Street
Hoboken, NJ 07030-5774
www.wiley.com

Copyright © 2011 Wiley, Hoboken, NJ
Published simultaneously in Canada

Library of Congress Control Number: 2011928428
ISBN: 978-0-470-87811-8 (pbk)
ISBN: 978-1-118-07729-0 (ebk)

Printed in the United States of America
10 9 8 7 6 5 4 3 2 1

For general information on our other products and services or to obtain technical support, please contact our Customer Care Department within the U.S. at 877-762-2974, outside the U.S. at 317-572-3993, or fax 317-572-4002.

Wiley also publishes its books in a variety of electronic formats. Some content that appears in print may not be available in electronic books. For more information about Wiley products, please visit our web site at www.wiley.com.

About the Authors

Northeast Editing, Inc., has been developing electronic and print products for educational publishers since 1992. Founded by Tracey Vasil Biscontini, the company works with clients to create high-quality, socially sensitive test-preparation and library-reference products, textbooks, teacher guides, and trade books for students of all ages. Located in a former rectory in Jenkins Township, nestled between Wilkes-Barre and Scranton in northeastern Pennsylvania, the company employs ten full-time editors, several part-time employees, and a large pool of local freelance authors and editors. The staff enjoys a relaxed work environment that feels like a home away from home. When they're not hard at work, the editors and writers at Northeast Editing, Inc., enjoy breaks in a large backyard and take time to scratch the bellies of the three rescued cats that live at the office.

Acknowledgments

Northeast Editing would like to extend special thanks to Greg Tubach, our acquisitions editor, and Elizabeth Kuball, our project editor, for their advice and patience during every step of this project.

Table of Contents

Civil Service Employment Opportunities 283

Benefits and Veteran Information 289

Introduction

The federal government is the single largest employer in the United States. With more than 2.7 million civilian employees across the country and thousands more in U.S. territories and foreign countries, the workforce of the federal government dwarfs that of any other employer.

As you can probably imagine, there is a great deal of competition for federal jobs. In order to ensure that all available positions are awarded to the most qualified and efficient candidates, the federal government requires all job applicants to take a test called the civil service exam.

The civil service exam is designed to test applicants' basic skills with respect to a number of different subjects, including reading, writing, and mathematics. Your performance on this test plays an important role in the hiring process and may determine whether you'll be considered for an open position.

About Civil Service Jobs

Civil service jobs encompass almost all types of jobs found in the private sector. Most civil service positions fall into one of seven primary categories:

- **Professional:** Professional positions require candidates to have knowledge related to a specialized field. In most cases, this means that candidates must have at least a college-level or postgraduate education. Some of the jobs in this category include engineers, lawyers, accountants, and scientists.

- **Administrative and managerial:** Administrative and managerial employees are charged with overseeing contracts with the private sector and buying goods and services on behalf of the government. Some administrative and managerial positions include purchasing officers, contract specialists, product control specialists, budget analysts, claims examiners, personnel officers, Internal Revenue Service agents, and administrative assistants.

- **Investigative and law enforcement:** Some government agencies employ police officers, investigators, and other law enforcement professionals in various positions that include everything from security guards to border patrol agents and intelligence officers. Among the government agencies that employ police officers and investigators are the Department of Justice, the Department of State, the Department of the Treasury, the Department of Homeland Security, Customs and Border Protection, the U.S. Postal Service, and the Federal Bureau of Investigation.

- **Technical:** Technical positions usually are filled by employees who provide support work in nonroutine professional or administrative fields, such as computers, electronics, and information technology.

- **Clerical:** As the largest category of civil service jobs, clerical positions account for almost half of all federal civil service jobs. There are hundreds of different types of clerical jobs, including secretaries, typists, machine operators, stenographers, telephone operators, and mail and file clerks.

- **Labor and mechanical:** The U.S. government is the nation's largest employer of mechanical, manual, and laboring workers. Some labor and mechanical positions include mechanics, maintenance workers, machine tool and metal workers, mobile equipment operators, and food preparation and service workers.

- **Unskilled:** There are many federal positions available to those with few skills or little training. These basic positions include janitors, housekeeping aides, mess attendants, and laundry workers.

About the Test

The hiring process for federal employees is governed by the Civil Service Act, which ensures that all new federal employees are hired on the basis of individual merit and personal fitness. In part, the Civil Service Act provides for competitive exams that allow federal agencies to hire new employees from a pool of only the most qualified candidates.

There are two primary types of civil service exams:

- **Competitive:** During competitive exams, all the candidates for a given position compete with one another. In this case, earning a higher score on the test will give you a better chance of getting the job.
- **Noncompetitive:** In noncompetitive exams, each candidate is tested only to determine how qualified he or she is for a certain position. You become eligible for the position simply by passing the test.

The goal of civil service exams is to recognize those applicants who have the capacity to learn quickly and do their jobs competently and efficiently. The specific subjects included on a given exam are closely related to the responsibilities of the position to be filled. Generally, the written exams required for federal jobs are designed to measure a candidate's verbal, clerical, and mathematical skills, as well as any other special skills that may be needed for a specific job. As such, most civil service exams are comprised of four basic components:

- **Verbal Ability test:** The verbal ability test is designed to test your basic language skills, including spelling, vocabulary, grammar, punctuation, reading, and writing. These skills are closely related to a wide variety of job responsibilities, like proofreading, copy editing, organizing files and documents, reading manuals, and following written instructions.
- **Mathematical Ability test:** Depending on the job you're applying for, your civil service exam may include a test that is specifically designed to test your basic mathematical skills. Many clerical jobs and manual trade jobs require basic math skills. Some of the topics frequently included on the mathematical ability test include fractions, decimals, ratios, proportions, percentages, graphs, tables, and reasoning.
- **Clerical Ability test:** Because so many federal jobs are related to clerical work, most civil service exams include a clerical ability test. This test is designed to measure your speed and accuracy in completing a number of different clerical tasks. As a result of this test's emphasis on speed and accuracy, you can expect the clerical ability test to be more closely timed than other sections of the civil service test. You may be penalized for incorrect answers. Some common skills covered in the clerical ability test include typing, alphabetic filing, stenography, and coding.
- **Other Abilities test:** Depending on what type of job you're applying for, you also may be tested on other topics. You may be asked to answer general aptitude questions related to the specific skills you'll need in order to perform a given job or questions pertaining to specific abilities not covered elsewhere on the civil service exam. Some question types you may encounter in this section include memory and following directions, judgment and decision-making, and mechanical aptitude.

The civil service exam also may contain a special section of personal experience questions. Although it's designed to look like a standard multiple-choice test, this section of the exam is meant to provide your potential employer with additional information about you and your personality. These questions help the employer to determine how well you might measure up to current employees.

In addition to federal civil service exams, all 50 states and many municipalities have their own civil service exams for state and local civil service jobs. In most cases, these tests are similar to federal exams, but their exact contents vary from state to state and municipality to municipality.

About This Book

The first step in preparing for the civil service exam is to determine how much time you have to study for the test. After that, you should select the appropriate cram plan: the two-month plan, the one-month plan, or the one-week plan. Each plan has a schedule for you to follow, along with estimates of how much time you'll need to complete each task.

Start by taking the Diagnostic Test, which will pinpoint your strengths and weaknesses. The answer explanations will indicate the areas of study in which you need the most practice. Each chapter includes practice exercises that will help strengthen your skills in various subject areas. At the end of the book, you'll find the Full-Length Practice Test, which will give you an idea of how you might perform on the civil service exam.

I. Diagnostic Test

Answer Sheet

Section 1

1 (A) (B) (C) (D)	26 (A) (B) (C) (D)
2 (A) (B) (C) (D)	27 (A) (B) (C) (D)
3 (A) (B) (C) (D)	28 (A) (B) (C) (D)
4 (A) (B) (C) (D)	29 (A) (B) (C) (D)
5 (A) (B) (C) (D)	30 (A) (B) (C) (D)
6 (A) (B) (C) (D)	31 (A) (B) (C) (D)
7 (A) (B) (C) (D)	32 (A) (B) (C) (D)
8 (A) (B) (C) (D)	33 (A) (B) (C) (D)
9 (A) (B) (C) (D)	34 (A) (B) (C) (D)
10 (A) (B) (C) (D)	35 (A) (B) (C) (D)
11 (A) (B) (C) (D)	36 (A) (B) (C) (D)
12 (A) (B) (C) (D)	37 (A) (B) (C) (D)
13 (A) (B) (C) (D)	38 (A) (B) (C) (D)
14 (A) (B) (C) (D)	39 (A) (B) (C) (D)
15 (A) (B) (C) (D)	40 (A) (B) (C) (D)
16 (A) (B) (C) (D)	41 (A) (B) (C) (D)
17 (A) (B) (C) (D)	42 (A) (B) (C) (D)
18 (A) (B) (C) (D)	43 (A) (B) (C) (D)
19 (A) (B) (C) (D)	44 (A) (B) (C) (D)
20 (A) (B) (C) (D)	45 (A) (B) (C) (D)
21 (A) (B) (C) (D)	46 (A) (B) (C) (D)
22 (A) (B) (C) (D)	47 (A) (B) (C) (D)
23 (A) (B) (C) (D)	48 (A) (B) (C) (D)
24 (A) (B) (C) (D)	49 (A) (B) (C) (D)
25 (A) (B) (C) (D)	50 (A) (B) (C) (D)

Section 2

1 (A) (B) (C) (D)	26 (A) (B) (C) (D)
2 (A) (B) (C) (D)	27 (A) (B) (C) (D)
3 (A) (B) (C) (D)	28 (A) (B) (C) (D)
4 (A) (B) (C) (D)	29 (A) (B) (C) (D)
5 (A) (B) (C) (D)	30 (A) (B) (C) (D)
6 (A) (B) (C) (D)	31 (A) (B) (C) (D)
7 (A) (B) (C) (D)	32 (A) (B) (C) (D)
8 (A) (B) (C) (D)	33 (A) (B) (C) (D)
9 (A) (B) (C) (D)	34 (A) (B) (C) (D)
10 (A) (B) (C) (D)	35 (A) (B) (C) (D)
11 (A) (B) (C) (D)	36 (A) (B) (C) (D)
12 (A) (B) (C) (D)	37 (A) (B) (C) (D)
13 (A) (B) (C) (D)	38 (A) (B) (C) (D)
14 (A) (B) (C) (D)	39 (A) (B) (C) (D)
15 (A) (B) (C) (D)	40 (A) (B) (C) (D)
16 (A) (B) (C) (D)	41 (A) (B) (C) (D)
17 (A) (B) (C) (D)	42 (A) (B) (C) (D)
18 (A) (B) (C) (D)	43 (A) (B) (C) (D)
19 (A) (B) (C) (D)	44 (A) (B) (C) (D)
20 (A) (B) (C) (D)	45 (A) (B) (C) (D)
21 (A) (B) (C) (D)	46 (A) (B) (C) (D)
22 (A) (B) (C) (D)	47 (A) (B) (C) (D)
23 (A) (B) (C) (D)	48 (A) (B) (C) (D)
24 (A) (B) (C) (D)	49 (A) (B) (C) (D)
25 (A) (B) (C) (D)	50 (A) (B) (C) (D)

CUT HERE

Section 3

1 Ⓐ Ⓑ Ⓒ Ⓓ		26 Ⓐ Ⓑ Ⓒ Ⓓ		
2 Ⓐ Ⓑ Ⓒ Ⓓ		27 Ⓐ Ⓑ Ⓒ Ⓓ		
3 Ⓐ Ⓑ Ⓒ Ⓓ		28 Ⓐ Ⓑ Ⓒ Ⓓ		
4 Ⓐ Ⓑ Ⓒ Ⓓ		29 Ⓐ Ⓑ Ⓒ Ⓓ		
5 Ⓐ Ⓑ Ⓒ Ⓓ		30 Ⓐ Ⓑ Ⓒ Ⓓ		
6 Ⓐ Ⓑ Ⓒ Ⓓ		31 Ⓐ Ⓑ Ⓒ Ⓓ		
7 Ⓐ Ⓑ Ⓒ Ⓓ		32 Ⓐ Ⓑ Ⓒ Ⓓ		
8 Ⓐ Ⓑ Ⓒ Ⓓ		33 Ⓐ Ⓑ Ⓒ Ⓓ		
9 Ⓐ Ⓑ Ⓒ Ⓓ		34 Ⓐ Ⓑ Ⓒ Ⓓ		
10 Ⓐ Ⓑ Ⓒ Ⓓ		35 Ⓐ Ⓑ Ⓒ Ⓓ		
11 Ⓐ Ⓑ Ⓒ Ⓓ		36 Ⓐ Ⓑ Ⓒ Ⓓ		
12 Ⓐ Ⓑ Ⓒ Ⓓ		37 Ⓐ Ⓑ Ⓒ Ⓓ		
13 Ⓐ Ⓑ Ⓒ Ⓓ		38		
14 Ⓐ Ⓑ Ⓒ Ⓓ		39 Ⓐ Ⓑ Ⓒ Ⓓ		
15 Ⓐ Ⓑ Ⓒ Ⓓ		40 Ⓐ Ⓑ Ⓒ Ⓓ		
16 Ⓐ Ⓑ Ⓒ Ⓓ		41 Ⓐ Ⓑ Ⓒ Ⓓ		
17 Ⓐ Ⓑ Ⓒ Ⓓ		42 Ⓐ Ⓑ Ⓒ Ⓓ		
18 Ⓐ Ⓑ Ⓒ Ⓓ		43 Ⓐ Ⓑ Ⓒ Ⓓ		
19 Ⓐ Ⓑ Ⓒ Ⓓ		44 Ⓐ Ⓑ Ⓒ Ⓓ		
20 Ⓐ Ⓑ Ⓒ Ⓓ		45 Ⓐ Ⓑ Ⓒ Ⓓ		
21 Ⓐ Ⓑ Ⓒ Ⓓ		46 Ⓐ Ⓑ Ⓒ Ⓓ		
22 Ⓐ Ⓑ Ⓒ Ⓓ		47 Ⓐ Ⓑ Ⓒ Ⓓ		
23 Ⓐ Ⓑ Ⓒ Ⓓ		48 Ⓐ Ⓑ Ⓒ Ⓓ		
24 Ⓐ Ⓑ Ⓒ Ⓓ		49 Ⓐ Ⓑ Ⓒ Ⓓ		
25 Ⓐ Ⓑ Ⓒ Ⓓ		50 Ⓐ Ⓑ Ⓒ Ⓓ		

Section 4

1 Ⓐ Ⓑ Ⓒ Ⓓ		26 Ⓐ Ⓑ Ⓒ Ⓓ		
2 Ⓐ Ⓑ Ⓒ Ⓓ		27 Ⓐ Ⓑ Ⓒ Ⓓ		
3 Ⓐ Ⓑ Ⓒ Ⓓ		28 Ⓐ Ⓑ Ⓒ Ⓓ		
4 Ⓐ Ⓑ Ⓒ Ⓓ		29 Ⓐ Ⓑ Ⓒ Ⓓ		
5 Ⓐ Ⓑ Ⓒ Ⓓ		30 Ⓐ Ⓑ Ⓒ Ⓓ		
6 Ⓐ Ⓑ Ⓒ Ⓓ		31 Ⓐ Ⓑ Ⓒ Ⓓ		
7 Ⓐ Ⓑ Ⓒ Ⓓ		32 Ⓐ Ⓑ Ⓒ Ⓓ		
8 Ⓐ Ⓑ Ⓒ Ⓓ		33 Ⓐ Ⓑ Ⓒ Ⓓ		
9 Ⓐ Ⓑ Ⓒ Ⓓ		34 Ⓐ Ⓑ Ⓒ Ⓓ		
10 Ⓐ Ⓑ Ⓒ Ⓓ		35 Ⓐ Ⓑ Ⓒ Ⓓ		
11 Ⓐ Ⓑ Ⓒ Ⓓ		36 Ⓐ Ⓑ Ⓒ Ⓓ		
12 Ⓐ Ⓑ Ⓒ Ⓓ		37 Ⓐ Ⓑ Ⓒ Ⓓ		
13 Ⓐ Ⓑ Ⓒ Ⓓ		38 Ⓐ Ⓑ Ⓒ Ⓓ		
14 Ⓐ Ⓑ Ⓒ Ⓓ		39 Ⓐ Ⓑ Ⓒ Ⓓ		
15 Ⓐ Ⓑ Ⓒ Ⓓ		40 Ⓐ Ⓑ Ⓒ Ⓓ		
16 Ⓐ Ⓑ Ⓒ Ⓓ		41 Ⓐ Ⓑ Ⓒ Ⓓ		
17 Ⓐ Ⓑ Ⓒ Ⓓ		42 Ⓐ Ⓑ Ⓒ Ⓓ		
18 Ⓐ Ⓑ Ⓒ Ⓓ		43 Ⓐ Ⓑ Ⓒ Ⓓ		
19 Ⓐ Ⓑ Ⓒ Ⓓ		44 Ⓐ Ⓑ Ⓒ Ⓓ		
20 Ⓐ Ⓑ Ⓒ Ⓓ		45 Ⓐ Ⓑ Ⓒ Ⓓ		
21 Ⓐ Ⓑ Ⓒ Ⓓ		46 Ⓐ Ⓑ Ⓒ Ⓓ		
22 Ⓐ Ⓑ Ⓒ Ⓓ		47 Ⓐ Ⓑ Ⓒ Ⓓ		
23 Ⓐ Ⓑ Ⓒ Ⓓ		48 Ⓐ Ⓑ Ⓒ Ⓓ		
24 Ⓐ Ⓑ Ⓒ Ⓓ		49 Ⓐ Ⓑ Ⓒ Ⓓ		
25 Ⓐ Ⓑ Ⓒ Ⓓ		50 Ⓐ Ⓑ Ⓒ Ⓓ		

CUT HERE

Section 1: Verbal Ability

Time: 45 minutes

50 questions

Directions (1–6): Choose the answer that best describes the meaning of the italicized word.

1. What is the meaning of *sever?*

   A. To widen
   B. To alter
   C. To divide
   D. To repair

2. What is the meaning of *construe?*

   A. To fear
   B. To deduce
   C. To appear
   D. To hope

3. What is the meaning of *inconspicuous?*

   A. Intelligent
   B. Strange
   C. Friendly
   D. Unnoticeable

4. What is the meaning of *eccentric?*

   A. Unusual
   B. Unstable
   C. Repetitive
   D. Circular

5. What is the meaning of *repudiate?*

   A. To disown
   B. To accuse
   C. To label
   D. To punish

6. What is the meaning of *inconceivable?*

   A. Untruthful
   B. Unwise
   C. Unbelievable
   D. Unshakable

Directions (7–12): Choose the correct answer solely on the basis of the corresponding passage.

Question 7 refers to the following passage.

The increasingly widespread use of cellphones and other handheld electronic devices has led to a noticeable rise in the number of annual traffic accidents. Drivers are easily distracted by their phones, frequently carrying on conversations and texting while attempting to drive. These distractions have led to many traffic accidents that might have been avoided.

7. Which of the following statements does the passage best support?

    A.   Cellphones should be used only in emergency situations.
    B.   Cellphones often distract drivers and lead to traffic accidents.
    C.   Cellphones should be used only by experienced drivers.
    D.   Cellphones have little impact on the way that drivers behave.

Question 8 refers to the following passage.

Over the years, television has become an increasingly large part of our lives. Years ago, only a handful of channels existed. Now there are hundreds of channels, featuring a wide variety of programs for every viewer. It is no surprise that as the medium has expanded, so has the amount of time we spend watching television.

8. Which of the following statements does the passage best support?

    A.   Television has become a significant part of daily life.
    B.   Television does not provide enough channels.
    C.   Television has not changed much over the years.
    D.   Television is for entertainment purposes only.

Question 9 refers to the following passage.

When treating a patient who is experiencing shock caused by severe blood loss, a paramedic's first priority is to stop the bleeding. The paramedic should immediately locate the source of the blood loss and take the appropriate steps to slow the blood flow as much as possible. Once the bleeding is under control, the paramedic should initiate transport to a nearby medical facility.

9. What is the most important element in treating a patient who is experiencing shock?

    A.   Determining how the patient was injured
    B.   Transporting the patient immediately
    C.   Keeping the patient calm
    D.   Slowing the loss of blood

Question 10 refers to the following passage.

Believe it or not, some historical records are inaccurate. Historians have long recognized that recorded history sometimes offers a skewed version of real events, often because writers insert their own points of view while relaying facts to readers. In order to develop an accurate account of a historical event, it is important to gather information from various sources. This will provide you with the most complete view of the event.

10. What is the main idea of this passage?

    A. Historians are experts at interpreting historical events.
    B. Historians do not include their own beliefs in their writings.
    C. Historical accounts from multiple sources are often more accurate than from a single source.
    D. Historical accounts should not be believed.

Question 11 refers to the following passage.

In recent years, many baseball players have come under scrutiny for their use of steroids and other performance-enhancing substances. This disturbing trend of drug use has led to public outcry over the legitimacy of these players' athletic accomplishments. This controversy has damaged the sport's image and led to widespread drug testing throughout Major League Baseball.

11. How has the use of performance-enhancing substances influenced public opinion of baseball players?

    A. The public does not believe that these players earned their accomplishments.
    B. The public no longer watches Major League Baseball.
    C. The public does not care about the use of performance-enhancing substances.
    D. The public feels that more drug testing is needed.

Question 12 refers to the following passage.

The price of movie tickets has skyrocketed over the last 30 years. Thanks to high production costs, the ballooning salaries of movie stars, and expensive advertising campaigns, most modern movies cost millions of dollars to make. The only way to recoup this investment is to make the money back at the box office. This has forced theater owners to raise the price of admission. With all this in mind, a cheap movie ticket seems like nothing but a distant memory.

12. What is the main idea of this passage?

    A. There has been a substantial increase in demand for new movies.
    B. Movie-ticket prices are related to the cost of making movies.
    C. Television has had no impact on the movie industry.
    D. The price of a movie ticket will decrease over time.

Directions (13–14): Choose the best revision for each underlined portion of the passage. If no change is required, select choice A.

In recent years, there has been a significant increase in the number of concussions sustained by football players at all levels of the sport. This alarming phenomenon has led doctors and other medical experts to

13
search for ways to prevent and treat these serious injuries. There work has led to the development of various

14
methods of preventing, diagnosing, and treating concussions, which includes advances in equipment technology and new rules of play designed to decrease the likelihood of a concussion.

13. **A.**   NO CHANGE
    B.   every level of the sport
    C.   every level
    D.   all levels of the sports

14. **A.**   NO CHANGE
    B.   They're
    C.   They
    D.   Their

Directions (15–16): Choose the best answer to complete each sentence.

15. _____ he ran faster than all his competitors, he did not break the world record.

    A.   Since
    B.   However
    C.   Because
    D.   Although

16. After his impressive piano recital, he was _____ the grand prize.

    A.   appraised
    B.   awarded
    C.   reviewed
    D.   respected

Directions (17–18): Choose the correct sentence order for the following paragraphs.

17. Although Benjamin Franklin was a diplomat, author, and inventor, he may best be remembered for his famous kite experiment, which proved that lightning was electricity.

   1. When an appropriate storm came along, Franklin took his kite to a field and began his experiment.
   2. After waiting some time for a result, Franklin touched the key and noticed a spark; his theory was correct!
   3. Franklin was convinced that electricity, a relatively new scientific discovery at the time, was directly related to the lightning.
   4. Hoping to find evidence to prove his theory correct, Franklin connected a metal key to the end of a kite, believing that the key would conduct electricity during a lightning storm.

   A. 1, 2, 4, 3
   B. 3, 4, 1, 2
   C. 2, 3, 4, 1
   D. 4, 1, 3, 2

18. While driving down a busy highway, Lenny Thomas witnesses two vehicles collide violently at an intersection.

   1. Taking a closer look, Lenny finds a severely damaged sedan with three occupants and a less damaged pickup truck with a single occupant.
   2. After witnessing the two cars collide, Lenny pulls over and climbs out of his car to offer assistance.
   3. After checking on the driver of the truck, who is unharmed, Lenny remains on the scene with the victims until help arrives.
   4. First, Lenny checks on the people in the sedan; he calls 911 after the occupants report several injuries.

   A. 3, 2, 1, 4
   B. 2, 1, 3, 4
   C. 2, 1, 4, 3
   D. 3, 4, 1, 2

Directions (19–21): Choose the word that best completes each sentence.

19. The nosy secretary was asked not to _____ in the affairs of her co-workers.

   A. metal
   B. medal
   C. mettle
   D. meddle

20. The new team members are preparing to undergo the _____ of initiation.

   A. rites
   B. rights
   C. writes
   D. wrights

21. The farmer woke up early because he knew it would take all day to _____ his fields.

   A. so
   B. sew
   C. sow
   D. sough

Directions (22–23): Choose the answer that reflects an error in capitalization.

22. David Murphy, the County Commissioner, has announced that he will hold a press conference at noon.

   A. noon
   B. David Murphy
   C. press conference
   D. County Commissioner

23. President Smith will be addressing congress tonight about restructuring the Department of Homeland Security in accordance with constitutional law.

   A. congress
   B. constitutional
   C. President Smith
   D. Department of Homeland Security

Directions (24–25): Choose the sentence that corrects the error in punctuation.

24. The manager explained the new office procedure to the clerk but she did not seem to understand.

   A. The manager explained the new office procedure to the clerk; but she did not seem to understand.
   B. The manager, explained the new office procedure to the clerk, but she did not seem to understand.
   C. The manager explained the new office procedure to the clerk but, she did not seem to understand.
   D. The manager explained the new office procedure to the clerk: but she did not seem to understand.

25. The elevator which needs to be repaired got stuck again this morning.

   A. The elevator; which needs to be repaired got stuck again this morning.
   B. The elevator which needs to be repaired, got stuck again this morning.
   C. The elevator which needs to be repaired; got stuck again this morning.
   D. The elevator, which needs to be repaired, got stuck again this morning.

Directions (26–32): Choose the word that is spelled incorrectly.

26. A. proved
    B. yeeld
    C. beggar
    D. descent

27. **A.** sargeant
    B. knowledge
    C. endeavor
    D. column

28. **A.** mournful
    B. freight
    C. pamphlet
    D. rythem

29. **A.** villege
    B. efficiency
    C. conscientious
    D. cemetery

30. **A.** mischievious
    B. dependent
    C. inoculate
    D. kindergarten

31. **A.** indefinitely
    B. campeign
    C. superintendent
    D. specimen

32. **A.** administration
    B. parrallel
    C. calendar
    D. education

Directions (33–38): Choose the answer that best demonstrates the relationship between the two capitalized words.

33. PILLOW : SOFT ::

    A. silk : rough
    B. rock : hard
    C. sandpaper : smooth
    D. blanket : bed

34. CAT : KITTEN ::

    A. mare : horse
    B. cow : bull
    C. goat : lamb
    D. frog : tadpole

35. GOLD : EXPENSIVE :: TIN :

    A. cheap
    B. plentiful
    C. rare
    D. pliable

36. ZEPPELIN : AIR :: BARGE :

    A. fishermen
    B. water
    C. highway
    D. boats

37. PROFESSOR : TEACHER ::

    A. pupil : parent
    B. student : dean
    C. parent : child
    D. pupil : student

38. RAVENOUS : EAT :: PARCHED :

    A. sleep
    B. drink
    C. run
    D. work

Directions (39–44): Choose the synonym for each italicized word.

39. The word *libation* most nearly means:

    A. Payment
    B. Freedom
    C. Slander
    D. Beverage

40. Which word has the same meaning as *noxious?*

    A. Difficult
    B. Poisonous
    C. Odorous
    D. Horrific

41. The word *absolve* most nearly means:

    A. To mislead
    B. To recall
    C. To forgive
    D. To dispel

42. Which word has the same meaning as *ramification?*

    A. Offense
    B. Consequence
    C. Compromise
    D. Obstruction

43. The word *impartial* means most nearly:

    A. Unbiased
    B. Uninteresting
    C. Frustrated
    D. Flexible

44. Which word has the same meaning as *friable?*

    A. Important
    B. Costly
    C. Brittle
    D. Docile

Directions (45–50): The following questions present a sentence, part or all of which is underlined. Beneath the sentence, you find three ways of rephrasing the sentence. Select the answer that represents the most effective revision of the sentence, paying attention to grammar, word choice, and clarity. If the original sentence is correct and as effective as possible, select choice D.

45. During the seminar, the speaker offered easy tips to increased productivity, reducing overhead, and making more simple the management of off-site staff.

    A. offered easy tips for increasing productivity, reducing overhead, and simplifying the management of off-site staff
    B. offered easy tips to increased productivity, to reduce overhead, and to make the management of off-site staff simple
    C. offered easy tips about increased productivity, reduced overhead, and simplified the management of off-site staff
    D. NO ERROR

46. The filing system at the post office is more complex than the police station.

    A. The filing system at the post office is more complex than the police station, which has a simple filing system.
    B. The filing system at the post office is more complex than the police station's system.
    C. The filing system at the police station is less complex than the filing system at the post office, which has a more difficult filing system.
    D. NO ERROR

47. The county offers many jobs for motivated individuals with competitive salaries and health benefits.

    A. Competitive salaries and health benefits are offered to motivated individuals with jobs in the county.
    B. For motivated individuals with competitive salaries and health benefits, the county offers many jobs.
    C. The country offers many jobs with competitive salaries and health benefits for motivated individuals.
    D. NO ERROR

48. One must be sure to file reports under the correct codes or you will find it difficult to locate the reports in the future.

    A. One must be sure to file the reports under the correct codes or he or she
    B. One must be sure to file the reports under the correct codes or one
    C. One must be sure to file the reports under the correct codes or everyone
    D. NO ERROR

49. The clerk filed the report; however, he did not record the report's record number.

    A. the report, he did not, however, record
    B. the report: but he did not record
    C. the report, and he did not record
    D. NO ERROR

50. The candidate who wins the position must be the candidate who has the most experience in the position.

    A. The candidate who wins the position must be the person who has the most experience in the position.
    B. The candidate who wins the position must have the most experience.
    C. The candidate who wins the position must be the candidate who has, in the position, the most experience.
    D. NO ERROR

IF YOU FINISH BEFORE TIME IS CALLED, CHECK YOUR WORK ON THIS SECTION ONLY. DO NOT WORK ON ANY OTHER SECTION IN THE TEST.

Section 2: Mathematical Ability

Time: 45 minutes

50 questions

Directions (1–50): Answer the questions solely on the basis of the information provided.

Question 1 refers to the following table.

School	Number of Students Who Buy Lunch	Number of Students Who Bring Lunch
Chancellor Academy	252	123
Duffy High School	455	274
McDonald Prep School	367	355

1. According to the table, how many more students bring their lunch to school at Duffy High School than at Chancellor Academy?

    A. 81
    B. 93
    C. 151
    D. 232

2. Convert $\frac{13}{5}$ to a mixed number.

    A. $2\frac{1}{5}$

    B. $2\frac{2}{5}$

    C. $2\frac{3}{5}$

    D. $2\frac{4}{5}$

Question 3 refers to the following figure.

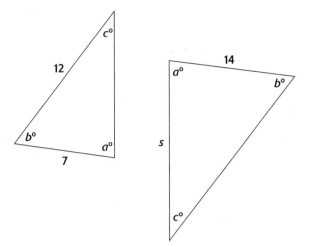

3. The triangles are similar. What is the value of *s*?

   A.   6
   B.   12
   C.   18
   D.   24

4. A bottle of water is left out in the sun for two days. After the first day, $\frac{2}{3}$ of the water has evaporated. After the second day, $\frac{1}{4}$ of the remainder evaporates. After two days, how much of the original amount of water still remains?

   A. $\frac{1}{5}$

   B. $\frac{1}{4}$

   C. $\frac{1}{2}$

   D. $\frac{3}{4}$

5. A federal agency replaces two computer monitors at a cost of $120 each. If the agency was expecting to be charged $150 per monitor, what percentage of the expected cost did the agency save?

   A.   10
   B.   15
   C.   20
   D.   25

6. As of the most recent census, the town of Smithville had a population of 24,000. Since that time, the population has increased by $\frac{1}{3}$. What is the present population of Smithville?

   A.   26,000
   B.   28,000
   C.   30,000
   D.   32,000

Question 7 refers to the following pie chart.

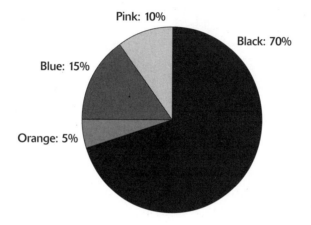

7. The pie chart shows the number of scarves ordered by a group of 300 women. How many more women ordered blue scarves than pink scarves?

   A.   15
   B.   30
   C.   45
   D.   50

8. How much is 18.7 divided by 5.3, rounded to three places after the decimal point?

   A.   3.526
   B.   3.527
   C.   3.528
   D.   3.529

Question 9 refers to the following graph.

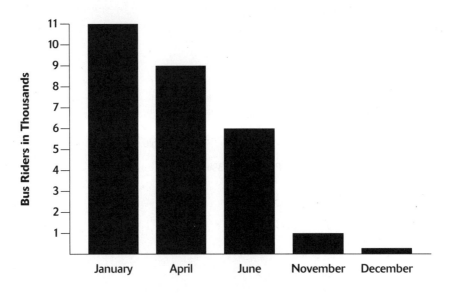

9. The graph shows the number of people who rode the bus during five months throughout a particular year. How many people rode the bus during November?

   A. 1,000
   B. 3,000
   C. 6,000
   D. 11,000

10. Solve for x: $4x + 3x = 99 + 2x + 1$.

    A. 10
    B. 15
    C. 20
    D. 25

11. A DVD player purchased at a retail store for 20% off sold for $125. What was the original price of the DVD player before the sale?

    A. $152.00
    B. $149.25
    C. $154.95
    D. $156.25

Question 12 refers to the following pie chart.

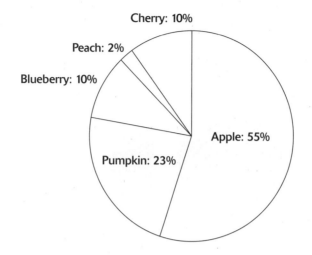

12. The chart shows the number of pie orders for a group of 200 teachers. How many teachers ordered pumpkin pie?

    A.   23
    B.   46
    C.   72
    D.   175

13. 81 : 9 ::

    A.   45 : 5
    B.   63 : 8
    C.   92 : 7
    D.   125 : 11

14. During a visit to the grocery store, a man spends $82.67 on food and $24.88 on toiletries. The man must pay $4.32 in tax. What was the total amount of the shopper's bill?

    A. $106.45
    B. $108.21
    C. $111.87
    D. $112.95

15. If 24 apples were sold at a rate of $1.35 for 3 apples, what would the total price be?

    A. $10.60
    B. $10.80
    C. $12.60
    D. $12.80

Question 16 refers to the following figure.

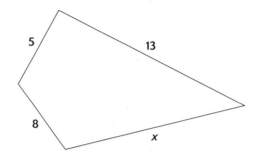

16. If the perimeter of the quadrilateral is 40, what is the value of x?

    A. 12

    B. 14

    C. 15

    D. 18

17. A diameter of a particular piece of piping is required to be 2.75 in. ± 0.017 in. Which of the following pipe diameters is NOT acceptable?

    A. 2.733 in.

    B. 2.742 in.

    C. 2.764 in.

    D. 2.768 in.

18. Reduce the fraction $\frac{7}{42}$ to the lowest possible terms.

    A. $\frac{1}{8}$

    B. $\frac{1}{7}$

    C. $\frac{1}{6}$

    D. $\frac{1}{5}$

Question 19 refers to the following graph.

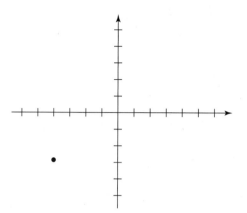

19. What are the coordinates of the point shown on the graph?

    A. (4, 3)
    B. (4, –3)
    C. (–4, 3)
    D. (–4, –3)

20. If 14 workers can complete a certain job in 20 days, how many workers would be needed to complete the job in 8 days?

    A. 18
    B. 22
    C. 30
    D. 35

Question 21 refers to the following figure.

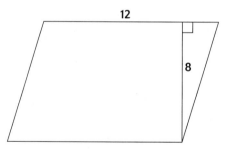

21. Determine the area of the parallelogram in the figure.

    A. 20
    B. 44
    C. 68
    D. 96

22. What is the ratio of 36 to 54?

    A.   3:8
    B.   2:3
    C.   4:7
    D.   5:6

23. Three machines can complete a certain job in five days. One machine breaks down, and now two machines will have to complete the same job. How many days will it take two machines to complete the job?

    A.   6
    B.   6.5
    C.   7
    D.   7.5

24. If 16 file clerks are able to file 2,056 papers in 20 minutes, approximately how many papers per minute does each clerk file?

    A.   6
    B.   6.2
    C.   6.4
    D.   6.6

25. A federal worker rents a car for three days and is charged $240. The rental company charges $20 per day and an extra 40¢ per mile. Based on the bill, how many miles did the worker drive?

    A.   250
    B.   375
    C.   400
    D.   450

26. An equal number of employees in two federal offices have been polled about a possible new overtime policy. In one office, $\frac{1}{4}$ of the employees favored the policy. In the other office, $\frac{1}{8}$ of the employees favored the policy. What is the average of the fractions of the employees in both offices who favored the policy?

    A. $\frac{3}{16}$
    B. $\frac{5}{16}$
    C. $\frac{3}{8}$
    D. $\frac{7}{10}$

27. If $x = 24$ and $y = 6$, what is the value of $2x(x - y)$?

   A. 626
   B. 864
   C. 942
   D. 1,464

28. A certain type of alloy is composed of copper and nickel at a ratio of 8:2. If an object made of this alloy weighs 250 pounds, how many pounds of nickel does it contain?

   A. 25
   B. 45
   C. 50
   D. 55

29. Lois has filed 15 fewer papers than 3 times the number of papers that Samantha has filed. If p represents the number of papers that Samantha has filed, which of the following expressions shows the number of papers that Lois filled?

   A. $3p - 15$
   B. $3p + 15$
   C. $4p - 15$
   D. $4p + 15$

30. What is 20% of 300?

   A. 30
   B. 40
   C. 50
   D. 60

31. A typist types a document with 80 pages in it. If she finishes the entire document in eight hours, how many minutes, on average, did the typist spend typing each page?

   A. 6
   B. 6.5
   C. 7
   D. 7.5

32. A clerk must file 500 papers. Assuming she can file 40 papers per hour, how many papers will the clerk have left to file after six hours?

   A. 230
   B. 240
   C. 260
   D. 280

Question 33 refers to the following diagram.

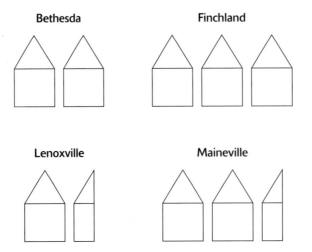

Each house = 46 residents

33. The diagram represents the number of residents living in four different cities. According to the diagram, how many residents live in Maineville?

    A. 69
    B. 92
    C. 115
    D. 138

34. If $x = 16$ and $y = 4$, what is the value of $4x(2x + y)$?

    A. 1,988
    B. 2,304
    C. 3,757
    D. 4, 490

35. $420 is being divided among three people according to the ratio 2:2:4. How much will each person receive?

    A. $75, $75, and $270
    B. $100, $100, and $220
    C. $105, $105, and $210
    D. $110, $110, and $200

36. A federal worker travels 270 miles in 4.5 hours. What is the worker's average speed during this trip?

    A.   50 miles per hour
    B.   55 miles per hour
    C.   60 miles per hour
    D.   65 miles per hour

Question 37 refers to the following figure.

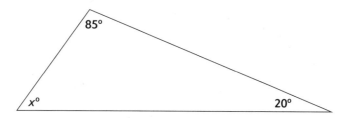

37. Determine the value of x in the figure.

    A.   75°
    B.   85°
    C.   95°
    D.   105°

38. If it takes three typists five days to complete seven reports, how many days will it take to complete the same number of reports if one typist is out sick for the week?

    A.   3.5
    B.   5
    C.   7.5
    D.   9

Question 39 refers to the following figure.

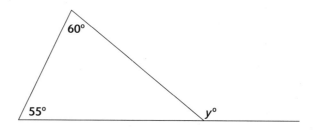

39. Determine the value of the exterior angle labeled y in the figure.

    A.   55°
    B.   65°
    C.   115°
    D.   130°

40. If a federal worker drives at a constant speed of 55 miles per hour for 4.5 hours, how many miles will the worker travel?

    A.   205
    B.   220.5
    C.   235
    D.   247.5

41. What is $\frac{7}{12}$ in decimal form, rounded to the nearest thousandth?

    A.   0.573
    B.   0.578
    C.   0.583
    D.   0.584

42. Three employees assigned to a particular job are working on equal parts of the job. One worker completes a portion in 115 minutes. The second worker completes a portion in 95 minutes. The third worker completes a portion in 120 minutes. What was the average time in which the job portions were completed?

    A.   100 minutes
    B.   105 minutes
    C.   110 minutes
    D.   115 minutes

43. Solve for n: $6n - 2 = n + 8$.

    A.   2
    B.   4
    C.   6
    D.   8

Question 44 refers to the following figure.

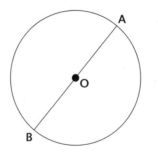

44. If $AO = 4$ and $\pi = 3.14$, what is the circumference of the circle shown?

    A.   12.56
    B.   18.84
    C.   25.12
    D.   31.40

Question 45 refers to the following graph.

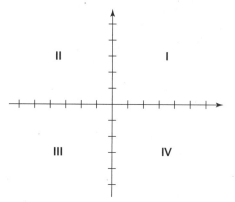

45. In which quadrant would a point with the coordinates (16, −22) appear?

    A. I
    B. II
    C. III
    D. IV

Question 46 refers to the following diagram.

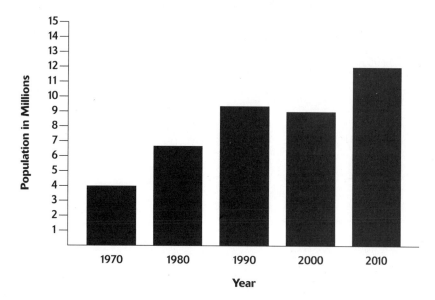

46. The diagram shows the number of people living in the city of Burbank from 1970 to 2010. Which decade experienced the greatest population increase?

    A. 1970
    B. 1980
    C. 1990
    D. 2010

Question 47 refers to the following figure.

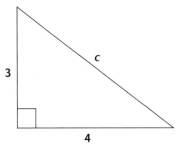

47. Determine the value of the hypotenuse.

    A.   3
    B.   4
    C.   5
    D.   6

Question 48 refers to the following table.

Coffee Shop	Coffee	Cappuccino	Latte
The Beanery	$1.00	$3.50	$4.00
The Coffee Bean	$1.29	$3.00	$4.25
Coffee Cafe	$1.09	$3.95	$3.95

48. According to the table, how much does a latte cost at The Coffee Bean?

    A. $3.50
    B. $3.95
    C. $4.00
    D. $4.25

Question 49 refers to the following graph.

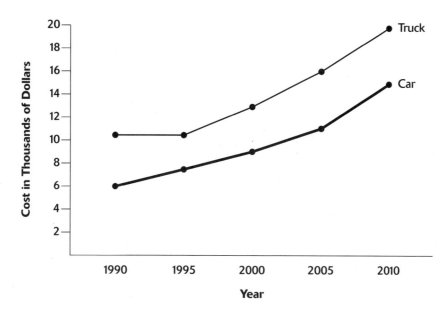

49. According to the graph, what is the difference between the cost of a truck in 2000 and the price of a car in 2000?

    A. $1,000
    B. $3,500
    C. $4,000
    D. $5,500

50. In order to pass his upcoming math test, Sam must earn at least a 75%. If the test has 40 questions, how many can Sam get wrong without failing?

    A. 8
    B. 9
    C. 10
    D. 11

IF YOU FINISH BEFORE TIME IS CALLED, CHECK YOUR WORK ON THIS SECTION ONLY. DO NOT WORK ON ANY OTHER SECTION IN THE TEST.

Section 3: Clerical Ability

Time: 45 minutes

50 questions

Directions (1–4): Each of the following questions contains a list of four names or numbers that may or may not be exactly alike. Compare the items and determine how many items are the same.

1. Richard L. Sellers

   Richard L. Sellers

   Richard I. Sellers

   Richard L. Sellers

   A. 0
   B. 2
   C. 3
   D. 4

2. Michael S. Sharpe

   Michael S. Sharp

   Michael S. Sharpe

   Michelle S. Sharpe

   A. 0
   B. 2
   C. 3
   D. 4

3. 6235488

   6325488

   6234588

   6235408

   A. 0
   B. 2
   C. 3
   D. 4

4. Neil A. Nutley

   Neil A. Nutley

   Neil A. Nutley

   Neal A. Nutley

   A. 0
   B. 2
   C. 3
   D. 4

Directions (5–15): Ask a friend or study partner to dictate the following passage while you take notes. Then, using your notes and the alphabetic word list that follows, fill in the blanks of the following transcript of the passage. Do not look at the passage itself. Then find the corresponding answer choice for each word and fill in your Answer Sheet with the correct letter.

Business success can be directly connected to the qualities of the employees who work for the company. (Period) Good employees make good businesses. (Period) The most important qualities to look for in any current or prospective employees are technical skills, social skills, and positive mental attitude. (Period) An employee who is strong in all three of these areas will be of great benefit to your company, whereas an employee lacking these qualities may be a detriment. (Period) The first of these three qualities, technical skill, is the most obvious and necessary element of a good employee. (Period) Clearly, employees need to understand their jobs and the tools they will use to complete various tasks. (Period) All employees must be adequately educated and capable of performing the tasks assigned to them. (Period) Ensuring that your employees are well trained and competent will be of great benefit to your company. (Period) Social skills often are just as important as technical skills. (Period) Whether an employee is responsible for interacting with customers or clients, strong social skills are a must. (Period) The ability to effectively interact and communicate with others is a very important part of business, and employees who possess excellent social skills are very valuable. (Period) This is especially true of employees who must interact with customers, as they become the face of your company. (Period) Finally, ideal employees also should exhibit a positive mental attitude. (Period) A happy, positive employee is a productive employee. (Period) Employees with positive mental attitudes are of great value because they are highly motivated to do well and accomplish their goals. (Period) These employees also can inspire their co-workers and improve the entire work environment. (Period) Conversely, an employee with a negative attitude will be far less productive and can damage the morale and productivity of other employees. (Period) An employee with a positive mental attitude is always a valuable member of the team. (Period) Of course, the truly ideal employee is one who possesses all three of these important qualities. (Period)

Alphabetic Word List			
Word	**Answer Choice**	**Word**	**Answer Choice**
Acting	C	face	A
accomplishing	B	tools	A
Accurately	A	instruments	D
Adequately	D	interacting	B
Business	C	intelligent	D
Capable	A	performing	A
Clients	D	positive	C
Company	B	professional	A
Competent	C	properly	B
Consumers	B	representative	C
Corporation	A	social	C
Customers	D	products	B
Effectively	C	technical	B
Efficiently	D	workers	A
Employers	D		

The first of these three qualities, _____ skill, is the most obvious and necessary element of a good
₅

employee. Clearly, employees need to understand their jobs and the _____ they will use to complete
₆

various tasks. All employees must be _____ educated and capable of _____ the tasks assigned to
₇ ₈

them. Ensuring that your employees are well trained and _____ will be of great benefit to your com-
₉

pany. Social skills often are just as important as technical skills. Whether an employee is responsible

for _____ with _____ or _____, strong social skills are a must. The ability to _____
₁₀ ₁₁ ₁₂ ₁₃

interact and communicate with others is a very important part of business, and employees who possess excel-

lent social skills are very valuable. This is especially true of employees who must interact with customers, as

they become the _____ of your _____.
₁₄ ₁₅

Directions (16–18): Choose the word that should follow the given word in alphabetical order.

16. REGULATION
    A. recitation
    B. remainder
    C. reprimand
    D. realization

17. SANGUINE
    A. sandals
    B. sanctity
    C. sanitize
    D. sampled

18. MEDIAL
    A. medal
    B. mechanic
    C. meadow
    D. menial

Directions (19–22): Use the following coding chart to determine the correct delivery route for the addresses given in each question.

Postal Route Guide	
Address Range	**Delivery Route**
101–1500 Main Street 301–600 Langley Avenue 701–1200 Dodsworth Drive	A
1201–1600 Dodsworth Drive 201–400 Carver Street 10–100 Blue Hill Road	B
101–200 Blue Hill Road 60–20 Mountain Spring Lane	C
All mail that cannot be delivered to any of the above address ranges	D

19. 1357 Dodsworth Drive

    A. A
    B. B
    C. C
    D. D

20. 102 Blue Hill Road

    A. A
    B. B
    C. C
    D. D

21. 1525 Main Street

    A. A
    B. B
    C. C
    D. D

22. 259 Carver Street

    A. A
    B. B
    C. C
    D. D

Directions (23–26): Each question contains a list of four names or numbers that may or may not be exactly alike. Compare the list items and determine how many items are the same.

23. Patricia M. O'Donnell

    Patricia M. O'Donnell

    Patricia M. O'Donnell

    Patricia M. O'Donnell

    A. 0
    B. 2
    C. 3
    D. 4

24. E. Allen Ashland

    E. Alan Ashland

    E. Allen Ashland

    E. Allen Ashlund

    A. 0
    B. 2
    C. 3
    D. 4

25. 82570145

    82576145

    82576145

    82576145

    A. 0
    B. 2
    C. 3
    D. 4

26. Mary Beth P. Leonard

    Mary Beth P. Leonardo

    Mary Beth P. Leonardi

    Mary Beth R. Leonard

    A. 0
    B. 2
    C. 3
    D. 4

Directions (27–29): Choose the space in which the given name would appear in the alphabetical list.

27. Leon, Martha J.

    A. _____

    Landry, William S.

    B. _____

    Lello, Nicholas R.

    C. _____

    Leroy, Thomas J.

    D. _____

    Lincombe, Martha M.

28. Milton, Lawrence

    A. _____

    Martin, Maurice

    B. _____

    Meeks, Francine

    C. _____

    Merle, Paul

    D. _____

    Morgan, Michelle

29. Jackson, Karen

    A. _____

    Jackson, Neil

    B. _____

    Jackson, Richard

    C. _____

    Jackson, Stella

    D. _____

    Jackson, Wayne

Directions (30–33): Use the following Document Filing Report Form and coding instructions to answer the questions.

Document Filing Report Form				
Year	**Department**	**Document Type**	**Classification**	**Status**

Codes for this form are developed using the following keys:

Year	Department	Document Type	Classification	Status
A. 2000	A. Administrative	A. Business report	A. Confidential	A. Active
B. 2001	B. Accounting	B. Financial report	B. Restricted	B. Inactive
C. 2002	C. Billing	C. Customer complaint	C. Interdepartmental	C. Under review
D. 2003	D. Customer Service	D. Legal document	D. Public	D. Incomplete
E. 2004	E. Human Resources	E. Internal management document		E. Destroyed
F. 2005	F. Public Relations			
G. 2006				
H. 2007				
I. 2008				
J. 2009				
K. 2010				

Code the information found in each question using the keys above. Be sure to use only the given information to determine the code. The code should be ordered in the same format as the Document Filing Report Form shown above, from left to right.

30. What is the code for a restricted 2003 financial report from the Accounting Department that is currently inactive?

    A. BBCAB
    B. DBBBC
    C. DBBBB
    D. CBACB

31. What is the code for an active, interdepartmental 2009 legal document from the Human Resources Department?

    A. JFDCA
    B. JEDCA
    C. JEEDA
    D. JCEBA

32. What is the code for an administrative internal management document written in 2010 that is confidential and currently under review?

    A. KAEAC
    B. KADAB
    C. KBEAC
    D. KCAEA

33. What is the code for a destroyed 2006 customer complaint from the Customer Service Department that was classified as restricted?

    A. GDBBE
    B. GCAEE
    C. GECAE
    D. GDCBE

Directions (34–37): Using the list of names provided, determine which position the bold name would be in if the list were alphabetized by last name.

34. Mary Samuels

    Franklin Samuel

    Paul Samuelson

    Peter Samuels

    A. First
    B. Second
    C. Third
    D. Fourth

35. Vincent D'Amonte

    Michael Damon

    Dr. Victor DeMonte

    Paul F. D'Amonte

    A. First
    B. Second
    C. Third
    D. Fourth

36. **Joseph Peters, Jr.**

Floyd Peterson

Dolores Peterson

Dr. Ralph Peters

A. First
B. Second
C. Third
D. Fourth

37. James McEllison

Fr. Eric McDonald

Jeffery MacPherson

Charles MacThomas

A. First
B. Second
C. Third
D. Fourth

Directions (38): Retype the following passage in its entirety. Continue typing for five minutes. If you come to the end of the passage before time is up, double-space once, and start again from the beginning.

A clerical typist can be an invaluable asset for any modern business. A truly capable typist must be able to type a significant amount of letters, numbers, and symbols in a short period of time with accuracy. In fact, accuracy is often just as important as speed. Typists who can replicate large blocks of text or entire documents at an accelerated rate with few, if any, errors serve an important function in many companies. When reproducing various written documents, typists also can act as impromptu editors, checking for and correcting any mistakes in the original documents. This helps business administrators ensure the quality of all business communications. In this capacity, a typist plays an important role in enhancing the company's credibility through its documentation.

In addition to taking dictation, today's typists also may be asked to participate in many other day-to-day operations of the company. Because of their specialized writing and typing skills, office managers or administrators may ask typists to write company memorandums or compose letters to customers and clients.

Finally, typists also may be required to help with the other secretarial duties involved in the daily operation of a business office. Typists may be responsible for answering phones, taking messages, keeping track of office supplies, making photocopies, and sending faxes. Whether they are responsible only for their basic typing duties or for an array of everyday office tasks, typists can be a vital part of any company's success.

Directions (39–42): Use the following table to determine the correct code for the file described in each question. Each code consists of a two-letter code, followed by a one-number code, followed by a two-letter code.

Filing Code		
Year	Originator	Department
AA – 2006	1 – Kevin Jones	AC – Accounting
AB – 2007	2 – Ana Torres	PR – Public Relations
BB – 2008	3 – Matthew Williams	CS – Customer Service
BC – 2009	4 – Harold Kelly	AD – Administrative

Document Filing Report Form		
Year	Originator	Department

39. What code would be used for a 2007 customer service file created by Harold Kelly?

   A. AB4CS
   B. AA4CS
   C. AB3AC
   D. AA1PR

40. What code would be used for a file created by Ana Torres in 2009 for the Accounting Department?

   A. BB1AD
   B. BC3PR
   C. BC2AC
   D. AA2AC

41. What code would be used for a public relations file created in 2008 by Matthew Williams?

   A. AB3PR
   B. BB3PR
   C. BB4PR
   D. AA2PR

42. What code would be correct for a file created by Kevin Jones for the Administrative Department in 2006?

   A. AB3AC
   B. AB1AD
   C. AA4AC
   D. AA1AD

Directions (43–45): Of the four names listed, choose the one that would be *third* if the list were put into alphabetical order.

43. **A.** 10th Avenue Diner
    B. Tenderson-Smith Corp.
    C. Tim Rose and Sons, Inc.
    D. Tin Roof Construction Co.

44. **A.** Randall Dunovan, Sr.
    B. Andre P. LeDunne
    C. Prof. Kevin Dunn
    D. Robert Van Dunn

45. **A.** Peter Charles
    B. MaryAnn Charleston
    C. Frank Charlotte
    D. Michael Charleson

Directions (46–50): Each question contains a list of four names or numbers that may or may not be exactly alike. Compare the list items and determine how many items are the same.

46. Arthur J. Masterson

    Arthur J. Masterson

    Arthur J. Masterson

    Arthur J. Masterson

    A. 0
    B. 2
    C. 3
    D. 4

47. 9133214

    9173314

    9173314

    9173214

    A. 0
    B. 2
    C. 3
    D. 4

48. Alexander D. Graham

    Alexander D. Graham

    Alexander D. Graham

    Alexander D. Graham

    A. 0
    B. 2
    C. 3
    D. 4

49. Maria G. Shavers

    Marie G. Shavers

    Maria G. Shaver

    Mara G. Shavers

    A. 0
    B. 2
    C. 3
    D. 4

50. L. T. Young, III

    L. T. Young, III

    L. T. Young, III

    L. I. Young, III

    A. 0
    B. 2
    C. 3
    D. 4

IF YOU FINISH BEFORE TIME IS CALLED, CHECK YOUR WORK ON THIS SECTION ONLY. DO NOT WORK ON ANY OTHER SECTION IN THE TEST.

Section 4: Other Abilities

Time: 45 minutes

50 questions

Directions (1–5): Study the photograph for ten minutes; then cover the photograph and answer the questions based on your memory.

1. Which of the following items is the man standing at the booth next to the woman wearing?

   A.   A tie
   B.   A hat
   C.   Jeans
   D.   A sweater

2. Which of the following is the phone number listed on the sign hanging above the stand?

   A. 423-9632
   B. 429-3269
   C. 426-2239
   D. 422-2362

3. How many people are working at the stand in the photograph?

   A. 1
   B. 2
   C. 3
   D. 4

4. Which of the following names is listed on the sign hanging above the stand?

   A. Ricky
   B. Charlene
   C. Raymond
   D. Cheryl

5. Which of the following symbols does NOT appear on the sign hanging above the stand?

   A. The sun
   B. Birds
   C. A cat
   D. Trees

Directions (6–9): Answer the following questions honestly and completely. These questions do not have correct or incorrect answers. They are used to gauge aspects of your personality.

6. You think it's important to stand up for yourself.

   A. Strongly agree
   B. Agree
   C. Disagree
   D. Strongly disagree

7. Which of these qualities best defines your personality?

   A. Outgoing
   B. Carefree
   C. Rigid
   D. Agreeable

8. Which of these situations would you like to see yourself in?

   A.   Resolving conflicts
   B.   Leading a team
   C.   Making key decisions
   D.   Working at your own pace

9. How often do you skip breaks and work through your lunch?

   A.   Very often
   B.   Often
   C.   Sometimes
   D.   Rarely

Directions (10–12): To achieve the full testing experience, don't simply read the following questions and select an answer. Instead, ask a friend to read these questions aloud to you and select the best answer based on what you hear. Have your friend pause before moving on to the next question to give you time to select the answer.

10. For question 10, select the answer choice that shows the time that Mark James, a mail carrier, most likely delivered his last stack of mail before ending his shift.

    A.   8:15 a.m.
    B.   12:30 p.m.
    C.   4:30 p.m.
    D.   10:45 p.m.

11. For question 11, select the answer choice that contains the initials of building inspector Larry Franklin Horowitz.

    A.   F. L. H.
    B.   L. F. H.
    C.   C. H. F.
    D.   H. F. C.

12. For question 12, select the answer choice that contains a house, a paw print, two people, and a sun.

A.

B.

C.

D.

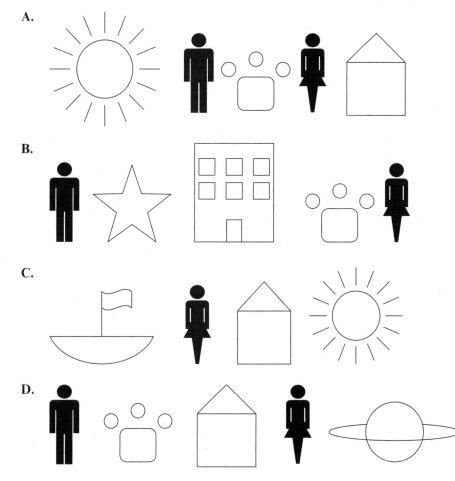

Directions (13–15): Answer the following questions based solely on the information provided.

The U.S. Postal Service employs people in many positions, including carriers, clerks, pre-sorters, and sorters. The following are rules for deciding who performs certain tasks:

- Pre-sorters are responsible for loading and unloading postal trucks and moving mail with either a forklift or a hand cart.
- Pre-sorters and sorters prepare mail for distribution.
- Sorters operate automated mail-processing equipment, while pre-sorters manually sort mail.
- Clerks provide direct sales and customer service services at retail postal offices and sell stamps, money orders, stationery, and mailing envelopes and boxes.
- Clerks are responsible for checking packages for mailing. They must weigh packages, determine postage, and check that the packages are in appropriate mailing condition.
- Carriers are responsible for delivering and picking up mail from residential and commercial mailboxes.

13. Which of the following positions would be responsible for emptying a mailbox located in a residential area?

    A. Carriers
    B. Clerks
    C. Pre-sorters
    D. Sorters

14. Which of the following positions would determine the appropriate postage for a 10-pound box?

    A. Carriers
    B. Clerks
    C. Pre-sorters
    D. Sorters

15. Which of the following positions would require a forklift license?

    A. Carriers
    B. Clerks
    C. Pre-sorters
    D. Sorters

Directions (16–23): Answer the following questions based solely on the information provided.

16. In a wheel-and-axle setup, if the radius of a wheel is 400 inches and the radius of its axle is 25 inches, what is the mechanical advantage?

    A. 6
    B. 16
    C. 28
    D. 50

17. An elevator technician arrives at a department store where four people are trapped in an elevator between the second and third floors. Firefighters have pried open the doors so that they can speak to the victims. As the technician begins to work, an elderly woman he recognizes as a frequent shopper at the department store approaches him and says that she saw him fix the same elevator last week. She questions his ability to fix the elevator and tells him he should consider early retirement or a change in occupation. She comments that the technician should hurry because her daughter is one of the people stuck on the elevator.

    How should the elevator technician respond?

    A. Ignore the woman and continue his work.
    B. Request that a nearby firefighter remove the woman from the store.
    C. Reassure the woman that he knows what he's doing and will get her daughter out soon.
    D. Tell the woman that her issue is with the department store and she should complain to the company.

18. Mr. Hoddle woke up in the morning and looked outside his window. He saw huge puddles of water, mounds of debris, and a fallen tree lying in his front yard. What can you infer happened?

    A. Mr. Hoddle was dreaming.
    B. A storm knocked down the tree.
    C. Mr. Hoddle's neighbor cut down the tree.
    D. A car hit the tree and it fell over.

Questions 19 through 21 refer to the following information.

Electricians are divided into four categories (industrial, lineman, residential, and journeyman), according to the amounts of voltage they are qualified to work with and the types of duties they may perform. The following are rules about which electricians can perform which jobs:

- An industrial electrician works on indoor electrical lines containing 120 to 13,800 volts in commercial and industrial settings.
- A lineman electrician is responsible for the transmission and distribution of utility power to residential, commercial, and industrial facilities. A lineman electrician works on outdoor electrical lines containing 4,600 to 375,000 volts.
- A residential electrician works on indoor electrical lines containing less than 240 volts in single- and multiple-family homes.
- A journeyman electrician installs electrical wiring in all types of buildings, including residential and commercial buildings, but is not permitted to design electrical systems.

19. An electrician in which of the following positions would work on the electrical wiring in a newly constructed home?

    A. Industrial
    B. Journeyman
    C. Lineman
    D. Residential

20. An electrician in which of the following positions would be sent to fix an outdoor electrical line after a storm?

    A. Industrial
    B. Journeyman
    C. Lineman
    D. Residential

21. An electrician in which of the following positions would be sent to a home to fix an electrical outlet that is not in working condition?

    A. Industrial
    B. Journeyman
    C. Lineman
    D. Residential

Questions 22 and 23 refer to the following figure.

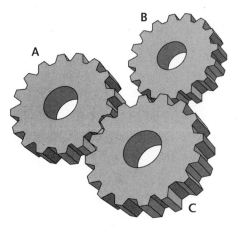

22. Based on the image, which of the following statements about the gears is true?

    A. Gear B makes more revolutions per minute than gear C.
    B. Gears A and B make the same number of revolutions per minute.
    C. Gear B makes fewer revolutions per minute than gear C.
    D. Gear A makes more revolutions per minute than gear B.

23. If gear A rotates counterclockwise, then which of the following statements is true?

    A. Gears B and C turn counterclockwise.
    B. Gear C turns clockwise.
    C. Gears B and C turn clockwise.
    D. Gear B turns clockwise.

Directions (24–26): Study the photograph for ten minutes; then cover the photograph and answer the questions based on your memory.

24. What of the following items is the boy in this photograph NOT wearing?

    A.   Shorts
    B.   A T-shirt
    C.   Sneakers
    D.   A hat

25. What does the sign hanging on the dunk tank read?

    A.   CLASS OF 2006 PHS
    B.   CLASS OF 2009 PHS
    C.   CLASS OF 2006 HSP
    D.   CLASS OF 2009 HSP

26. How many fire hydrants appear in this photograph?

    A.   1
    B.   2
    C.   3
    D.   4

Directions (27–29): Study the passage for ten minutes; then cover the passage and answer the questions based on your memory.

Date: January 19, 2010
To: All Employees
From: Sally Hernandez, XYZ Plant Safety Manager
Subject: Safety Regulations

This is a reminder to all employees regarding safety regulations. It has come to my attention that some employees are not following the proper safety protocols in place at XYZ Plant. Anyone caught not following the rules will receive a written warning. A second offense will result in termination. While on the clock, you should observe the following rules:

- A hard hat should be worn at all times.
- Hair should be tied back or a hairnet should be worn.
- Boots or sneakers should be worn at all times.
- No open-toe shoes or sandals are permitted.
- No loose clothing or jewelry is permitted.
- Safety goggles or glasses should be worn at all times.
- Spills should be cleaned immediately and reported to a supervisor.

If you have questions about these or other safety regulations, please contact me or your direct supervisor.

Sincerely,

Sally Hernandez
XYZ Plant Safety Manager

---

27. What is the date listed on the safety regulations memo?

   A. January 19, 2009
   B. January 9, 2010
   C. January 19, 2010
   D. January 9, 2009

28. What happens to an employee if he or she violates the safety regulations a second time?

    A. The employee is terminated.
    B. The employee is given a verbal warning.
    C. The employee is put on probation.
    D. The employee is given a written warning.

29. An employee is not permitted to wear which of the following items?

    A. A hard hat
    B. Flip-flops
    C. A T-shirt
    D. Glasses

Directions (30–34): Answer the following questions based solely on the information provided.

30. You are a newly hired police officer patrolling what is a normally quiet neighborhood by yourself at 11:40 p.m. on Sunday. You pass by a few dark houses and see nothing out of the ordinary. You then pass by a brightly lit house and hear arguing and a baby crying inside. You stop your vehicle. What should you do next?

    A. Ignore the situation and keep patrolling your beat.
    B. Call Child Protective Services.
    C. Knock on the door and check out the situation.
    D. Enter the home by force.

31. At 1:30 p.m., Bethany Maloney approaches a mail clerk in the post office and reports that a man attacked her in the parking lot and then stole her car. She tells the clerk the man was approximately 6'2". He was wearing a dark green sweatshirt and jeans and carrying a red backpack. Ms. Maloney says that she watched the man speed out of the parking lot and turn left on Main Street. The clerk must report the incident to the police. Which of the following expresses the information most clearly and accurately?

    A. It's 1:30 p.m. and the man who took Bethany Maloney's car was last seen driving on Main Street.
    B. A 6'2" male stole Bethany Maloney's car and started speeding. This happened at the post office. No one was hurt.
    C. Bethany Maloney's car was stolen from the parking lot of the post office at 1:30 p.m. The man who took the car is wearing a green sweatshirt and is carrying a red backpack. He was last seen making a left turn onto Main Street.
    D. A vehicle was stolen by a man wearing jeans. The incident occurred outside the local post office. Bethany Maloney is the owner of the vehicle. The man hit her first, and then he put his red backpack in the car and drove away.

32. As a police officer, you're called to the scene of a mugging. As you approach the scene, you notice that the victim is wearing a long white lab coat with a giant smiling mouth stitched onto the pocket. What can you infer from this situation?

    A. The victim is a dentist.
    B. The victim is a podiatrist.
    C. The victim is doing laundry today.
    D. The victim is ready for Halloween.

Question 33 refers to the following diagram.

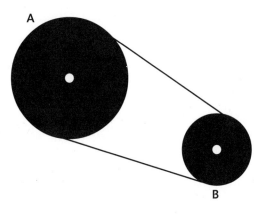

33. If wheel A is twice the size of wheel B and wheel A makes 90 revolutions per minute, how many revolutions per minute does wheel B make?

    A. 45
    B. 90
    C. 135
    D. 180

34. Which of these tools uses a circular blade to cut through wood?

    A. Axe
    B. Chisel
    C. Rotary saw
    D. Reciprocating saw

Directions (35–37): Answer the following questions honestly and completely. These questions do not have correct or incorrect answers. They are used to gauge aspects of your personality.

35. You prefer to work in groups rather than alone.

    A. Strongly agree
    B. Agree
    C. Disagree
    D. Strongly disagree

36. How often are you able to manage your time effectively during projects?

    A. Very often
    B. Often
    C. Sometimes
    D. Rarely

37. What best describes your current working situation?

    A. Stressful
    B. Hard
    C. Tiring
    D. Simple

Directions (38–42): Answer the following questions based solely on the information provided.

38. You arrive home after spending a weekend out of town. Your front door is wide open and you notice that your television is missing, as are some other items. What can you infer happened while you were gone?

    A. Someone broke into your house.
    B. You forgot to lock your door.
    C. You misplaced your house keys and someone found them.
    D. No one checked on your house while you were away.

39. Your company has hired a new young woman. She is assigned to sit at the desk next to yours and wears a type of perfume that bothers your allergies. The smell makes you sneeze and your eyes swell. It's impossible to finish your work. How should you respond to this situation?

    A. Tell her about your allergy and ask her not to wear perfume.
    B. Leave an anonymous note on her desk threatening her.
    C. Tell your supervisor and let him decide the best course of action.
    D. Quit your job because your health is more important than the job.

Question 40 refers to the following figure.

40. What would this tool most likely be used to do?

    A. Change a flat tire on a car.
    B. Cut through metal or wire.
    C. Hold objects together.
    D. Drive or remove nails.

Question 41 refers to the following figure.

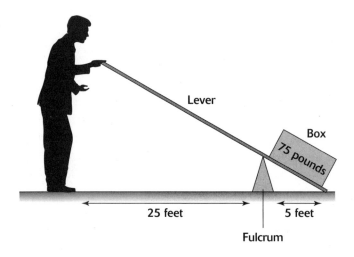

41. Based on the illustration, how many pounds of force must be applied to the lever to lift the box? Use the following equation to answer the question:

Weight of the Object · Distance from the Object to the Fulcrum =
Force · Distance from You to the Fulcrum

$$w \cdot d_1 = f \cdot d_2$$

    A. 15
    B. 25
    C. 35
    D. 50

42. When changing a vehicle's oil, which of the following should you do first?

    A. Take off the oil cap.
    B. Remove the drain plug.
    C. Drain the old oil.
    D. Fill the car with new oil.

Directions (43–45): Answer the following questions honestly and completely. These questions do not have correct or incorrect answers. They are used to gauge aspects of your personality.

43. You have many friends at work.

    A. Strongly agree
    B. Agree
    C. Disagree
    D. Strongly disagree

44. Which of the following best describes your ideal working conditions?

    A. Laid back
    B. Structured
    C. Busy
    D. Unstructured

45. How often are you on time for work?

    A. Very often
    B. Often
    C. Sometimes
    D. Rarely

Directions (46–50): Answer the following questions based solely on the information provided.

46. You've been assigned to deliver mail on a new route for the day because one of your co-workers called in sick. You're on your last delivery for the day. You place envelopes in a house's mailbox and you notice through an open screen door that an elderly man is lying on the floor near the door. How should you proceed?

    A. Call 911 and return to the post office.
    B. Knock on a neighbor's door for help.
    C. Ignore the situation and go home for the day.
    D. Call 911 and wait with the man until help arrives.

47. Trevor Daniels has just finished pruning a tree in the Hansons' backyard and is putting away his tools when Mr. Hanson comes out and asks Trevor where he's going. Trevor tells Mr. Hanson that he's finished pruning the tree and has to move on to his next appointment. Mr. Hanson studies the tree and tells Trevor that it doesn't look like he's done anything to it. "It's still too thick," he tells Trevor. Mr. Hanson then tells Trevor that he's not paying him until he thins the crown and removes a few more of the lower branches. It's 2:30 p.m. and Trevor has another appointment across town at 3 p.m. What should he do?

    A. Take out his tools and finish the job without question.
    B. Tell Mr. Hanson he can't finish the job today and leave.
    C. Call to tell the people at the next appointment that he'll be late, and finish pruning the tree.
    D. Leave for the day and come back unannounced to surprise Mr. Hanson by finishing the job.

48. After arriving on the scene of a house fire, you notice a man standing across the street, smoking a cigarette. He looks excited and interested in what the firefighters are doing, and his pants are wet. When you approach your fellow firefighters, you're told that someone set the fire and then exited the house through a second-floor window. There's a large pile of snow alongside the house and footprints leading away from the building. They assume someone jumped off the roof and into the snow bank below. What can you infer from this situation?

    A.   The man is in shock.
    B.   The man saw who started the fire.
    C.   The man started the fire and stayed to watch.
    D.   The man lived in the home and escaped from the second-floor window.

49. An electrician should wear all the following EXCEPT:

    A.   Rubber boots
    B.   A hard hat
    C.   Tight-fitting pants
    D.   A gold watch

50. What is one of the disadvantages of lithium batteries?

    A.   They last longer than alkaline batteries.
    B.   They cost more than alkaline batteries.
    C.   They have a higher voltage than alkaline batteries.
    D.   They are only available in AAA and AA sizes.

IF YOU FINISH BEFORE TIME IS CALLED, CHECK YOUR WORK ON THIS SECTION ONLY. DO NOT WORK ON ANY OTHER SECTION IN THE TEST.

Answer Key

Section 1: Verbal Ability

1. C	14. D	27. A	40. B
2. B	15. D	28. D	41. C
3. D	16. B	29. A	42. B
4. A	17. B	30. A	43. A
5. A	18. C	31. B	44. C
6. C	19. D	32. B	45. A
7. B	20. A	33. B	46. B
8. A	21. C	34. D	47. C
9. D	22. D	35. A	48. B
10. C	23. A	36. B	49. D
11. A	24. B	37. D	50. B
12. B	25. D	38. B	
13. C	26. B	39. D	

Section 2: Mathematical Ability

1. C	14. C	27. B	40. D
2. C	15. B	28. C	41. C
3. D	16. B	29. A	42. C
4. B	17. D	30. D	43. A
5. C	18. C	31. A	44. C
6. D	19. D	32. C	45. D
7. A	20. D	33. C	46. D
8. C	21. D	34. B	47. C
9. A	22. B	35. C	48. D
10. C	23. D	36. C	49. C
11. D	24. C	37. A	50. C
12. B	25. D	38. C	
13. A	26. A	39. C	

Section 3: Clerical Ability

1. C	14. A	27. C	39. A
2. B	15. B	28. D	40. C
3. A	16. B	29. A	41. B
4. C	17. C	30. C	42. D
5. B	18. A	31. B	43. D
6. A	19. B	32. A	44. B
7. D	20. C	33. D	45. B
8. A	21. D	34. C	46. D
9. C	22. B	35. D	47. B
10. B	23. D	36. A	48. D
11. D	24. B	37. C	49. A
12. C	25. C	38. See answer explanations.	50. C
13. C	26. A		

Section 4: Other Abilities

1. B	13. A	28. A	41. A
2. A	14. B	29. B	42. A
3. A	15. C	30. A	43. See answer explanations.
4. D	16. B	31. C	44. See answer explanations.
5. C	17. C	32. A	45. See answer explanations.
6. See answer explanations.	18. B	33. D	46. D
7. See answer explanations.	19. B	34. C	47. C
8. See answer explanations.	20. C	35. See answer explanations.	48. C
9. See answer explanations.	21. D	36. See answer explanations.	49. D
10. C	22. B	37. See answer explanations.	50. B
11. B	23. B	38. A	
12. A	24. D	39. C	
	25. B	40. A	
	26. A		
	27. C		

Answer Explanations

Section 1: Verbal Ability

1. **C** The word *sever* means "to divide." *Sever* does not mean "to widen," "to alter," or "to repair." *(See Chapter V, Section A.)*

2. **B** The word *construe* means "to deduce." *Construe* does not mean "to fear," "to appear," or "to hope." *(See Chapter V, Section A.)*

3. **D** The word *inconspicuous* means "unnoticeable." *Inconspicuous* does not mean "intelligent," "strange," or "friendly." *(See Chapter V, Section A.)*

4. **A** The word *eccentric* means "unusual." *Eccentric* does not mean "unstable," "repetitive," or "circular." *(See Chapter V, Section A.)*

5. **A** The word *repudiate* means "to disown." *Repudiate* does not mean "to accuse," "to label," or "to punish." *(See Chapter V, Section A.)*

6. **C** The word *inconceivable* means "unbelievable." *Inconceivable* does not mean "untruthful," "unwise," or "unshakable." *(See Chapter V, Section A.)*

7. **B** The passage best supports the statement that cellphones often distract drivers and lead to traffic accidents. The sentence "These distractions have led to many traffic accidents that might have been avoided" helps you conclude that cellphones are distracting to drivers and can cause accidents. The passage does not state that cellphones should be used only in emergencies or by experienced drivers, nor does it say that cellphones have little impact on drivers. *(See Chapter V, Section B.)*

8. **A** The passage best supports the statement that television has become a significant part of daily life. Nothing in the passage states that television does not have enough channels or has not changed over the years. It also states that television's purpose has expanded. *(See Chapter V, Section B.)*

9. **D** According to the passage, the most important element in treating shock is slowing the loss of blood. Choices A, B, and C are incorrect because they are not the most important steps to take when treating a person who is in shock. *(See Chapter V, Section B.)*

10. **C** The main idea of this passage is that historical accounts from multiple sources are often more accurate. Choices A, B, and D do not accurately reflect the main idea of this passage. *(See Chapter V, Section B.)*

11. **A** Because of the use of performance-enhancing substances, the public does not believe that these players earned their accomplishments. Nothing in this passage states that the public no longer watches Major League Baseball or feels more drug testing is needed. *(See Chapter V, Section B.)*

12. **B** The main idea of this paragraph is that movie-ticket prices are related to the cost of making movies. No details in the passage support the statements that there has been a substantial increase in demand for new movies, television has had no impact on the movie industry, or the price of movie tickets will decrease over time. *(See Chapter V, Section B.)*

13. **C** The correct usage would be "every level." The other variations, including the original text, are excessively wordy. Choice C conveys the same meaning in a more concise manner. *(See Chapter V, Section C.)*

14. **D** *Their* is a possessive adjective. *They're* is a contraction for "they are," and *they* is a pronoun, so choices B and C are incorrect. *(See Chapter V, Section C.)*

15. **D** The correct word to begin this sentence is *although.* The other transition words do not fit the context of the sentence. *(See Chapter V, Section C.)*

16. **B** The correct word to complete this sentence is *awarded.* The other verbs do not fit the context of the sentence. *(See Chapter V, Section D1.)*

17. **B** The correct sentence order is 3, 4, 1, 2: Franklin was convinced that electricity, a relatively new scientific discovery at the time, was directly related to the lightning. Hoping to find evidence to prove his theory correct, Franklin connected a metal key to the end of a kite, believing that the key would conduct electricity during a lightning storm. When an appropriate storm came along, Franklin took his kite to a field and began his experiment. After waiting some time for a result, Franklin touched the key and noticed a spark; his theory was correct! *(See Chapter V, Section C.)*

18. **C** The correct sentence order is 2, 1, 4, 3: After witnessing the two cars collide, Lenny pulls over and climbs out of his car to offer assistance. Taking a closer look, Lenny finds a severely damaged sedan with three occupants and a less damaged pickup truck with a single occupant. First, Lenny checks on the people in the sedan; he calls 911 after the occupants report several injuries. After checking on the driver of the truck, who is unharmed, Lenny remains on the scene with the victims until help arrives. *(See Chapter V, Section C.)*

19. **D** The correct answer is *meddle,* which means "to interfere with." *Medal* is a noun that refers to a small metallic object that is awarded to commemorate a person or event. *Metal* is a noun that refers to a solid chemical element. *Mettle* is a noun that can mean "strength of spirit" or "stamina." *(See Chapter V, Section D6.)*

20. **A** The correct answer is *rites,* which is a noun that refers to ceremonial acts. *Rights* are ideas or things to which a person has just claim. *Wrights* are workers who are skilled in particular fields. *Writes* is a verb that means "to compose." *(See Chapter V, Section D6.)*

21. **C** The correct answer is *sow,* which is a verb that means "to plant seed." Although it has various meanings and usages, *so* cannot be used as a verb. As a verb, *sough* means "to groan or make noise." *Sew* is a verb that means "to attach by stitching." *(See Chapter V, Section D6.)*

22. **D** *County Commissioner* should not be capitalized. Occupational titles are capitalized only when they precede a person's name. *(See Chapter V, Section D6.)*

23. **A** The word *congress* should be capitalized because it is a proper noun. *(See Chapter V, Section D6.)*

24. **B** A comma should be placed after *clerk* to separate the two independent clauses joined by the coordinating conjunction *but.* *(See Chapter V, Section D6.)*

25. **D** The phrase *which needs to be repaired* is a nonrestrictive element. Therefore, it should be set off by commas. *(See Chapter V, Section D6.)*

26. **B** *Yeeld* is spelled incorrectly. The correct spelling is *yield.* *(See Chapter V, Section E.)*

27. **A** *Sargeant* is spelled incorrectly. The correct spelling is *sergeant.* *(See Chapter V, Section E.)*

28. **D** *Rythem* is spelled incorrectly. The correct spelling is *rhythm.* *(See Chapter V, Section E.)*

29. **A** *Villege* is spelled incorrectly. The correct spelling is *village*. *(See Chapter V, Section E.)*

30. **A** *Mischievious* is spelled incorrectly. The correct spelling is *mischievous*. *(See Chapter V, Section E.)*

31. **B** *Campeign* is spelled incorrectly. The correct spelling is *campaign*. *(See Chapter V, Section E.)*

32. **B** *Parrallel* is spelled incorrectly. The correct spelling is *parallel*. *(See Chapter V, Section E.)*

33. **B** A pillow would be described as soft, and a rock would be described as hard. The other choices do not reflect the relationship between pillow and soft. *(See Chapter V, Section F.)*

34. **D** The relationship between cat and kitten is that a kitten is a young cat. The best choice is D because a tadpole is a young frog. *(See Chapter V, Section F.)*

35. **A** The word *expensive* refers to the cost of gold, and the word *cheap* refers to the cost of tin. *(See Chapter V, Section F.)*

36. **B** A *zeppelin* is a vehicle, and *air* is where the vehicle travels. The word that describes where a barge travels is *water*. *(See Chapter V, Section F.)*

37. **D** In this analogy, the words *professor* and *teacher* are set up as synonyms. The only choice that includes two synonyms is choice D. *Pupil* is a synonym for *student*. *(See Chapter V, Section F.)*

38. **B** A person would eat if he or she was feeling ravenous, whereas a person who was feeling parched would *drink* something to satisfy his or her thirst. *(See Chapter V, Section F.)*

39. **D** The word *beverage* is a synonym for the word *libation*. *Libation* is not similar in meaning to *payment, freedom,* or *slander*. *(See Chapter V, Section G.)*

40. **B** A synonym for the word *noxious* is *poisonous*. *Noxious* is not similar in meaning to *difficult, odorous,* or *horrific*. *(See Chapter V, Section G.)*

41. **C** A synonym of the word *absolve* is *forgive*. *Absolve* does not mean "to mislead," "to recall," or "to dispel." *(See Chapter V, Section G.)*

42. **B** The word *consequence* is a synonym for *ramification*. *Offense, compromise,* and *obstruction* do not have the same meaning as *ramification*. *(See Chapter V, Section G.)*

43. **A** The word *unbiased* is a synonym for *impartial*. *Impartial* does not mean "uninteresting," "frustrated," or "flexible." *(See Chapter V, Section G.)*

44. **C** A synonym for the word *friable* is *brittle*. *Important, costly,* and *docile* do not have the same meaning as *friable*. *(See Chapter V, Section G.)*

45. **A** The original sentence is awkward and contains an error in parallelism. Choice A corrects the awkward phrasing by changing the word *to* to *for* and balancing the ideas at the end of the sentence. Choice B attempts to correct the error in parallelism, but it makes the sentence even more awkward. Choice C is incorrect because it is awkward and the meaning of the sentence is unclear. *(See Chapter V, Section H.)*

46. **B** The original sentence is an example of an incomplete comparison. The sentence doesn't tell you if the author is comparing the post office's filing system to the entire police station or if the author is comparing the post office's filing system to the police station's filing system. Choices A and C create an awkward sentence by adding the words *which has*. Choice B makes the comparison clear by adding the words *the police station's system*. *(See Chapter V, Section H.)*

47. **C** The original sentence contains a misplaced modifier. After reading this sentence, you would assume that the county offers jobs only to motivated individuals who have competitive salaries and health benefits. Choice A confuses the intended meaning of the original sentence. The rearranging of the sentence in choice B does nothing to correct the original error. Choice C places the modifier *(with competitive salaries and health benefits)* next to the word it's modifying *(jobs)* and clears up any confusion within the sentence. *(See Chapter V, Section H.)*

48. **B** The original sentence contains a shift in person. The subject of the sentence changes from *one* to *you.* Choices A and C do not correct the shift in person. Only Choice B corrects this shift. *(See Chapter V, Section H.)*

49. **D** The original sentence is correct. Choice A creates a comma splice. Choice B incorrectly uses a colon. The use of the word *and* in choice C does not effectively convey the clerk's error. *(See Chapter V, Section H.)*

50. **B** The original sentence is wordy and redundant. There is no need to repeat the word *candidate* or *position* in this sentence. Choices A and C do not correct these errors. Choice B is concise and clearly demonstrates the author's intended meaning. *(See Chapter V, Section H.)*

Section 2: Mathematical Ability

1. **C** To solve this problem, subtract the number of students who bring their lunch to school at Chancellor Academy from the number of students who bring their lunch to school at Duffy High School: $274 - 123 = 151$. *(See Chapter VI, Section F2.)*

2. **C** To reach the correct answer, divide the numerator by the denominator: $13 \div 5 = 2\frac{6}{10}$. Then, simplify the fraction $\frac{6}{10}$ to $\frac{3}{5}$. This results in an answer of $2\frac{3}{5}$. *(See Chapter VI, Section A1.)*

3. **D** To find the value of s, solve using proportions. Because the triangles are similar, they have equal angles and proportional sides. Use the proportion $\frac{ab}{ab} = \frac{bc}{bc}$ and solve:

$$\frac{ab}{ab} = \frac{bc}{bc}$$
$$\frac{7}{14} = \frac{12}{s}$$
$$7s = 12 \cdot 14$$
$$7s = 168$$
$$s = 24$$

(See Chapter VI, Section E2.)

4. **B** The correct answer is $\frac{1}{4}$. Following the first day's evaporation, $\frac{1}{3}$ of the original water remains. After the second day's evaporation, $\frac{3}{4}$ of the water left from the first day remains. So, $\frac{1}{3} \cdot \frac{3}{4} = \frac{1}{4}$. As a result, $\frac{1}{4}$ of the original water remains. *(See Chapter VI, Section A1.)*

5. **C** The first step in the problem is to find the difference between the expected cost and the actual cost: $150 - $120 = $30. Then, divide the difference in costs ($30) by the expected cost ($150) to find the percent of the savings: $30 \div $150 = 0.20$, or 20%. So, the agency saved 20% off its expected cost. *(See Chapter VI, Section B1.)*

6. **D** To find the current population, first determine by how much the population has increased since the census. To find the amount of increase, multiply 24,000 by $\frac{1}{3}$:

$$24,000 \cdot \frac{1}{3} = 8,000$$

Then, add the population increase to the original population to find the current population:

$$24,000 + 8,000 = 32,000$$

(See Chapter VI, Section A1.)

7. **A** To find the answer, first multiply the percentage of people who ordered blue scarves by the total number of women, and then multiply the percentage of people who ordered pink scarves by the total number of women:

$$\text{Blue: } 15\% \text{ or } 0.15 \cdot 300 = 45$$
$$\text{Pink: } 10\% \text{ or } 0.10 \cdot 300 = 30$$

Then subtract the number of women who ordered pink scarves from the number of women who ordered blue scarves: $45 - 30 = 15$. *(See Chapter VI, Section F1.)*

8. **C** To find the correct answer, simply divide 18.7 by 5.3: $18.7 \div 5.3 = 3.5283$. Then round the answer to the third number after the decimal point: 3.5283 rounds to 3.528. *(See Chapter VI, Section A2.)*

9. **A** According to the bar graph, 1,000 people rode the bus during November. *(See Chapter VI, Section F1.)*

10. **C** To solve, first simplify like terms to create the equation $7x = 100 + 2x$. Then subtract $2x$ from both sides. This leaves you with $5x = 100$. Divide both sides by 5 to find $x = 20$. *(See Chapter VI, Section D2.)*

11. **D** The sale price of $125 represents 80% of the original price. To find what 80% of the original price is, divide $125 by 0.80: $125 \div 0.80 = \$156.25$. *(See Chapter VI, Sections A2 and B1.)*

12. **B** To find the answer, multiply the percentage of teachers who ordered pumpkin pies (23%) by the total number of teachers: $0.23 \cdot 200 = 46$. *(See Chapter VI, Section F1.)*

13. **A** You can rewrite ratios as fractions. The ratios $\frac{81}{9}$ and $\frac{45}{5}$ can both be reduced to $\frac{9}{1}$ or 9. Therefore, these number groups are similar. *(See Chapter VI, Section B2.)*

14. **C** To find the total amount of the bill, add the amount the man spent on food, the amount he spent on toiletries, and the amount he spent on taxes: $\$82.67 + \$24.88 + \$4.32 = \$111.87$. *(See Chapter VI, Section A2.)*

15. **B** You can determine the total cost of the apples using the following equation:

$$\frac{3}{24} = \frac{1.35}{P}$$
$$3P = 1.35 \cdot 24$$
$$P = 10.8$$

(See Chapter VI, Section A2.)

16. **B** To find the value of x, you need to solve for x. The perimeter of a quadrilateral is equal to the total of all four of its sides. Therefore, $40 = 5 + 8 + 13 + x$. To solve for x, add the three known values: $40 = 26 + x$, so $x = 14$. *(See Chapter VI, Section E3.)*

17. **D** The maximum diameter of the pipe is 2.75 + 0.017 = 2.767 in., and the minimum diameter of the pipe is 2.75 – 0.017 = 2.733. So, the pipe measuring 2.768 inches exceeds the maximum allowable diameter. *(See Chapter VI, Section E4.)*

18. **C** The correct answer is $\frac{1}{6}$. This answer is found by dividing both the numerator and the denominator by the greatest common divisor (GCD)—in this case, 7. This will reduce the fraction to $\frac{1}{6}$. *(See Chapter VI, Section A1.)*

19. **D** The coordinates of the point in the figure are (–4, –3). Since the point lands in Quadrant III, both the x- and y-coordinates are negative. *(See Chapter VI, Section E5.)*

20. **D** Based on the information provided, you can determine that it would take one worker 280 days to complete the job. Therefore, 280 ÷ 8 = 35 workers. *(See Chapter VI, Section B2.)*

21. **D** To find the area of the parallelogram, multiply the length of the shape's base by its height:

$$A = bh$$
$$= 12 \cdot 8$$
$$= 96$$

(See Chapter VI, Section E3.)

22. **B** Written as a fraction, $\frac{36}{54}$ could be reduced to $\frac{2}{3}$, which, as a ratio, would be 2:3. *(See Chapter VI, Section B2.)*

23. **D** To find the number of days it will take one machine to complete the job, multiple 3 by 5: 3 · 5 = 15 days. To find the number of days it will take for two machines to complete the same job, divide 15 days by 2 machines: 15 ÷ 2 = 7.5 days. *(See Chapter VI, Section C1.)*

24. **C** 2,056 papers ÷ 16 clerks = 128.5 papers filed by each clerk in 20 minutes. Then 128.5 papers ÷ 20 minutes ≈ 6.4 papers per minute. *(See Chapter VI, Section C1.)*

25. **D** The worker rented the car for three days, and the rental company charges $20 per day plus mileage. To answer the question, first subtract the per-day charges ($20 · 3 = $60) from the total bill: $240 – $60 = $180. To find the number of miles the worker drove, divide the remaining part of the bill ($180) by the cost per mile ($0.40): $180 ÷ $0.40 = 450 miles. *(See Chapter VI, Section C1.)*

26. **A** The average of the two fractions can be found by adding the fractions and dividing the total number of fractions, which is 2. Before adding the fractions together, you must make sure they have a common denominator: $\frac{1}{4} + \frac{1}{8} = \frac{2}{8} + \frac{1}{8} = \frac{3}{8}$. Then find the average by dividing by 2: $\frac{3}{8} \div \frac{2}{1} = \frac{3}{8} \cdot \frac{1}{2} = \frac{3}{16}$. *(See Chapter VI, Section A1.)*

27. **B** To solve this problem, replace letters x and y with the numeric values 24 (for x) and 6 (for y): 2(24)(24 – 6) = (48)(18) = 864. *(See Chapter VI, Section D3.)*

28. **C** With eight parts copper and two parts nickel, the alloy has a total of ten parts. To find how many pounds are in each part, divide 250 pounds by ten parts: 250 ÷ 10 = 25. Then, to solve the problem, multiply 25 pounds by two parts: 25 · 2 = 50 pounds. *(See Chapter VI, Section B2.)*

29. **A** If p stands for the number of files Samantha filed, and Lois filed 15 fewer than 3 times the number Samantha filed, you should multiply the number of reports Samantha filed by 3 and subtract 15 from the sum. So, 3p – 15. *(See Chapter VI, Section D1.)*

30. **D** Rate = Percentage · Base, so 0.20 · 300 = 60. *(See Chapter VI, Section B1.)*

31. **A** To solve this problem, first convert eight hours into minutes: 8 hours · 60 minutes/hour = 480 minutes. Then, divide the total number of minutes (480) by 80 pages: 480 ÷ 80 = 6. *(See Chapter VI, Section C1.)*

32. **C** If the clerk can file 40 papers in one hour, then he can file 240 papers in six hours (40 · 6 = 240). To the find the number of papers the clerk has left to file, subtract 240 papers from the total: 500 − 240 = 260 remaining papers. *(See Chapter VI, Section C1.)*

33. **C** According to the diagram, each house represents 46 residents and Maineville has $2\frac{1}{2}$ houses. To solve this problem, first divide 46 by 2 to get the value for the half of house: 46 ÷ 2 = 23. Then add two houses to this number: 46 + 46 + 23 = 115. *(See Chapter VI, Section F1.)*

34. **B** To solve this problem, replace the letters x and y with the numeric values 16 (for x) and 4 (for y): 4(16)(2[16] + 4) = (64)(32 + 4) = (64)(36) = 2,304. *(See Chapter VI, Section D3.)*

35. **C** To find the answer, divide the total amount of money by the number of parts: 420 ÷ (2 + 2 + 4) = 420 ÷ 8 = 52.5. Then, multiply that number by the number of parts that each person receives: 52.5 · 2 = 105 and 52.5 · 4 = 210. Therefore, two people receive $105 and one person receives $210. *(See Chapter VI, Section B2.)*

36. **C** The answer can be determined using the equation Rate = Distance ÷ Time. To solve, divide the distance the worker drove (270 miles) by the time he spent driving (4.5 hours): r = 270 miles ÷ 4.5 hours = 60. So, the rate is 60 miles per hour. *(See Chapter VI, Section C1.)*

37. **A** To find x, you have to remember that a triangle's three interior angles always will equal 180° when they're added together. To find the value of the triangle's third, unknown angle, add together the two known angles: 85° + 20° = 105°. Then, take the sum and subtract it from 180°: 105° − 180° = 75°. Therefore, $x°$ = 75. *(See Chapter VI, Sections E1–E2.)*

38. **C** To solve this problem, multiply the number of typists by the time it takes to complete the seven reports: 3 · 5 = 15. So, one typist can complete seven reports in 15 days. Next, divide the number of days it takes one typist to complete the seven reports by the total number of typists: 15 ÷ 2 = 7.5. So, it would take two typists 7.5 days to complete seven reports. *(See Chapter VI, Section C1.)*

39. **C** To find y, you must remember that an exterior angle of a triangle is equal to the sum of its remote interior angles. The remote interior angles in this figure are 60° and 55°. Adding these together will give you the value of $y°$. So, 60° + 55° = 115°, and $y°$ = 115. *(See Chapter VI, Sections E1–E2.)*

40. **D** To solve this problem, use the formula Distance = Rate · Time = 55 · 4.5. So, d = 247.5. *(See Chapter VI, Section C1.)*

41. **C** To find the answer, first divide 7 by 12: 7 ÷ 12 = 0.58333. Then, round the answer to the third number after the decimal point: 0.58333 rounds to 0.583. *(See Chapter VI, Section A2.)*

42. **C** This can be determined by using the equation Average = Sum Time ÷ Number of Workers. To solve, first add the three workers' times: 115 minutes + 95 minutes + 120 minutes = 330 minutes. Then, divide that total by the number of workers (3): 330 minutes ÷ 3 = 110. *(See Chapter VI, Section C1.)*

43. **A** Simplify the equation by adding 2 to each side, which gives you $6n = n + 10$. Then, subtract n from both sides, and reduce the equation to $5n = 10$. Finally, divide both sides by 5 to find that $n = 2$. *(See Chapter VI, Section D2.)*

44. **C** To find the circumference of the circle, you have to use the formula $C = \pi d$. You know that AO, a radius, is equal to 4. A circle's diameter is two times its radius, so you should use the equation $d = 2r = 2 \cdot 4 = 8$. Then, use the information you know to complete the formula: $C = \pi d = \pi \cdot 8 = 3.14 \cdot 8 = 25.12$. *(See Chapter VI, Section E4.)*

45. **D** A point with the coordinates of (16, –22) would appear in Quadrant IV. To plot this point, you would count positive 16 units on the x-axis and negative 22 units on the y-axis. *(See Chapter VI, Section E5.)*

46. **D** Since the bar chart shows the greatest jump in population from 2000 to 2010, Burbank saw the greatest population increase during 2010. *(See Chapter VI, Section F1.)*

47. **C** To find the hypotenuse of the right triangle in the figure, you have to use the Pythagorean theorem ($a^2 + b^2 = c^2$). To find the value of the hypotenuse, or c, replace a and b with the values from the diagram:

$$a^2 + b^2 = c^2$$
$$3^2 + 4^2 = c^2$$
$$9 + 16 = c^2$$
$$25 = c^2$$
$$5 = c$$

(See Chapter VI, Section E2.)

48. **D** According to the table, a latte costs $4.25 at the Coffee Bean. *(See Chapter VI, Section F2.)*

49. **C** According to the line graph, a truck cost $13,000 in 2000 and a car cost $9,000 in 2000, so the difference between the cost of a truck and car in 2000 is $13,000 – $9,000 = $4,000. *(See Chapter VI, Section F1.)*

50. **C** To find the number of questions Sam can answer incorrectly, multiply the 40 questions by 25%, or 0.25: $40 \cdot 0.25 = 10$ questions. *(See Chapter VI, Section B1.)*

Section 3: Clerical Ability

1. **C** Three of the names are written as "Richard L. Sellers," while one is written as "Richard I. Sellers." *(See Chapter VII, Section D.)*

2. **B** Two of the names are written as "Michael S. Sharpe." The other two are written as "Michael S. Sharp" and "Michelle S. Sharpe." *(See Chapter VII, Section D.)*

3. **A** None of the choices is the same. *(See Chapter VII, Section D.)*

4. **C** Three of the names are written as "Neil A. Nutley," while one is written as "Neal A. Nutley." *(See Chapter VII, Section D.)*

5. **B** The correct answer is choice B, *technical.* *(See Chapter VII, Section A2.)*

6. **A** The correct answer is choice A, *tools.* *(See Chapter VII, Section A2.)*

7. **D** The correct answer is choice D, *adequately.* *(See Chapter VII, Section A2.)*

8. **A** The correct answer is choice A, *performing.* *(See Chapter VII, Section A2.)*

9. **C** The correct answer is choice C, *competent.* *(See Chapter VII, Section A2.)*

10. **B** The correct answer is choice B, *interacting. (See Chapter VII, Section A2.)*

11. **D** The correct answer is choice D, *customers. (See Chapter VII, Section A2.)*

12. **C** The correct answer is choice C, *clients. (See Chapter VII, Section A2.)*

13. **C** The correct answer is choice C, *effectively. (See Chapter VII, Section A2.)*

14. **A** The correct answer is choice A, *face. (See Chapter VII, Section A2.)*

15. **B** The correct answer is choice B, *company. (See Chapter VII, Section A2.)*

16. **B** *Remainder* would follow the word *regulation* in alphabetical order. *(See Chapter VII, Section B2.)*

17. **C** *Sanitize* would follow the word *sanguine* in alphabetical order. *(See Chapter VII, Section B2.)*

18. **A** *Megabyte* would follow the word *medial* in alphabetical order. *(See Chapter VII, Section B2.)*

19. **B** The address 1357 Dodsworth Drive is part of route B. *(See Chapter VII, Section C1.)*

20. **C** The address 102 Blue Hill Road is a part of route C. *(See Chapter VII, Section C1.)*

21. **D** The address 1525 Main Street is not included in the assigned delivery routes and would be classified as route D. *(See Chapter VII, Section C1.)*

22. **B** The address 259 Carver Street is part of route B. *(See Chapter VII, Section C1.)*

23. **D** All four are the same. *(See Chapter VII, Section D1.)*

24. **B** Two of the names are written as "E. Allen Ashland." The other two are written as "E. Alan Ashland" and "E. Allen Ashlund." *(See Chapter VII, Section D.)*

25. **C** Three of the numbers are written as "82576145," while one is written as "82570145." *(See Chapter VII, Section D.)*

26. **A** None of the choices is the same. *(See Chapter VII, Section D.)*

27. **C** *Leon, Martha J.* would be placed between *Lello, Nicholas R.* and *Leroy, Thomas J. (See Chapter VII, Section B1.)*

28. **D** *Milton, Lawrence* would be placed between *Merle, Paul* and *Morgan, Michelle. (See Chapter VII, Section B1.)*

29. **A** *Jackson, Karen* would be the first name on the list. *(See Chapter VII, Section B1.)*

30. **C** The correct code for this document is DBBBB. *(See Chapter VII, Section C2.)*

31. **B** The correct code for this document is JEDCA. *(See Chapter VII, Section C2.)*

32. **A** The correct code for this document is KAEAC. *(See Chapter VII, Section C2.)*

33. **D** The correct code for this document is GDCBE. *(See Chapter VII, Section C2.)*

34. **C** *Peter Samuels* would be third in an alphabetical list. *(See Chapter VII, Section B2.)*

35. **D** *Dr. Victor DeMonte* would be fourth in an alphabetical list. *(See Chapter VII, Section B2.)*

36. **A** *Joseph Peters, Jr.,* would be first in an alphabetical list. *(See Chapter VII, Section B2.)*

37. **C** *Fr. Eric McDonald* would be third in an alphabetical list. *(See Chapter VII, Section B2.)*

38. The minimum speed for the typing test will vary from state to state. The number of errors allowed also will vary. Contact your local testing facility for more information on the requirements for the typing test. *(See Chapter VII, Section A1.)*

39. **A** The correct code for this file is AB4CS. *(See Chapter VII, Section C2.)*

40. **C** The correct code for this file is BC2AC. *(See Chapter VII, Section C2.)*

41. **B** The correct code for this file is BB3PR. *(See Chapter VII, Section C2.)*

42. **D** The correct code for this file is AA1AD. *(See Chapter VII, Section C2.)*

43. **D** *Tin Roof Construction Co.* would be third in an alphabetical list. *(See Chapter VII, Section B1.)*

44. **B** *Andre P. LeDunne* would be third in an alphabetical list. *(See Chapter VII, Section B1.)*

45. **B** *MaryAnn Charleston* would be third in an alphabetical list. *(See Chapter VII, Section B1.)*

46. **D** All four are the same. *(See Chapter VII, Section D.)*

47. **B** Two of the numbers are written as "9173314." The other numbers are written as "9133214" and "9173214." *(See Chapter VII, Section D.)*

48. **D** All four are the same. *(See Chapter VII, Section D.)*

49. **A** None of the choices is the same. *(See Chapter VII, Section D.)*

50. **C** Three of the names are written as "L. T. Young, III," while one is written as "L. I. Young, III." *(See Chapter VII, Section D.)*

Section 4: Other Abilities

1. **B** The man standing at the booth next to the woman in this photograph is wearing a short-sleeved shirt, shorts, and a hat. *(See Chapter VIII, Section A1.)*

2. **A** The phone number listed on the sign above the booth is 423-9632. *(See Chapter VIII, Section A1.)*

3. **A** One person, a man wearing a short-sleeved shirt and light-colored shorts, appears to be positioned inside the stand. His back is turned toward his customers, but it's safe to assume he's responsible for the stand. *(See Chapter VIII, Section A1.)*

4. **D** The name *Cheryl* is on the sign, along with the name *Richard*. *(See Chapter VIII, Section A1.)*

5. **C** The sign contains symbols of trees, houses, suns, and birds, but it doesn't contain a cat symbol. *(See Chapter VIII, Section A1.)*

6. This personality question has no correct or incorrect answer. This type of question is designed to test your ability to work with others. *(See Chapter VIII, Section D.)*

7. This personality question has no correct or incorrect answer. This type of question is designed to identify your personality traits. *(See Chapter VIII, Section D.)*

8. This personality question has no correct or incorrect answer. This type of question is designed to test your leadership skills. *(See Chapter VIII, Section D.)*

9. This personality question has no correct or incorrect answer. This type of question is designed to test your ability to manage time. *(See Chapter VIII, Section D.)*

10. **C** Most mail carriers end their shifts in the late afternoon or early evening; therefore, Mark James most likely delivered his last stack of mail at 4:30 p.m. It would be odd to see a mail carrier finishing his route at 10:30 p.m., so choice D is incorrect. At 8:15 a.m., the mail carrier is likely just beginning his shift, so choice A is incorrect. Mark James is more likely to be on his lunch at 12:30 p.m. than delivering mail to his last stop, so choice B is incorrect. *(See Chapter VIII, Section B.)*

11. **B** Building inspector Larry Franklin Horowitz's initials are *L. F. H. (See Chapter VIII, Section A2.)*

12. **A** Choice A contains a house, a paw print, two people, and the sun. Choice B is incorrect because it includes a star and an apartment building instead of the sun and a house. Choice C is incorrect because it includes a boat instead of a paw print. Choice D is incorrect because it includes a depiction of a planet instead of the sun. *(See Chapter VIII, Section A1.)*

13. **A** Carriers are responsible for picking up mail from residential mailboxes. *(See Chapter VIII, Section A2.)*

14. **B** Clerks are responsible for checking packages for mailing, such as determining the appropriate postage for these items. *(See Chapter VIII, Section A2.)*

15. **C** Pre-sorters are required to have a forklift license because people in this position use forklifts to load and unload postal trucks. *(See Chapter VIII, Section A2.)*

16. **B** To determine the mechanical advantage of a wheel-and-axle setup, divide the radius of the wheel by the radius of the axle: $400 \div 25 = 16$. *(See Chapter VIII, Section C.)*

17. **C** The elevator technician should reassure the woman that he knows what he's doing and will get her daughter out soon. By politely guaranteeing the woman that her daughter will be safe, the technician is avoiding angering or further upsetting the woman. *(See Chapter VIII, Section B2.)*

18. **B** Because Mr. Hoddle sees puddles and debris, including the tree, you can infer that a storm knocked down the tree. A car may have hit the tree, but because of the puddles and other debris, it's more likely that a storm passed through and caused the tree to fall. *(See Chapter VIII, Section B1.)*

19. **B** A journeyman electrician is responsible for the installation of electrical wiring in all types of buildings, including newly constructed homes. *(See Chapter VIII, Section A2.)*

20. **C** Since a lineman works on outdoor electrical lines, he or she would be sent to fix an outdoor electrical line after a storm. *(See Chapter VIII, Section A2.)*

21. **D** A residential electrician would be sent to a home to fix an electrical outlet that is not in working condition because he or she is responsible for working on indoor electrical lines in home settings. *(See Chapter VIII, Section A2.)*

22. **B** Gears with the same number of teeth have the same ratio. Even though gear B is smaller than gear A, each has 16 cogs, which means that both gear A and gear B will make the same number of revolutions per minute. *(See Chapter VIII, Section C.)*

23. **B** If gear A rotates counterclockwise, gear C will turn clockwise and gear B will turn counterclockwise. *(See Chapter VIII, Section C.)*

24. **D** The child in the foreground of this photograph is wearing shorts, a T-shirt, socks, and sneakers, but he is not wearing a hat. *(See Chapter VIII, Section A1.)*

25. **B** The sign hanging on the dunk tank reads class of 2009 phs. *(See Chapter VIII, Section A1.)*

26. **A** This photograph features one fire hydrant located to the left of the dunk tank. *(See Chapter VIII, Section A1.)*

27. **C** The memo is dated January 19, 2010. *(See Chapter VIII, Section A1.)*

28. **A** If an employee violates the safety regulations a second time, the punishment is termination. *(See Chapter VIII, Section A1.)*

29. **B** According to the memo, "no open-toe shoes or sandals are permitted," so an employee would not be permitted to wear flip-flops while working. *(See Chapter VIII, Section A1.)*

30. **C** You should knock on the door and check out the situation before you do anything else. The arguing and baby crying might not warrant police intervention, but you don't know unless you intervene. You should not ignore the situation, or jump the gun and call Child Protective Services or knock down the door until you know exactly what's going on inside the house. *(See Chapter VIII, Section B2.)*

31. **C** The most clear and accurate information the mail clerk can report is that Bethany Maloney's car was stolen from the parking lot of the post office at 1:30 p.m. The man who took the car is wearing a green sweatshirt and is carrying a red backpack. He was last seen making a left onto Main Street. This information includes the time of the incident, the location of the incident, who was involved, what the suspect looked like, and in which direction he was last seen traveling. Choices A, B, and D are incorrect because these reports are either inaccurate or don't contain enough useful information. *(See Chapter VIII, Section B1.)*

32. **A** After seeing the white lab coat with the smiling mouth patch, you can infer that the victim is a dentist. *(See Chapter VIII, Section B1.)*

33. **D** Since wheel A is twice the size of wheel B, it spins half as fast. If wheel A makes 90 revolutions per minute, then wheel B makes twice as many revolutions, so it makes 180 revolutions per minute. *(See Chapter VIII, Section C.)*

34. **C** A rotary saw is a power-operated saw with circular, removable blades used to cut through materials such as wood, plastic, or metal. An axe and chisel are hand tools used to cut through materials such as wood or stone; they do not have circular blades. A reciprocating saw is a power-operated saw with a short, straight blade. *(See Chapter VIII, Section C.)*

35. This personality question has no correct or incorrect answer. This type of question is designed to test your ability to work with others. *(See Chapter VIII, Section D.)*

36. This personality question has no correct or incorrect answer. This type of question is designed to test your ability to manage time. *(See Chapter VIII, Section D.)*

37. This personality question has no correct or incorrect answer. This type of question is designed to test your honesty. *(See Chapter VIII, Section D.)*

38. **A** Because your door is open and your television is missing, you can infer that someone broke into your home. *(See Chapter VIII, Section B1.)*

39. **A** The best course of action in this situation is to tell your co-worker that you're allergic to perfume and ask her not to wear it. If this doesn't work, then you should talk to your supervisor. You should not leave a threatening note or quit your job. *(See Chapter VIII, Section B2.)*

40. **A** The tool pictured is a cross wrench, which is used to change a flat tire on a car. Cutting pliers are used to cut through metal or wire. A clamp is used to hold objects together. A hammer is used to drive or remove nails. *(See Chapter VIII, Section C.)*

41. **A** You would have to apply 15 pounds of force to lift the box. To answer this question, use the information you know to complete the equation. The weight of the object is 75 pounds, so $w = 75$. The distance from the object to the fulcrum is 5 feet, so $d_1 = 5$. The distance from the person to the fulcrum is 25 feet, so $d_2 = 25$. First, multiply the weight of the object by the distance from the object to the fulcrum: $75 \cdot 5 = 375$. Then, divide each side by 25 to get 15:

$$w \cdot d_1 = f \cdot d_2$$
$$75 \cdot 5 = f \cdot 25$$
$$375 = 25f$$
$$15 = f$$

(See Chapter VIII, Section C.)

42. **A** Before draining the old oil, you should open the oil filler cap on the engine under the hood. This will allow air flow and enable the oil to drain quickly. *(See Chapter VIII, Section C.)*

43. This personality question has no correct or incorrect answer. This type of question is designed to test your ability to get along with others. *(See Chapter VIII, Section D.)*

44. This personality question has no correct or incorrect answer. This type of question is designed to test your honesty. *(See Chapter VIII, Section D.)*

45. This personality question has no correct or incorrect answer. This type of question is designed to test your ability to follow rules. *(See Chapter VIII, Section D.)*

46. **D** You should call 911 and wait with the man until help arrives. Because you don't know what is wrong with the man and he is unconscious, you should stay with him until emergency help arrives. You should not leave the man, ignore the situation, or go to a neighbor's house for help. *(See Chapter VIII, Section B2.)*

47. **C** Trevor should agree to finish pruning the tree and call to tell the people at the next appointment that he'll be late. Mr. Hanson clearly doesn't like the work that Trevor has done thus far, so Trevor must politely agree to finish the job. Because he has other people waiting for him, the most responsible action to take would be to call ahead and tell the next homeowner that he'll be a bit late. This ensures that neither Mr. Hanson nor the next homeowner will be upset. Trevor shouldn't offer to come back at the end of the day because it may be dark by then and he should not be operating saws and other tools in the dark. *(See Chapter VIII, Section B2.)*

48. **C** You can infer that the man started the fire and stayed to watch. He not only shows an interest in the growing flames but also appears to be excited about the firefighters' activities. The firefighters assume that whoever started the fire jumped into the snow bank alongside the building. Because the man's pants are wet, it may be safe to suspect that it's because he was knee-deep in snow. Although this may be true, you can't immediately act on this suspicion. Your first step should be to question the man, not immediately assume he is to blame. *(See Chapter VIII, Section B1.)*

49. **D** An electrician should wear rubber boots, a hard hat, and tight-fitting clothing to protect himself or herself when working with electrical currents. Electricians should not wear any jewelry such as gold watches, because gold and other metals conduct electricity. *(See Chapter VIII, Section C.)*

50. **B** One of the drawbacks of lithium batteries is that they cost more than alkaline batteries. But lithium batteries also last much longer than alkaline batteries do. *(See Chapter VIII, Section C.)*

II. Two-Month Cram Plan

	Verbal Ability	Mathematical Ability	Clerical Ability	Other Abilities
8 weeks before the test	**Study Time:** 2½ hours ❏ Take the **Diagnostic Test** and review the answer explanations. ❏ Based on your errors on the Diagnostic Test, identify difficult topics and their corresponding chapters. These are your targeted areas.			

7 weeks before the test	**Study Time:** 1 hour
	❏ Chapter V
	  ❏ Read sections A–D.
	  ❏ Do practice questions 1–5 in each section.
	  ❏ For targeted areas, do practice questions 1–7 in each section.
		Study Time: 1 hour
		❏ Chapter VI
		  ❏ Read sections A–B.
		  ❏ Do practice questions 1–5 in each section.
		  ❏ For targeted areas, do practice questions 1–7.
			Study Time: 1 hour
			❏ Chapter VII
			  ❏ Read sections A–B.
			  ❏ Do practice question 1–15 in Section A.
			  ❏ Do practice questions 1–5 in Section B.
			  ❏ If Section B is a targeted area, do practice questions 1–7.
				Study Time: 1 hour
				❏ Chapter VIII
				  ❏ Read sections A–B.
				  ❏ Do practice questions 1–5 in each section.
				  ❏ For targeted areas, do practice questions 1–7 in each section.

6 weeks before the test	**Study Time:** 1 hour
	❏ Chapter V
	  ❏ Review sections A–D.
	  ❏ Do practice questions 6–10 in each section.
		Study Time: 1 hour
		❏ Chapter VI
		  ❏ Review sections A–B.
		  ❏ Do practice questions 6–10 in each section.
			Study Time: 1 hour
			❏ Chapter VII
			  ❏ Review Section B.
			  ❏ Do practice questions 6–10 in Section B.
				Study Time: 1 hour
				❏ Chapter VIII
				  ❏ Review sections A–B.
				  ❏ Do practice questions 6–10 in each section.

5 weeks before the test	**Study Time:** 1 hour
	❏ Chapter V
	  ❏ Read sections E–F.
	  ❏ Do practice questions 1–5 in each section.
	  ❏ For targeted areas, do practice questions 1–7 in each section.
		Study Time: 1 hour
		❏ Chapter VI
		  ❏ Read sections C–D.
		  ❏ Do practice questions 1–5 in each section.
		  ❏ For targeted areas, do practice questions 1–7.
			Study Time: 1 hour
			❏ Chapter VII
			  ❏ Read sections C–D.
			  ❏ Do practice questions 1–5 in each section.
			  ❏ For targeted areas, do practice questions 1–7.
				Study Time: 1 hour
				❏ Chapter VIII
				  ❏ Read sections C–D.
				  ❏ Do practice questions 1–5 in each section.
				  ❏ For targeted areas, do practice questions 1–7 in each section.

continued

	Verbal Ability	Mathematical Ability	Clerical Ability	Other Abilities

4 weeks before the test	**Study Time:** 1 hour
	 ❑ Chapter V
	     ❑ Review sections E–F.
	     ❑ Do practice questions 6–10 in each section.
		Study Time: 1 hour
		 ❑ Chapter VI
		     ❑ Review sections C–D.
		     ❑ Do practice questions 6–10 in each section.
			Study Time: 1 hour
			 ❑ Chapter VII
			     ❑ Review sections C–D.
			     ❑ Do practice questions 6–10 in each section.
				Study Time: 1 hour
				 ❑ Chapter VIII
				     ❑ Review sections C–D.
				     ❑ Do practice questions 6–10 in each section.

3 weeks before the test	**Study Time:** 1 hour
	 ❑ Chapter V
	     ❑ Read sections G–H.
	     ❑ Do practice questions 1–5 in each section.
	     ❑ For targeted areas, do practice questions 1–7 in each section.
		Study Time: 1 hour
		 ❑ Chapter VI
		     ❑ Read sections E–F.
		     ❑ Do practice questions 1–5 in each section.
			Study Time: 1 hour
			 ❑ Chapter VII
			     ❑ Review sections A–D.
				Study Time: 1 hour
				 ❑ Chapter VIII
				     ❑ Review sections A–D.

2 weeks before the test	**Study Time:** 2½ hours ❑ Take the **Practice Test** and review the answer explanations. ❑ Based on your errors on the Practice Test, identify difficult topics and their corresponding chapters. These are your targeted areas.			
	Study Time: 1 hour ❑ Based on the Practice Test, review any sections in Chapter V that remain problematic. ❑ Redo any Verbal questions that you answered incorrectly on the Practice Test.	**Study Time:** 1 hour ❑ Based on the Practice Test, review any sections in Chapter VI that remain problematic. ❑ Redo three practice problems in each section of Chapter VI.	**Study Time:** 1 hour ❑ Based on the Practice Test, review any sections in Chapter VII that remain problematic. ❑ Redo any Clerical Ability problems that you answered incorrectly on the Practice Test.	**Study Time:** 1 hour ❑ Based on the Practice Test, review any sections in Chapter VIII that remain problematic. ❑ Review any Other Abilities questions that you answered incorrectly on the Practice Test.

7 days before the test	**Study Time:** 1 hour
	 ❑ Chapter V
	     ❑ Review sections G–H.
	     ❑ Do practice questions 6–10 in each section.
		Study Time: 1 hour
		 ❑ Chapter VI
		     ❑ Review sections E–F.
		     ❑ Do practice questions 6–10 in each section.
			Study Time: 30 minutes
			 ❑ Chapter VII
			     ❑ Review Section A.
				Study Time: 30 minutes
				 ❑ Chapter VIII
				     ❑ Review sections A–B.
				     ❑ Redo practice questions 1–3 in each section.

	Verbal Ability	Mathematical Ability	Clerical Ability	Other Abilities

6 days before the test	**Study Time:** 30 minutes
	❑ Chapter V
	   ❑ Review sections A–B.
	   ❑ Redo practice questions 6–10.
		Study Time: 30 minutes
		❑ Chapter VI
		   ❑ Review sections A–B.
		   ❑ Redo practice questions 1–3 in each section.
			Study Time: 30 minutes
			❑ Chapter VII
			   ❑ Review Section B.
			   ❑ Redo practice questions 8–10.
				Study Time: 30 minutes
				❑ Chapter VIII
				   ❑ Review sections C–D.
				   ❑ Redo practice questions 4–7 in each section.

5 days before the test	**Study Time:** 30 minutes
	❑ Chapter V
	   ❑ Review sections C–D.
	   ❑ Redo practice questions 1–5.
		Study Time: 30 minutes
		❑ Chapter VI
		   ❑ Review sections C–D.
		   ❑ Redo practice questions 4–7 in each section.
			Study Time: 30 minutes
			❑ Chapter VII
			   ❑ Review Section B.
			   ❑ Redo practice questions 5–7.
				Study Time: 30 minutes
				❑ Chapter VIII
				   ❑ Review sections A–B.
				   ❑ Redo practice questions 4–7 in each section.

4 days before the test	**Study Time:** 30 minutes
	❑ Chapter V
	   ❑ Review sections E–F.
	   ❑ Redo practice questions 6–10.
		Study Time: 30 minutes
		❑ Chapter VI
		   ❑ Review sections E–F.
		   ❑ Redo practice questions 8–10 in each section.
			Study Time: 30 minutes
			❑ Chapter VII
			   ❑ Review sections C–D.
			   ❑ Redo practice questions 1–5 in each section.
				Study Time: 30 minutes
				❑ Chapter VIII
				   ❑ Review sections C–D.
				   ❑ Redo practice questions 1–3 in each section.

3 days before the test	**Study Time:** 30 minutes
	❑ Chapter V
	   ❑ Review sections G–H.
	   ❑ Redo practice questions 1–5.
		Study Time: 30 minutes
		❑ Chapter VI
		   ❑ Review sections A–F.
			Study Time: 30 minutes
			❑ Chapter VII
			   ❑ Review Section B.
			   ❑ Redo practice questions 4–7.
				Study Time: 30 minutes
				❑ Chapter VIII
				   ❑ Review sections A–B.
				   ❑ Redo practice questions 8–10 in each section.

2 days before the test	**Study Time:** 30 minutes
	❑ Chapter V
	   ❑ Review sections C–D.
	   ❑ Redo practice questions 6–10.
		Study Time: 30 minutes
		❑ Chapter VI
		   ❑ Redo two practice problems in sections A–F.
			Study Time: 30 minutes
			❑ Chapter VII
			   ❑ Review sections C–D.
			   ❑ Redo practice questions 1–5 in each section.
				Study Time: 30 minutes
				❑ Chapter VIII
				   ❑ Review sections C–D.
				   ❑ Redo practice questions 8–10 in each section.

1 day before the test	❑ Take a break! You're well prepared for the test. ❑ Get a good night's rest.			

Morning of the test	**Reminders:**
	❑ Eat a healthy breakfast.
	❑ Take with you to the testing facility:
	   ❑ Two forms of identification, including photo ID
	   ❑ Several no. 2 pencils
	   ❑ Any documentation that is required by the testing facility
	❑ Try to arrive at the testing facility early to give yourself time to prepare for the test.
	❑ Stay calm during the test and take deep breaths if you feel nervous.
	❑ Have confidence in your ability to do well on the test.			

III. One-Month Cram Plan

	Verbal Ability	Mathematical Ability	Clerical Ability	Other Abilities
4 weeks before the test	**Study Time:** 2½ hours ❏ Take the **Diagnostic Test** and review the answer explanations. ❏ Based on your errors on the Diagnostic Test, identify difficult topics and their corresponding chapters. These are your targeted areas.			

	Study Time: 2 hours
	❏ Chapter V
	  ❏ Read sections A–D.
	  ❏ Do practice questions 1–5 in each section.
	  ❏ For targeted areas, do practice questions 1–7 in each section.
		Study Time: 2 hours
		❏ Chapter VI
		  ❏ Read sections A–B.
		  ❏ Do practice questions 1–5 in each section.
		  ❏ For targeted areas, do practice questions 1–7 in each section.
			Study Time: 2 hours
			❏ Chapter VII
			  ❏ Read Section A.
			  ❏ Do practice questions 1–15.
			  ❏ Review any practice questions that you answered incorrectly.
				Study Time: 2 hours
				❏ Chapter VIII
				  ❏ Read sections A–B.
				  ❏ Do practice questions 1–5 in each section.
				  ❏ For targeted areas, do practice questions 1–6.

3 weeks before the test	**Study Time:** 3 hours
	❏ Chapter V
	  ❏ Review sections A–D.
	  ❏ Do practice questions 6–10 in each section.
	  ❏ Read sections E–H.
	  ❏ Do practice questions 1–5 in each section.
	  ❏ For targeted areas, do practice questions 1–7 in each section.
		Study Time: 2 hours
		❏ Chapter VI
		  ❏ Read sections C–D.
		  ❏ Do practice questions 1–5 in each section.
		  ❏ For targeted areas, do practice questions 1–7 in each section.
			Study Time: 2 hours
			❏ Chapter VII
			  ❏ Read sections B–D.
			  ❏ Do practice questions 1–5 in each section.
			  ❏ For targeted areas, do practice questions 1–7 in each section.
				Study Time: 2 hours
				❏ Chapter VIII
				  ❏ Read sections C–D.
				  ❏ Do practice questions 1–5 in each section.
				  ❏ For targeted areas, do practice questions 1–6.

2 weeks before the test	**Study Time:** 2 hours
	❏ Chapter V
	  ❏ Review sections E–H.
	  ❏ Do practice questions 6–10 in each section.
		Study Time: 2 hours
		❏ Chapter VI
		  ❏ Read sections E–F.
		  ❏ Do practice questions 1–5 in each section.
		  ❏ For targeted areas, do practice questions 1–7 in each section.
			Study Time: 2 hours
			❏ Chapter VII
			  ❏ Review sections B–D.
			  ❏ Complete the remaining practice questions in each section.
				Study Time: 2 hours
				❏ Chapter VIII
				  ❏ Review sections A–D.
				  ❏ Complete the remaining practice questions in each section.

	Verbal Ability	Mathematical Ability	Clerical Ability	Other Abilities
7 days before the test	**Study Time:** 2½ hours ❑ Take the **Practice Test** and review the answer explanations. ❑ Based on your errors on the Practice Test, identify difficult topics and their corresponding chapters. These are your targeted areas.			
6 days before the test	**Study Time:** 1 hour ❑ Based on the Practice Test, review any sections in Chapter V that remain problematic. ❑ Redo any Verbal questions that you answered incorrectly on the Practice Test.	**Study Time:** 1 hour ❑ Based on the Practice Test, review any sections in Chapter VI that remain problematic. ❑ Redo three practice problems in each section of Chapter VI.	**Study Time:** 1 hour ❑ Based on the Practice Test, review any sections in Chapter VII that remain problematic. ❑ Redo any Clerical Ability problems that you answered incorrectly on the Practice Test.	**Study Time:** 1 hour ❑ Based on the Practice Test, review any sections in Chapter VIII that remain problematic. ❑ Review any Other Abilities questions that you answered incorrectly on the Practice Test.

5 days before the test	**Study Time:** 30 minutes
	 ❑ Chapter V
	   ❑ Read sections A–B.
	   ❑ Redo practice questions 8–10 in each section.
		Study Time: 1 hour
		 ❑ Chapter VI
		   ❑ Review sections A–B.
		   ❑ Do practice questions 6–10 in each section.
			Study Time: 30 minutes
			 ❑ Chapter VII
			   ❑ Review Section A.
			   ❑ Redo practice questions 7–15.
				Study Time: 30 minutes
				 ❑ Chapter VIII
				   ❑ Review Section A.
				   ❑ Redo practice questions 1–3.

4 days before the test	**Study Time:** 30 minutes
	 ❑ Chapter V
	   ❑ Read sections C–D.
	   ❑ Redo practice questions 1–3 in each section.
		Study Time: 1 hour
		 ❑ Chapter VI
		   ❑ Review sections C–D.
		   ❑ Do practice questions 6–10 in each section.
			Study Time: 30 minutes
			 ❑ Chapter VII
			   ❑ Review Section B.
			   ❑ Redo practice questions 1–3.
				Study Time: 30 minutes
				 ❑ Chapter VIII
				   ❑ Review Section B.
				   ❑ Redo practice questions 4–6.

3 days before the test	**Study Time:** 30 minutes
	 ❑ Chapter V
	   ❑ Read sections E–F.
	   ❑ Redo practice questions 4–7 in each section.
		Study Time: 1 hour
		 ❑ Chapter VI
		   ❑ Review sections E–F.
		   ❑ Do practice questions 6–10 in each section.
			Study Time: 30 minutes
			 ❑ Chapter VII
			   ❑ Review Section C.
			   ❑ Redo practice questions 9–12.
				Study Time: 30 minutes
				 ❑ Chapter VIII
				   ❑ Review Section C.
				   ❑ Redo practice questions 7–9.

2 days before the test	**Study Time:** 30 minutes
	 ❑ Chapter V
	   ❑ Read sections G–H.
	   ❑ Redo practice questions 8–10 in each section.
		Study Time: 30 minutes
		 ❑ Chapter VI
		   ❑ Review sections A–F.
		   ❑ Redo one practice question in each section.
			Study Time: 30 minutes
			 ❑ Chapter VII
			   ❑ Review Section D.
			   ❑ Redo practice questions 4–7.
				Study Time: 30 minutes
				 ❑ Chapter VIII
				   ❑ Review Section D.
				   ❑ Redo practice questions 8–10.

	Verbal Ability	Mathematical Ability	Clerical Ability	Other Abilities
1 day before the test	❏ Take a break! You're well prepared for the test. ❏ Get a good night's rest.			

Morning of the test	**Reminders:**
	 ❏ Eat a healthy breakfast.
	 ❏ Take with you to the testing facility:
	      ❏ Two forms of identification, including photo ID
	      ❏ Several no. 2 pencils
	      ❏ Any documentation that is required by the testing facility
	 ❏ Try to arrive at the testing facility early to give yourself time to prepare for the test.
	 ❏ Stay calm during the test and take deep breaths if you feel nervous.
	 ❏ Have confidence in your ability to do well on the test.			

IV. One-Week Cram Plan

	Verbal Ability	Mathematical Ability	Clerical Ability	Other Abilities
7 days before the test	**Study Time:** 2½ hours ❏ Take the **Diagnostic Test** and review the answer explanations. ❏ Based on your errors on the Diagnostic Test, identify difficult topics and their corresponding chapters. These are your targeted areas.			

6 days before the test	**Study Time:** 1 hour
	❏ Chapter V
	   ❏ Read sections A–B.
	   ❏ Do practice questions 1–5 in each section.
	   ❏ For targeted areas, do practice questions 1–7.
		Study Time: 1 hour
		❏ Chapter VI
		   ❏ Read sections A–B.
		   ❏ Do practice questions 4–8 in Section A.
		   ❏ If Section A is a targeted area, do practice questions 3–9.
		   ❏ Do practice questions 1–5 in Section B.
		   ❏ If Section B is a targeted area, do practice questions 1–7.
			Study Time: 1 hour
			❏ Chapter VII
			   ❏ Read Section A.
			   ❏ Do practice questions 1–15.
				Study Time: 1 hour
				❏ Chapter VIII
				   ❏ Read Section A.
				   ❏ Do practice questions 1–10.

5 days before the test	**Study Time:** 1 hour
	❏ Chapter V
	   ❏ Read sections C–D.
	   ❏ Do practice questions 1–10 in each section.
		Study Time: 1 hour
		❏ Chapter VI
		   ❏ Read sections C–D.
		   ❏ Do practice questions 1–5 in both sections.
		   ❏ For targeted areas, do practice questions 1–7.
			Study Time: 1 hour
			❏ Chapter VII
			   ❏ Read sections B and D.
			   ❏ Do practice questions 1–5 in each section.
			   ❏ For targeted areas, do practice questions 1–7.
				Study Time: 1 hour
				❏ Chapter VIII
				   ❏ Read sections B–C.
				   ❏ Do practice questions 1–5 in each section.
				   ❏ For targeted areas, do practice questions 1–7.

4 days before the test	**Study Time:** 1 hour
	❏ Chapter V
	   ❏ Read sections F and H.
	   ❏ Do practice questions 1–5 in both sections.
	   ❏ For targeted areas, do practice questions 1–7.
		Study Time: 1 hour
		❏ Chapter VI
		   ❏ Read sections E–F.
		   ❏ Do practice questions 1–5 in both sections.
		   ❏ For targeted areas, do practice questions 1–7.
			Study Time: 1 hour
			❏ Chapter VII
			   ❏ Read Section C.
			   ❏ Do practice questions 1–5.
			   ❏ If Section C is a targeted area, do practice questions 1–7.
				Study Time: 30 minutes
				❏ Chapter VIII
				   ❏ Read Section D.
				   ❏ Do practice questions 1–10.

	Verbal Ability	Mathematical Ability	Clerical Ability	Other Abilities
3 days before the test	**Study Time:** 2½ hours ❏ Take the **Practice Test** and review the answer explanations. ❏ Based on your errors on the Practice Test, identify difficult topics and their corresponding chapters. These are your targeted areas.			

2 days before the test	**Study Time:** 1 hour
	 ❏ Chapter V
	    ❏ Read sections E and G.
	    ❏ Do practice questions 1–5 in both sections.
	    ❏ For targeted areas, do practice questions 1–7.
	    ❏ Note any practice questions that you answered incorrectly.
		Study Time: 1 hour
		 ❏ Chapter VI
		    ❏ Review sections A–C.
		    ❏ Do practice questions 1–2 and 9–10 in Section A.
		    ❏ Do practice questions 6–10 in sections B–C.
		    ❏ Redo any practice questions that you answered incorrectly in sections A–C.
			Study Time: 30 minutes
			 ❏ Chapter VII
			    ❏ Review sections A–B.
			    ❏ Do practice questions 6–10 in Section B.
			    ❏ Redo any practice questions that you answered incorrectly in sections A–B.
				Study Time: 30 minutes
				 ❏ Chapter VIII
				    ❏ Review sections A–B.
				    ❏ Redo any practice questions that you answered incorrectly in Section A.
				    ❏ Do practice questions 6–10 in Section B.

1 day before the test	**Study Time:** 1 hour
	 ❏ Chapter V
	    ❏ Briefly review sections A–H.
	    ❏ Redo any practice questions that you answered incorrectly in sections A–H.
	    ❏ Redo any questions that you answered incorrectly on the Practice Test.
		Study Time: 1 hour
		 ❏ Chapter VI
		    ❏ Briefly review sections D–F.
		    ❏ Do practice questions 7–10 in each section.
		    ❏ Redo any practice questions that you answered incorrectly in sections D–F.
			Study Time: 30 Minutes
			 ❏ Chapter VII
			    ❏ Briefly review sections C–D.
			    ❏ Redo any practice questions that you answered incorrectly in sections C–D.
			    ❏ Redo any questions that you answered incorrectly on the Practice Test.
				Study Time: 30 minutes
				 ❏ Chapter VIII
				    ❏ Briefly review sections C–D.
				    ❏ Do practice questions 6–10 in Section C.
				    ❏ Redo any practice problems that you answered incorrectly in Section C.
				    ❏ Redo any questions that you answered incorrectly on the Practice Test.

Morning of the test	**Reminders:**
	 ❏ Eat a healthy breakfast.
	 ❏ Take with you to the testing facility:
	    ❏ Two forms of identification, including photo ID
	    ❏ Several no. 2 pencils
	    ❏ Any documentation that is required by the testing facility
	 ❏ Try to arrive at the testing facility early to give yourself time to prepare for the test.
	 ❏ Stay calm during the test and take deep breaths if you feel nervous.
	 ❏ Have confidence in your ability to do well on the test.			

V. Verbal Ability

Your ability to read and understand written information significantly affects your chances of securing a civil service job. Many civil service positions, especially those in clerical settings, involve tasks such as proofreading, organizing files, following written instructions, and correcting written text. The employees responsible for these tasks must have strong verbal skills. For this reason, an entire part of the civil service exam is devoted to assessing your verbal abilities.

Questions in this section of the civil service exam are specifically designed to test your ability to read and understand the English language, follow the basic rules of grammar, demonstrate adequate writing skills, and more.

Though the exact components of the Verbal Ability test may vary from exam to exam, most civil service exams will include the following:

- Vocabulary
- Reading comprehension
- Writing
- English grammar and usage
- Spelling
- Analogies
- Synonyms
- Effective expression

As with other types of questions on the civil service exam, practice is the key to success. Use the practice exercises in this chapter to familiarize yourself with the types of questions you'll likely encounter on the Verbal Ability test. Doing so will help you sharpen your skills and perform better on test day.

A. Vocabulary

Most civil service jobs require employees to read letters, memos, and other documents. To correctly comprehend these documents, civil service employees must have strong vocabulary skills.

The vocabulary section of the civil service exam is designed to test your knowledge of word meanings and your ability to decipher the meaning of a word you may not recognize. In each question, you'll be given a word and four possible definitions. You must choose the correct definition of the given word.

EXAMPLE:

What is the meaning of *submerge?*

A. To sink
B. To join
C. To float
D. To divide

In this question, you're asked to determine the meaning of the word *submerge.* If you're familiar with this word, you should easily be able to determine that the correct meaning is choice A, to sink. If you don't recognize this word (or others on the exam), you may be able to determine the correct meaning using some of the following helpful techniques:

- **Recall a sentence in which you've heard or seen the word used.** Sometimes remembering a sentence that includes the word you're asked to define can help you to figure out its meaning. Thinking about how a word would fit into sentence can provide context to help you to determine its meaning.

- **Ask yourself if the word is positive or negative.** Some words have a naturally positive or negative sense. For example, words like *brash, callous,* and *seethe* all sound negative. On the other hand, words like *mellow, genteel,* and *laud* all sound positive. Thinking about how a word sounds can help you determine its meaning.

- **Pay attention to roots, prefixes, and suffixes.** Many of the more challenging words on the civil service exam contain prefixes or suffixes that can provide hints to their meanings. The word *submerge* in the example question contains the prefix *sub–*. Knowing that *sub–* means under or below, you can correctly guess that *submerge* means to go under something or sink. Many English words also contain roots based on other languages, especially Spanish, French, and Italian. If you're familiar with a word's root, you may be able to more easily determine its meaning.

As you prepare for the vocabulary section of the Verbal Ability test, it may be helpful to practice figuring out the meanings of unfamiliar words. Try finding a few words you don't recognize and work on determining their meanings. When you're finished, look them up in the dictionary and find out if you were right. Doing this quick exercise once a day helps you learn how to decipher the meaning of new words and builds your vocabulary.

You also can study for these questions and learn word meanings using flash cards, memory devices, or other similar methods. *Remember:* The best thing you can do to ensure that you're ready for the exam is to practice, practice, practice!

Practice

Directions (1–10): Choose the answer that best describes the meaning of the italicized word.

---

1. What is the meaning of *erroneous?*

   A. Smelly
   B. Vulgar
   C. Common
   D. Incorrect

2. What is the meaning of *uncouth?*

   A. Crude
   B. Random
   C. Strange
   D. Playful

3. What is the meaning of *barter?*

   A. To argue
   B. To serve
   C. To seize
   D. To trade

4. What is the meaning of *vivacious?*

   A. Lively
   B. Modest
   C. Confused
   D. Dangerous

5. What is the meaning of *regale?*

   A. To award
   B. To honor
   C. To amuse
   D. To comfort

6. What is the meaning of *capitulate?*

   A. To give in
   B. To put off
   C. To take hold
   D. To get started

7. What is the meaning of *luster?*

   A. Scent
   B. Shine
   C. Desire
   D. Bravery

8. What is the meaning of *decrepit?*

   A. Honest
   B. Feeble
   C. Indifferent
   D. Respectable

9. What is the meaning of *abhorrent?*

    A.   Frightening
    B.   Imaginary
    C.   Agreeable
    D.   Repulsive

10. What is the meaning of *procure?*

    A.   To solve
    B.   To repair
    C.   To invent
    D.   To acquire

Answers

1. **D** The word *erroneous* means "incorrect."

2. **A** The word *uncouth* means "crude."

3. **D** The word *barter* means "to trade."

4. **A** The word *vivacious* means "lively."

5. **C** The word *regale* means "to amuse."

6. **A** The word *capitulate* means "to give in."

7. **B** The word *luster* means "shine."

8. **B** The word *decrepit* means "feeble."

9. **D** The word *abhorrent* means "repulsive."

10. **D** The word *procure* means "to acquire."

B. Reading Comprehension

The reading comprehension section of the Verbal Ability test is designed to assess your ability to answer questions based on information presented in a short paragraph. Each item in this section consists of a brief paragraph followed by a single question about that paragraph.

There are two main types of reading comprehension questions: main idea questions and detail questions. Each type of question is designed to test your understanding of the information in the paragraph in a unique way.

- **Main idea questions:** Main idea questions test your overall understanding of the passage. Simply put, these questions ask you to identify the main idea of the paragraph. Most main idea questions on the civil service exam are very straightforward and may simply ask, "What is the main idea of this paragraph?" Though the actual question stem may be worded differently from test to test, main idea questions always ask for the same information: the main idea of the paragraph.

    When answering main idea questions, read the paragraph carefully and select the answer that most accurately reflects the primary idea expressed by the paragraph.

- **Detail questions:** Detail questions ask you to pick out specific pieces of information from within the paragraph. They may ask you to identify a fact or other detail found in the paragraph. These questions always are based on information that is included in the paragraph, so you'll never have to rely on any outside information or knowledge to answer correctly.

  When answering detail questions, read the question stem carefully and be sure you understand what information you must find in the paragraph. It also may be helpful to try reading the question stem first and then searching the paragraph for the information you need.

When you encounter reading comprehension questions on the Verbal Ability portion of the civil service exam, it may be helpful to remember the following tips:

- **Read the question stem carefully.** This is the most important part of answering a reading comprehension question. You must be sure that you understand what the question is asking. Does it ask you to determine the main idea of the paragraph or to find a specific detail in the paragraph? If you don't fully understand the question, you may not be likely to choose the correct answer.

- **Scan the paragraph.** Once you know what the question is asking, quickly scan through the paragraph to find the information you need. If you know what you're looking for, you may not need to spend time reading or rereading the whole paragraph. This is especially important for detail questions.

- **Predict the correct answer.** You don't want to spend too much time trying to come up with an exact answer. Instead, focus on thinking about the basic premise of what you need to know. This will help guide you to the correct answer choice.

- **Pick the most accurate answer choice.** Quickly look over the choices and select the one that best reflects what you believe to be the correct answer. If you're still not sure which choice is correct, try eliminating the incorrect choices. You can disregard choices that are irrelevant or contradictory or that simply don't make sense. Once you eliminate the incorrect choices, you'll be left with the correct answer choice.

Practice

Directions (1–10): Choose the correct answer based on the corresponding paragraph.

Question 1 refers to the following paragraph.

The hectic pace of our modern lives has had a distinctly negative impact on our eating habits. As our days have grown busier and faster, our eating habits have grown noticeably worse. Faced with increasingly tight schedules, we have come to rely more and more on fast food and other quick meals that, although they may be convenient, are usually low on health benefits. Sometimes we even resort to skipping meals altogether. This kind of behavior can only be harmful, so we should make more of an effort to eat properly and stay healthy.

1. What is the main idea of this paragraph?

   A. Fast food is unhealthy and should be avoided.
   B. The pace of our lives has negatively affected our eating habits.
   C. We should focus more attention on healthy living and good nutrition.
   D. Eating properly can better prepare us for tackling our busy daily schedules.

Question 2 refers to the following paragraph.

The 1960 presidential election proved that personal appearance plays an important role in a candidate's chances of success. In the early stages of the election, which pitted John F. Kennedy against Richard Nixon, many voters found themselves leaning in favor of Nixon. Nixon's performance in radio debates won him many supporters, and it seemed as though he would be victorious in November. When Nixon and Kennedy took part in the first televised debate, however, viewers could see Nixon was sweaty and uncomfortable. Nixon's visible behavior changed many people's impressions of him and helped Kennedy win the election.

2. Nixon's loss in the 1960 election was influenced by

    A. Kennedy's strong speaking ability
    B. Nixon's conservative political viewpoints
    C. Kennedy's overwhelming popularity
    D. Nixon's questionable personal appearance

Question 3 refers to the following paragraph.

Many of today's movies have far less substance than those of the past. While most movies were once built on strong plots, engaging characters, and innovative filmmaking, many modern films are composed simply of flashy special effects, uninspiring celebrity actors, and simplistic or recycled plots. Filmmakers today need to get back to basics and focus on the fundamental elements of a good movie.

3. The paragraph best supports which of the following statements?

    A. Older movies are of higher quality than more recent ones.
    B. Well-executed special effects can only improve a movie.
    C. Today's actors are less talented than those of the past.
    D. The bigger its budget, the better a movie will be.

Question 4 refers to the following paragraph.

Over the years, the Super Bowl broadcast has become the most coveted advertising event of the year. Because this event has a larger viewership than any other single television program, companies from around the world vie for a Super Bowl advertising spot every year. Even as the cost for such a spot has risen into the millions, advertisers are still eager to put their products in the spotlight during this national event.

4. Advertisers are willing to pay for expensive Super Bowl ad time because

    A. They are offered incentives from the networks.
    B. The audience for this game is incredibly large.
    C. Football fans generate more sales than others.
    D. The price is affordable for major corporations.

Question 5 refers to the following paragraph.

Recent studies have shown that the repeated blows endured by boxers often have serious consequences that can affect the long-term quality of their lives. These studies have indicated that the large number of heavy blows most boxers take directly to the head can lead to multiple concussions and other brain injuries. These injuries, which accumulate over time, can lead to permanent brain damage or various mental conditions that may result in serious impairment. Boxing officials should be mindful of this situation and institute more effective safety measures.

5. What is the main idea of this paragraph?

   A. Boxers should fight more defensively in the ring.
   B. Boxing can have serious, long-term health effects.
   C. Boxing has become too dangerous and should be banned.
   D. Boxers should be better compensated for the risks they take.

Question 6 refers to the following paragraph.

Motorists today are driving more aggressively than ever before. Pressed for time because of our busy schedules, we often seem to be in a constant rush to get from one place to another. We exceed speed limits daily, ignore many of the simple rules of the road for the sake of saving time, and become instantly enraged at even the slightest amount of traffic congestion. Too often, we disregard our safety and the safety of others. We need to learn to be more relaxed behind the wheel and drive more carefully.

6. The paragraph best supports which of the following statements?

   A. Aggressive driving has become a serious modern problem.
   B. Current speed limits on many roads are too high for safety.
   C. The authorities should enforce traffic laws more carefully.
   D. High traffic volume leads to an increase in car accidents.

Question 7 refers to the following paragraph.

The cost of tickets to major-league sporting events is becoming much too great. Over the last 20 years, ticket prices for baseball, football, basketball, and hockey games have risen dramatically. Astronomical player salaries are mostly to blame, but overly extravagant arenas and stadiums, as well as staffing costs and corporate greed, also have served to fuel the increase in ticket prices. If measures to lower prices aren't taken soon, sports teams will likely see thinner and less enthusiastic crowds.

7. The rise in ticket prices is primarily due to

   A. Support-staff costs
   B. Severe corporate greed
   C. Excessive player salaries
   D. Extravagant playing facilities

Question 8 refers to the following paragraph.

A child's behavior is influenced by many sources, including peers, media, and adult acquaintances. No source is more important, however, than a child's parents. Children spend more time and form deeper bonds with their parents than with any other figures in their early lives. As a result, a child will most likely emulate the behavior demonstrated by his or her parents. For this reason, it is vitally important for parents to always display proper behavior in front of their children and set a good example.

8. The passage best supports which of the following statements?

    A. Parents should enforce strict rules of behavior.
    B. Children are directly influenced by parental behaviors.
    C. Parental influence on a child's behavior wanes with age.
    D. Children learn most social behaviors from their peers.

Question 9 refers to the following paragraph.

Over time, we have made great advances in the field of medicine. We have found cures for countless diseases and ailments and even developed effective means to prevent many illnesses. Sometimes, though, medical advances can have unexpected results. Antibiotics, for example, have great health benefits, but they can increase our vulnerability to sickness if we use them improperly. In some cases, developing an immunization for a certain type of disease can cause the formation of a more serious form of the disease. The point is, although we should always encourage medical advancements, we should do so cautiously.

9. The passage best supports which of the following statements?

    A. Some diseases would be better left untreated.
    B. Medicine is often a very complicated science.
    C. Some medical advances have negative effects.
    D. Medications should be tested more thoroughly.

Question 10 refers to the following paragraph.

In 1492, Christopher Columbus embarked on his famous voyage that led to the discovery of the New World across the Atlantic Ocean. Believing that he would find a water route to Asia if he sailed west from Europe, Columbus persuaded King Ferdinand and Queen Isabella of Spain to finance his expedition. He took three ships—the *Nina,* the *Pinta,* and the *Santa Maria*—and traveled across the ocean, landing on an island in the Caribbean. His discovery introduced Europeans to the Americas and would forever change the world.

10. For which country did Columbus make his voyage?

    A. Italy
    B. Spain
    C. England
    D. Portugal

Answers

1. **B** The main idea of the paragraph is that the pace of our lives has negatively affected our eating habits.

2. **D** Nixon's loss in the 1960 election was influenced by his questionable personal appearance.

3. **A** The paragraph best supports the statement that older movies are of higher quality than more recent ones.

4. **B** Advertisers are willing to pay for expensive Super Bowl ad time because the audience for this game is incredibly large.

5. **B** The main idea of this paragraph is that boxing can have serious, long-term health effects.

6. **A** The paragraph best supports the statement that aggressive driving has become a serious modern problem.

7. **C** The rise in ticket prices is primarily due to excessive player salaries.

8. **B** The passage best supports the statement that children are directly influenced by parental behaviors.

9. **C** The passage best supports the statement that some medical advances have negative effects.

10. **B** Columbus made his voyage for Spain.

C. Writing

Writing is an important part of every job. Even if you think that your job might not involve much writing, you need to know how to use the written word to communicate effectively with co-workers, supervisors, and clients. Carefully worded e-mails and reports are essential in any office.

A number of questions test your writing abilities on the civil service exam. Although every test differs from state to state and municipality to municipality, there are a few types of questions that you should review as you prepare for the test.

For **scrambled paragraph** questions, you'll be asked to choose the best order of the sentences in a paragraph. Each question begins with a topic sentence, which is followed by four other sentences in no particular order. Based on the topic sentence and the logical sequence of ideas, you'll need to decide how the other four sentences should be arranged.

> **Tip:** Look for transitional words such as *first, next,* and *finally* to help you determine the order of the sentences in scrambled paragraph questions. Other transitional words and phrases, such as *however, for example,* and *as a result,* also may help you identify the correct order of sentences.

Try the following example question before moving on to the next section. Choose the correct sentence order for the paragraph.

EXAMPLE:

> For years, people have dismissed television as a mindless form of entertainment.
>
> 1. Television has provided information on wars, rebellions, and triumphs of the human spirit.
> 2. These critics, however, forget all the momentous events that television has brought to millions of viewers.
> 3. Television has allowed us to soar to the moon and travel across the globe.
> 4. Still, reality shows and sensationalized news stories overshadow all the good that television has done.
>
>   **A.** 2, 4, 1, 3
>   **B.** 1, 4, 3, 2
>   **C.** 2, 3, 1, 4
>   **D.** 1, 3, 4, 2

Choice C is correct. The correct order of the paragraph is 2, 3, 1, 4: These critics, however, forget all the momentous events that television has brought to millions of viewers. Television has allowed us to soar to the moon and travel across the globe. Television has provided information on wars, rebellions, and triumphs of the human spirit. Still, reality shows and sensationalized news stories overshadow all the good that television has done.

Sentence completion questions also test your writing skills. For these types of questions, you'll be asked to choose the best word or phrase to fill in the blank. If the question includes more than one blank, you'll need to make sure that both words in the answer choice fit the context of the sentence.

Review the following examples of sentence completion questions.

EXAMPLES:

> 1. _____ most employees don't have to go to work on Friday, essential personnel should report to the office.
>
>   **A.** Because
>   **B.** Although
>   **C.** Therefore
>   **D.** Since

Choice B is correct. The word *Although* should be used to show the contrast between the two clauses.

> 2. Before the snow storm started, public works _____ salted the roads.
>
>   **A.** employees
>   **B.** helpers
>   **C.** candidates
>   **D.** managers

Choice A is correct. The word *employees* fits best in the context of the sentence.

You also may encounter questions that involve **identifying errors** within a paragraph. These questions may ask you to find errors in grammar, sentence structure, and word choice. It's important for you to review various grammar rules, discussed later in this chapter, before you answer these questions.

Each question refers to a numbered and underlined portion of the paragraph. You need to select the word or phrase that would correct the error. If you find no error, you should select choice A, NO CHANGE.

The following is an example of this type of question.

EXAMPLES:

On Monday night, the parks and recreation committee proposed a number of projects for the next calendar year. Ms. Sullivan, deputy director of parks and recreation, discussed these changes with town council members and citizens. Sullivan explained that a number of area parks <u>are in need of repair</u>. When several

1
council members <u>voice</u> their concerns, Sullivan provided a detailed report explaining how the parks and rec-

2
reation committee would raise the money for the repairs.

---

1. **A.**   NO CHANGE
    B.   needing repairs
    C.   are needed repair
    D.   are in needs of repair

Choice A is correct. There is no need to change the underlined portion of the sentence.

---

2. **A.**   NO CHANGE
    B.   voicing
    C.   voices
    D.   voiced

Choice D is correct. The entire paragraph is written in the past tense. Therefore, you should change the word *voice* to *voiced.*

Now that you understand the types of writing questions you may encounter on the civil service exam, try this practice exercise. Remember to review the answer explanations to help you identify any areas that need additional practice.

Practice

Directions (1–2): Choose the correct sentence order for the following paragraphs.

1. The new coding procedures involve a series of steps that employees must follow to ensure that all reports are filed correctly.

   1. Next, the employee should locate the name of the document's creator.
   2. Finally, the report can be color-coded and filed.
   3. After that, the date the report was created should be recorded.
   4. First, the employee should identify the type of report that needs to be filed.

   A. 4, 1, 3, 2
   B. 2, 1, 3, 4
   C. 4, 3, 2, 1
   D. 2, 4, 3, 1

2. Although most people don't realize it, the right to vote is not explicitly guaranteed by the U.S. Constitution.

   1. While this shocks some people, many scholars argue that the right to vote is implied in the Constitution.
   2. These amendments guaranteed that states cannot prevent citizens from voting based on their race, gender, or age.
   3. However, nowhere in the Constitution do the Founding Fathers provide citizens with the legal right to vote.
   4. This implication allowed for the passage of the 15th, 19th, and 26th amendments.

   A. 1, 3, 2, 4
   B. 2, 1, 4, 3
   C. 1, 4, 2, 3
   D. 4, 3, 1, 2

Directions (3–7): Choose the word that best completes each sentence.

3. The director of the public works committee was _____ Public Official of the Year.

   A. given
   B. named
   C. awarded
   D. prized

4. Courthouse officials _____ a notice for typists and clerical workers in last Sunday's newspaper.

   A. created
   B. drew
   C. wrote
   D. posted

5. Civil service candidates must _____ adequate verbal, mathematical, and clerical skills to pass the test.

   A. study
   B. encourage
   C. demonstrate
   D. form

6. The post office will be closed on Friday, _____ it will have extended hours on Thursday evening.

   A. still
   B. but
   C. while
   D. and

7. _____ it was the driver's first traffic violation, the officer let her go with a warning.

   A. Since
   B. While
   C. Although
   D. However

Directions (8–10): Choose the best revision for each underlined portion of the paragraph. If no change is required, select choice A.

All citizens who are remodeling or adding to any preexisting structures must contact the building inspector for permits before <u>any work completes</u>. Failure to do so will result in <u>an initial fine</u> of $200. Additional fines
  8   9
will be incurred for every day that the homeowner goes without obtaining a permit. Projects that <u>required</u>
                                                                                                        10
homeowners to file permits with the building inspector include electrical and plumbing work, removal of walls or windows, resurfacing of a driveway or sidewalk, and the addition of any new structure on the home-owner's property.

8. **A.** NO CHANGE
   B. completing any work
   C. any completed work
   D. having any completed work

9. **A.** NO CHANGE
   B. a initial fine
   C. an initial change
   D. a first fine

10. **A.** NO CHANGE
    B. require
    C. requires
    D. requiring

Answers

1. **A** The correct sentence order is 4, 1, 3, 2: First, the employee should identify the type of report that needs to be filed. Next, the employee should locate the name of the document's creator. After that, the date the report was created should be recorded. Finally, the report can be color coded and filed.

2. **C** The correct sentence order is 1, 4, 2, 3: While this shocks some people, many scholars argue that the right to vote is implied in the Constitution. This implication allowed for the passage of the 15th, 19th, and 26th amendments. These amendments guaranteed that states cannot prevent citizens from voting based on their race, gender, or age. However, nowhere in the Constitution do the Founding Fathers provide citizens with the legal right to vote.

3. **B** The word *named* best fits the context of the sentence.

4. **D** The correct word to complete this sentence is *posted.*

5. **C** The word *demonstrate* best fits the context of the sentence.

6. **B** The correct word to complete this sentence is *but.*

7. **A** The word *Since* best fits the context of the sentence.

8. **B** The correct usage here would be *completing work.* This paragraph is in the present tense, so the answer choice you select also should be in the present tense.

9. **A** There is no need to change the original portion of the sentence. The words *an initial fine* are grammatically correct.

10. **B** Because this paragraph is in the present tense, the word *required* should be changed to *require* to fix the error in tense.

D. English Grammar and Usage

Throughout much of the Verbal Ability portion of the civil service exam, you'll need to exhibit a strong understanding of proper grammar and word usage. When preparing for the Verbal Ability test, you should take some time to review the fundamentals and rules of grammar.

The following brief guide will illustrate some of the concepts you should review in preparation for the Verbal Ability test.

1. Parts of Speech

The most fundamental elements of English grammar are the different parts of speech, the words we use to construct sentences. Here is a list of the most important parts of speech:

- **Nouns:** A noun is a person, place, or thing (for example, *boy, hospital, clock*).
- **Pronouns:** Pronouns serve as replacements for nouns (for example, *he, she, it, they*).
- **Verbs:** Verbs depict an action or a state of being (for example, *run, pull, is*).
- **Adjectives:** Adjectives modify nouns (for example, *loud, messy, boring*).
- **Adverbs:** Adverbs modify verbs, adjectives, or other adverbs (for example, *quickly, proudly, sadly*).
- **Conjunctions:** Conjunctions connect words, phrases, and sentences (for example, *but, and, or*).
- **Prepositions:** Prepositions express a position in space or time (for example, *over, under, around*).

2. Sentence Structure

Three important rules govern sentence structure:

- **All sentences have verbs.** A sentence is not complete if it doesn't have a verb. Without a verb, it is only a fragment.
- **All sentences have a subject**. Every sentence must have a subject, which can be a noun, a pronoun, or a phrase that acts as a noun. You should note, however, that in commanding sentences, the subject is usually not defined, but rather assumed to be *you.*
- **Subordinate clauses are not complete sentences.** Subordinate clauses are never complete sentences, though they do contain verbs and subjects. These clauses can function as nouns, adjectives, or adverbs.

3. Agreement

There are also special rules concerning subject-verb agreement and verb tense:

- A verb must agree in number with its subject.
- A verb should never be made to agree with any noun that is included in a phrase following the subject.
- A subject that is composed of two or more nouns connected by a coordinating conjunction should always take a plural verb.
- When you use conjunctions like *or,* the number of the verb should agree with the last subject.

- When words introduced by *as well as, with,* or other similar terms are added to the subject of a sentence, the number of the verb is not changed.
- In a sentence that starts with *there is* or *there are,* the verb should agree with the noun that follows it.
- Any statements that are just as true in the present as in the past should be written in the present tense.
- The subjunctive form *were* should be used to express a condition opposed to a fact or desire.

4. Capitalization

It's also very important to know when to capitalize certain words. Following is a brief overview of when you should and should not capitalize certain words.

You should capitalize the following:

- The opening word of a sentence
- Any proper names
- Professional titles that precede a person's name
- Days, months, years, and holidays
- The opening word and any critical subsequent words in a title
- Common nouns used as, or as part of, a proper name
- Compass points when referencing a particular place or region
- Languages and place names that are used as modifiers
- The opening word of a direct quotation

You should *not* capitalize

- The seasons
- Professional titles that do not precede a person's name
- Points of a compass in reference to a direction
- School subjects other than those that use languages and place names as modifiers
- The first word of the second half of a broken quote

5. Punctuation

Finally, you should review the basic rules of punctuation. The common types of punctuation you might encounter on the Verbal Ability test include the following:

- Period (.)
- Question mark (?)
- Exclamation point (!)
- Comma (,)
- Apostrophe (')
- Colon (:)

- Semicolon (;)
- Em dash (—)
- En dash (–)
- Hyphen (-)
- Quotation marks (" ")

As you prepare for the Verbal Ability test, be sure that you're familiar with all the fundamental rules of grammar. Having a firm grasp of grammar can go a long way toward ensuring a satisfactory score on the Verbal Ability test.

6. Types of English Grammar and Usage Questions

Though the exact nature of the grammar and usage questions you may encounter on the Verbal Ability test may vary, the most common types of these questions focus on capitalization, punctuation, and sentence completion.

a. Capitalization Questions

In each capitalization question, you'll be presented with a sentence that contains a capitalization error. You'll also be provided with four answer choices, each of which represents a possible capitalization error. You must select the answer choice that represents the true capitalization error in the sentence.

EXAMPLE:

> Senator Byron is expected to discuss his income tax proposal during his campaign speech at the Lester convention center.
>
> A. Senator
> B. income tax
> C. Lester
> D. convention center

The correct answer is choice D, convention center. Because these words are part of the proper name *Lester Convention Center,* they should be capitalized.

When you're answering a capitalization question, remember to read the sentence carefully and pay close attention to those words that *are* capitalized when they shouldn't be, or are *not* capitalized when they should be.

b. Punctuation Questions

Punctuation questions present you with a sentence that contains some form of punctuation error. Each of the answer choices will include a version of the same sentence written in a different way in order to correct the error. You must select the sentence that corrects the original error and is free of any other errors.

EXAMPLE:

> The grocery store stocks three kinds of green beans; fresh, frozen, and canned.
>
> A. The grocery store stocks three kinds of green beans, fresh, frozen, and canned.
> B. The grocery store stocks three kinds of green beans: fresh, frozen, and canned.
> C. The grocery store stocks three kinds of green beans fresh, frozen, and canned.
> D. The grocery store stocks three kinds of green beans; fresh frozen and canned.

The correct answer is choice B. The original sentence incorrectly uses a semicolon instead of a colon. Choices A, C, and D all use some other incorrect form of punctuation.

When you're answering punctuation questions, remember to read the given sentence very carefully and be sure you understand what the error is. Once you know what's wrong with the sentence, you can select the answer choice that best addresses the problem.

c. Sentence Completion Questions

In sentence completion questions, you'll be given a sentence in which one word has been left out. You must choose the word that best fits in the blank. In most cases, the words you'll have to choose from are homophones—words that sound alike, but are spelled differently.

EXAMPLE:

> The guards were ordered to _____ the imposters.
>
> A. seas
> B. sees
> C. cees
> D. seize

The correct answer is choice D, seize. This sentence is best completed using the word *seize,* which means to take hold of or capture.

When answering sentence completion questions, remember to read the given sentence and think carefully about the meanings of each of the words in the answer choices. Be sure to select the answer choice that fits best within the sentence.

Practice

Directions (1–2): Choose the word that best completes each sentence.

1. When Maria returned from the market, she realized she had forgotten to purchase a _____.

   A. caret
   B. karat
   C. carat
   D. carrot

2. The teacher asked her students to each present a speech on civil _____.

   A. rites
   B. rights
   C. writes
   D. wrights

Directions (3–6): Choose the answer that reflects an error in capitalization.

3. In the Spring, President Williams is scheduled to visit Miami, Florida.

   A. President
   B. Miami
   C. Florida
   D. Spring

4. A brave group of explorers headed North on an expedition to the Arctic tundra.

   A. explorers
   B. North
   C. Arctic
   D. tundra

5. Samuel Down, our town's incoming Mayor, is set to be inaugurated tonight at City Hall.

   A. Samuel
   B. Down
   C. Mayor
   D. City

6. Mrs. Sanderson teaches english and literature at Blackwood High School.

   A. Sanderson
   B. english
   C. literature
   D. School

Directions (7–10): Choose the sentence that corrects the error in punctuation.

7. In response to Johns question, Vincent offered no reply.

   A. In response to Johns question: Vincent offered no reply.
   B. In response, to Johns question, Vincent offered no reply.
   C. In response to Johns question Vincent offered no reply.
   D. In response to John's question, Vincent offered no reply.

8. The game was near its end: there remained only one play before victory was achieved.

    A. The game was near its end, there remained only one play before victory was achieved.
    B. The game was near its end; there remained only one play before victory was achieved.
    C. The game was near its end there remained only one play before victory was achieved.
    D. The game was near its end-there remained only one play before victory was achieved.

9. The parade is expected to start at 11:30 am.

    A. The parade is expected to start at 11.30 am.
    B. The parade is expected to start, at 11:30 am.
    C. The parade is expected to start at 11:30 a.m.
    D. The parade is expected to start at 11 30 am.

10. We are going to Professor Cox's lecture with Jan, Chris, and, Bob.

    A. We are going to Professor Cox's lecture with Jan, Chris, and Bob.
    B. We are going to Professor Coxs lecture with Jan, Chris, and Bob.
    C. We are going to Professor Cox's lecture with Jan Chris and Bob.
    D. We are going to Professor Cox's lecture with, Jan, Chris, and Bob.

Answers

1. **D** The correct answer is *carrot,* which is a type of vegetable. A *caret* is a mark used in proofreading. *Carat* and *karat* both refer to a measurement of the concentration of gold.

2. **B** The correct answer is *rights,* which refers to something to which one is entitled. *Rites* is another word for rituals. *Writes* refers to the action of writing. *Wrights* are people who build or make things.

3. **D** *Spring* should not be capitalized. The names of seasons are never capitalized.

4. **B** *North* should not be capitalized. Compass points should be capitalized only when they refer to a specific place or region.

5. **C** *Mayor* should not be capitalized. Professional titles should be capitalized only when they precede a proper name.

6. **B** *English* should be capitalized. Language names should always be capitalized.

7. **D** Since *John's* is possessive, it should have an apostrophe.

8. **B** The two clauses should be separated by a semicolon.

9. **C** The abbreviation *a.m.* should always include periods.

10. **A** The original sentence contains an unnecessary comma after *and.*

E. Spelling

Another component of the civil service exam's Verbal Ability test is the spelling portion. Because civil service employees are often responsible for a great deal of writing and editing work, it's important that they have strong spelling skills. To test the spelling skills of potential job candidates, the civil service exam contains questions that are specifically designed to test their ability to spell properly.

Each question will contain four answer choices. Three of the choices will contain correctly spelled words, while one choice contains an incorrectly spelled word.

EXAMPLE:

1. **A.** confidential
   B. inscendiary
   C. invocation
   D. colloquial

In the example question above, the correct answer is choice B, inscendiary. This word is properly spelled as *incendiary.*

When answering spelling questions, remember to read all four words carefully and pay close attention to the letters in each. If you aren't sure which word is misspelled, take your best guess. There are no penalties for wrong answers on the Verbal Ability test, so you won't have to worry about losing points for guessing incorrectly.

To prepare for the spelling portion of the Verbal Ability test, try some of these helpful techniques:

- **Visualize the word.** Some words are frequently spelled incorrectly because of the way they sound. After reading the answer choices, try imagining the way each word looks. Spell each word in your mind.

- **Make a list of commonly misspelled words.** Many spelling questions use frequently misspelled words, so making and studying a list of these words will help you to recognize their correct spelling.

- **Answer sample questions.** One of the best ways you can prepare for spelling questions is to answer sample questions. This will give you the chance to familiarize yourself with the format of the questions and learn how best to answer them. Try answering the sample questions provided in this chapter or create some of your own.

- **Study basic spelling rules.** Knowing the basic rules of spelling will help you to recognize incorrectly spelled words. For example, many words are misspelled based on the use of word endings, like *–ing* or *–ly.* You also may encounter words that are spelled incorrectly on the basis of the "*i* before *e,* except after *c*" rule. Keeping these simple rules in mind can be very helpful when answering spelling questions.

- **Write a list of difficult words.** If you encounter any words that you have a particularly hard time spelling, write them down and study them frequently. Learning how to spell one difficult word can help you to spell many others correctly.

Practice

Directions (1–10): Choose the word that is spelled incorrectly.

1. **A.** occurance
   B. rebuttal
   C. predecessor
   D. cordial

2. **A.** repetitive
   B. precipitation
   C. transistional
   D. lethargic

3. **A.** graciousness
   B. competance
   C. liability
   D. maintenance

4. **A.** intersperse
   B. colander
   C. towerring
   D. propel

5. **A.** reputation
   B. unscrupulous
   C. dislocate
   D. litagate

6. **A.** grating
   B. libelous
   C. remady
   D. philander

7. **A.** navigate
   B. misdemeanor
   C. frolick
   D. frigate

8. **A.** tremulous
   B. genteel
   C. crater
   D. boysterous

9. **A.** parlimentary
   B. treble
   C. reprimand
   D. ostrich

10. **A.** plentiful
    B. grievence
    C. raucous
    D. quagmire

Answers

1. **A** *Occurance* is spelled incorrectly. The correct spelling is *occurrence.*

2. **C** *Transistional* is spelled incorrectly. The correct spelling is *transitional.*

3. **B** *Competance* is spelled incorrectly. The correct spelling is *competence.*

4. **C** *Towerring* is spelled incorrectly. The correct spelling is *towering.*

5. **D** *Litagate* is spelled incorrectly. The correct spelling is *litigate.*

6. **C** *Remady* is spelled incorrectly. The correct spelling is *remedy.*

7. **C** *Frolick* is spelled incorrectly. The correct spelling is *frolic.*

8. **D** *Boysterous* is spelled incorrectly. The correct spelling is *boisterous.*

9. **A** *Parlimentary* is spelled incorrectly. The correct spelling is *parliamentary.*

10. **B** *Grievence* is spelled incorrectly. The correct spelling is *grievance.*

F. Analogies

In addition to vocabulary questions, your vocabulary skills also will be tested on the civil service exam through analogy questions. These questions are specifically designed to test your vocabulary and assess your ability to recognize and comprehend word relationships.

Each analogy question is made up of two pairs of related words. In some questions, you'll be provided with the first pair of words in full. You'll also be given the first half of the second pair of words. To answer the question, you'll have to choose the word that best completes the second pair and the analogy itself.

EXAMPLE:

FIRE : HOT :: ICE :

A. warm
B. water
C. cold
D. slippery

Notice that the relationship in this question is between a subject and a characteristic. Since *fire* is to *hot,* you can correctly determine that *ice* is to *cold.* Thus, the correct answer is choice C.

Some analogy questions are structured a little differently. You may be given a single pair of related words and asked to select the second pair of related words that best completes the analogy.

EXAMPLE:

BULL : COW ::

A. doe : fawn
B. man : woman
C. chicken : hen
D. dog : cat

In this question, the relationship between *bull* and *cow* is that of a male to a female. This clearly means that choice B is the correct answer.

As you may have noticed, the most important element of answering an analogy question is understanding the relationship shared between pairs of words. This relationship is the key to any analogy, and recognizing it is vitally important to answering the question correctly.

The analogy questions you'll encounter on the civil service exam are based on a number of relationships. Here are some common relationships:

- **Classifications:** Analogy questions based on classifications include comparisons between the following:
  - A broad category and a narrow category
  - A person and a characteristic
  - The general and the specific
  - A word and an antonym of itself
  - A word and a synonym of itself
  - A word and its definition
  - A male and a female
  - A family relationship and a like-family relationship
  - A virtue and a failing
  - An element and an extreme of itself
  - A lesser degree and a greater degree
  - A plural and a singular
- **Structurals:** Some structural analogies include comparisons between the following:
  - A part and a whole
  - A part and a part
- **Components:** Some analogies based on components include comparisons between the following:
  - An ingredient and a finished product
  - An element and a compound that it's a part of

- **Operationals:** Some analogies based on operationals include comparisons between the following:
  - One element of time and another element of time
  - A beginning and an end
  - A complete operation and a stage of that operation

When answering analogy questions, remember the following helpful tips:

- **Determine the relationship.** When you first encounter an analogy question, carefully examine the first pair of words, and try to determine their relationship. Once you know how they're related, you can move on to the second pair.
- **Keep in mind that the word order must be identical in both pairs.** Some answer choices may include word pairs that share the same relationship as the pair you're given, but in reverse order. Don't forget to pay close attention to word order.
- **Remember that the parts of speech in each pair should be the same.** If the first pair of words are a noun and an adjective, the second pair should also be a noun and an adjective.
- **Be aware that the subject of each pair may be different, though the relationship in each pair is the same.** For example, an analogy may compare a house and a door with a car and a wheel. Although buildings and vehicles are separate subjects, both pairs compare a whole with a part.
- **Examine all the answer choices for each question quickly.**
- **Eliminate incorrect answers, remembering to look for the best possible choice.**

Practice

Directions (1–10): Choose the answer that best demonstrates the relationship between the two capitalized words.

1. KNOB : DOOR ::

   A. house : room
   B. county : state
   C. lock : key
   D. feet: toes

2. WEIGHTLIFTER : STRONG ::

   A. dancer : limber
   B. weights : heavy
   C. arm : graceful
   D. muscles : big

3. HOUR : MINUTE :: MINUTE :

   A. hour
   B. day
   C. time
   D. second

4. SCENE : MOVIE :: STUDENT :

    A. class
    B. teacher
    C. book
    D. library

5. DAYBREAK : DUSK ::

    A. night : day
    B. breakfast : brunch
    C. introduction : epilogue
    D. thunder : lightning

6. WIND : TORNADO ::

    A. snow : flurry
    B. rain : drizzle
    C. drought : desert
    D. wave : tsunami

7. VILLIAN : EVIL :: HERO :

    A. victorious
    B. good
    C. strong
    D. mysterious

8. CALF : CALVES ::

    A. deer : fawn
    B. fungus : fungi
    C. knives : knife
    D. kitten : cat

9. RISE : FALL ::

    A. offer : rescind
    B. plummet : drop
    C. run : sprint
    D. shout: yell

10. SEDAN : AUTOMOBILE :: SNARE :

    A. captive
    B. beat
    C. drum
    D. band

Answers

1. **B** A knob is a part of a door, much as a county is part of a state.

2. **A** The word *strong* refers to a characteristic of a weightlifter. Choice A is correct because the word *limber* refers to a characteristic of a dancer.

3. **D** An hour is composed of 60 minutes. Likewise, a minute is composed of 60 seconds.

4. **A** A scene is part of a movie, whereas a student is part of a class.

5. **C** In this analogy, *daybreak* and *dusk* refer to the beginning and end of a day. Similarly, *introduction* and *epilogue* refer to the beginning and end of a book.

6. **D** A tornado is an extreme form of wind, whereas a tsunami is an extreme type of wave.

7. **B** A villain can be characterized as evil, and a hero can be characterized as good.

8. **B** *Calves* is the plural form of *calf,* much like *fungi* is the plural form of *fungus.*

9. **A** *Rise* is an antonym of *fall.* This relationship indicates that choice A is correct because *offer* is an antonym of *rescind.*

10. **C** A sedan is a type of automobile, whereas a snare is a type of drum.

G. Synonyms

As you take the civil service exam, you also may encounter synonym questions. Synonyms are words that share the same meaning. These questions are similar to vocabulary questions because you need to have an idea of what the words mean. Synonym questions differ from vocabulary questions, however, because synonym questions require you to not only know the definition of the word, but also another word that means the same thing. When answering a synonym question, you'll need to select the answer choice most similar in meaning to the given word.

EXAMPLE:

The word *fragile* most nearly means:

A. Sturdy
B. Flexible
C. Delicate
D. Dangerous

You're presented with the word *fragile* and asked to select the word with the same meaning. The correct answer is choice C, delicate. Both *fragile* and *delicate* are words used to describe something that is weak or that may break easily. *Sturdy* (choice A) and *flexible* (choice B) both have different meanings from *fragile.* *Dangerous* (choice D) is not related to *fragile* at all.

When you're answering synonym questions on the civil service exam, keep the following tips in mind:

- **Carefully read the question and pay close attention to the given word.**
- **Eliminate incorrect answers.** You may immediately recognize some answers as being wrong. If so, simply eliminate these answers and concentrate on the others.
- **Choose the word with the meaning closest to that of the given word.** Remember that the correct answer may not always be a word that you would ordinarily use or even a perfect synonym for the word in the question.
- **If you aren't sure of a word's meaning, try using it in a sentence.** You can then try using the answer choice words in the same sentence to figure out which one fits best. This process should give you a clue to the correct answer.
- **Sometimes, prefixes or suffixes can help you determine the meaning of a word.** If you come across a difficult word, try breaking it down into its basic parts. This analysis also can give you a clue to the correct answer.

Practice

Directions (1–10): Choose the synonym for each italicized word.

1. The word *rapture* most nearly means:

   A. Explosion
   B. Delight
   C. Disturbance
   D. Reaction

2. The word *fictitious* most nearly means:

   A. Genuine
   B. Frightening
   C. Confusing
   D. Imaginary

3. Which word has the same meaning as *conspicuous?*

   A. Obvious
   B. Strange
   C. Hidden
   D. Intelligent

4. The word *meticulous* most nearly means:

   A. Boring
   B. Careful
   C. Repetitive
   D. Decisive

5. The word *interrogate* means most nearly:

   A. Search
   B. Enclose
   C. Question
   D. Recall

6. Which word has the same meaning as *dirigible?*

   A. Boat
   B. Raft
   C. Glider
   D. Blimp

7. Which word has the same meaning as *vociferous?*

   A. Angry
   B. Loud
   C. Chaotic
   D. Crafty

8. The word *organic* most nearly means:

   A. Synthetic
   B. Natural
   C. Common
   D. Original

9. The word *rectify* most nearly means:

   A. Remember
   B. Challenge
   C. Repair
   D. Play

10. Which word has the same meaning as *miscreant?*

   A. Assistant
   B. Scoundrel
   C. Juvenile
   D. Citizen

Answers

1. B The word *delight* is a synonym for the word *rapture.*

2. D The word *imaginary* is a synonym for the word *fictitious.*

3. **A** The word *obvious* is a synonym for the word *conspicuous.*

4. **B** The word *careful* is a synonym for the word *meticulous.*

5. **C** The word *question* is a synonym for the word *interrogate.*

6. **D** The word *blimp* is a synonym for the word *dirigible.*

7. **B** The word *loud* is a synonym for the word *vociferous.*

8. **B** The word *natural* is a synonym for the word *organic.*

9. **C** The word *repair* is a synonym for the word *rectify.*

10. **B** The word *scoundrel* is a synonym for the word *miscreant.*

H. Effective Expression

In this section, we'll review effective expression questions, which require you to utilize all your verbal skills at once.

When answering effective expression questions, you must use your punctuation, grammar, word usage, and reading comprehension skills to determine if a sentence expresses an idea effectively. All the skills you've learned in this chapter will help you answer effective expression questions.

Although some civil service exams may not include effective expression questions, practicing these questions will strengthen your verbal abilities.

Effective expression questions ask you to read a sentence, part or all of which is underlined. Beneath the sentence you'll find three answer choices that rephrase the underlined portion of the sentence. The fourth answer choice (choice D) will read NO ERROR. Your task is to select the answer choice that represents the most effective revision while paying close attention to grammar, word choice, and clarity. For some questions, the original sentence will be the most effective expression of the author's idea. If this is the case, you should select choice D.

Effective expression questions are challenging. However, you can improve your chances of answering the questions correctly by reading each question carefully and following a few simple rules.

Follow these steps when answering effective expression questions:

1. **Read the entire sentence carefully.**
2. **Reread the underlined portion of the sentence.**
3. **If you feel that there is an error in grammar, word choice, or punctuation in the underlined portion, you must choose the most effective revision of the sentence from the three answer choices listed below the question.**

    It's important to note that spelling errors don't commonly occur in effective expression questions. Try not to focus too much on the spelling of words and concentrate on the structure of the sentence itself.

4. **If you feel that the underlined portion of the sentence is correct as written and effectively presents the author's idea, select choice D, NO ERROR.**

As you answer effective expression questions, ask yourself if the sentence makes sense. If the sentence is unclear or confusing, you should choose one of the revisions. Once you determine that the sentence is unclear or has an error, read through the revisions carefully. You want to choose the revision that not only corrects the original error but also expresses the author's idea clearly and effectively.

Before you move on to the practice, look at the following example questions. These questions present a sentence, part or all of which is underlined. Beneath the sentence, you'll find three ways of rephrasing the sentence. Select the answer that represents the most effective revision of the sentence, paying attention to grammar, word choice, and clarity. If the original sentence is correct and as effective as possible, select choice D, NO ERROR.

Examples:

> 1. All employees should hand in his or her vacation requests by January 30.
>
>   **A.**   All employees should hand in our vacation requests by January 30.
>   **B.**   All employees should hand in his or her vacation request for January 30.
>   **C.**   All employees should hand in their vacation requests by January 30.
>   **D.**   NO ERROR

The correct answer is C. *All employees* is plural and requires the plural form of the possessive adjective. Therefore, *his or her* must be changed to *their* to make this sentence correct.

> 2. Starting next Monday, all employees must sign in at the start of their shifts using the new computer system.
>
>   **A.**   Starting next Monday; all employees
>   **B.**   Starting next Monday: all employees
>   **C.**   Starting next Monday all employees
>   **D.**   NO ERROR

The correct answer is D. The original sentence is correct as written. There is no need to change the punctuation because the comma correctly separates the introductory phrase from the rest of the sentence.

Now that you have an idea of what effective expression questions look like, try the following practice exercise.

Practice

Directions (1–10): The following questions will present a sentence, part or all of which is underlined. Beneath the sentence, you'll find three ways of rephrasing the sentence. Select the answer that represents the most effective revision of the sentence, paying attention to grammar, word choice, and clarity. If the original sentence is correct and as effective as possible, select choice D, NO ERROR.

1. All employees that want to sign up for the optional vision plan, must do so by next week.

    A. All employees which want to sign up for the optional vision plan, must do so by next week.
    B. All employees who want to sign up for the optional vision plan must do so by next week.
    C. All employees that want to sign up for the optional vision plan; must do so by next week.
    D. NO ERROR

2. All expenditure reports must be filed according to the coding procedures which had been established in last Monday's meeting.

    A. that were established in last Monday's meeting
    B. which have been established during last Monday's meeting
    C. established during last Monday's meeting
    D. NO ERROR

3. The office will be closed if the governor declares a state of emergency, however, all supervisors should contact the regional manager by 9 a.m.

    A. The office will be closed if the governor declares a state of emergency; however, all supervisors should contact the regional manager by 9 a.m.
    B. The office will be closed if the governor declares a state of emergency, therefore, all supervisors should contact the regional manager by 9 in the morning.
    C. The office will be closed if the governor declares a state of emergency: however, all supervisors should contact the regional manager by 9 a.m.
    D. NO ERROR

4. Employees, that are participating in the company retreat in Ithaca, New York, must attend a safety meeting.

    A. Employees that are participating in the company retreat in Ithaca, New York, must attend a safety meeting.
    B. Employees who are participating in the company retreat in Ithaca, New York, must attend a safety meeting.
    C. Employees—who are participating in the company retreat in Ithaca, New York, must attend a safety meeting.
    D. NO ERROR

5. Safety officers check fire extinguishers, create emergency protocols, and ensure that all employees leave the building in the event of a fire or other emergency.

    A. Safety officers check fire extinguishers, creating emergency protocols, and ensure that all employees leave the building in the event of a fire or other emergency.
    B. Safety officers check fire extinguishers, create emergency protocols, and ensuring that all employees leaving the building in the event of a fire or other emergency.
    C. Safety officers checking fire extinguishers, create emergency protocols, and ensure that all employees leave the building in the event of a fire or other emergency.
    D. NO ERROR

6. A comprehensive benefits package that includes prescription, dental, and vision coverage is offered to state employees.

   A. State employees, who receive a comprehensive benefits package, are offered prescription, dental, and vision coverage.
   B. State employees receive a comprehensive benefits package that includes prescription, dental, and vision coverage.
   C. Prescription, dental, and vision coverage, which is part of a comprehensive benefits package, is offered to state employees.
   D. NO ERROR

7. Office clerks are responsible for the following tasks: scheduling meetings, transcribing notes, taking messages, and filing reports.

   A. following tasks, scheduling meetings, transcribing notes, taking messages, and filing reports.
   B. following tasks schedule meetings, transcribe notes, take messages, and file reports.
   C. following tasks; scheduling meetings, transcribing notes, taking messages, and filing reports.
   D. NO ERROR

8. All employees must leave the building if they hear the fire alarm, it may signal a real emergency.

   A. if anyone hears the fire alarm, it may signal a real emergency.
   B. if they hear the fire alarm, but it may signal a real emergency.
   C. if they hear the fire alarm because it may signal a real emergency.
   D. NO ERROR

9. Monday's seminar on effective time management mandatory for office supervisors.

   A. Monday's seminar on effective time management is mandatory for office supervisors.
   B. Monday's seminar on effective time management, which is mandatory for office supervisors.
   C. Monday's seminar on effective time management that is mandatory for office supervisors.
   D. NO ERROR

10. The meeting is for new employees on office e-mail policies.

   A. The meeting, which is for new employees, on office e-mail policies.
   B. The meeting on office e-mail policies is for new employees.
   C. For new employees, the meeting is on office e-mail policies.
   D. NO ERROR

Answers

1. **B** Because employees are people, you should use the word *who* instead of *that* or *which*. Also, the comma in this sentence is unnecessary and should be removed.

2. **C** The most effective way to rephrase the underlined portion of this sentence is to remove the phrase *which had been* and change the word *in* to *during*. This makes the sentence easy to understand and concise.

3. **A** A semicolon is used to join two independent clauses within a compound sentence. There is no need to change the word *however* or the abbreviation *a.m.*

4. **B** The word *who* should be used when referring to employees. In addition, the phrase *who are participating in the company retreat in Ithaca, New York* is restrictive. This means that the phrase should not be set off by commas. However, a comma should be placed after Ithaca and after New York to set off the individual elements of the place name.

5. **D** The original sentence is grammatically correct and effectively expresses the author's idea. There is no need to change the tense of any of the verbs within the sentence.

6. **B** Although there is no grammatical error in the original sentence, other than the awkward use of passive voice, it's confusing and doesn't present the author's idea in the most effective manner. The sentence must be rearranged to make it clear that the benefits package includes prescription, dental, and vision coverage.

7. **D** The original sentence is grammatically correct and effectively expresses the author's idea. There is no need to change the colon or the form of the verbs that follow the colon.

8. **C** The original sentence contains a comma splice, meaning that two independent clauses are spliced together using only a comma. The best way to fix this error is to remove the comma and join the two independent clauses with the conjunction *because*.

9. **A** The original sentence is a fragment. This error can be fixed by adding the verb *is* between *management* and *mandatory*. This addition turns the fragment into a complete sentence.

10. **B** The original sentence contains a misplaced modifier. The phrase *on office e-mail policies* modifies *employees* when it should modify *meeting*.

VI. Mathematical Ability

Though it may not always be apparent, math skills play an important role in our everyday lives. Whether we're paying bills, measuring ingredients for a recipe, or slicing a cake, we're relying on our math skills.

For civil service employees, a strong foundation in basic mathematics is critically important. Civil service workers often need to rely on their mathematical abilities to complete various daily tasks. With this in mind, the civil service exam always includes a Mathematical Ability test. This test is designed to assess your basic math skills and your ability to complete various math-related tasks.

Math can be difficult. For this reason, you may find the prospect of a Mathematical Ability test intimidating. Although this test is an important part of the civil service exam, you shouldn't stress about it. The math concepts you'll encounter are relatively basic. With a little study and practice, you can easily earn a passing score.

On most civil service exams, there are six types of mathematics questions:

- Fractions and decimals
- Percents, ratios, and proportions
- Reasoning
- Algebra
- Geometry
- Graphs and tables

These questions require you to have a basic understanding of a wide variety of simple mathematical concepts, including the following:

- **Real number:** A number that can identify a position on a number line; all real numbers, except zero, are positive or negative.
- **Rational number:** A number that can be written as a ratio of two integers; includes integers, repeating decimals, and terminating decimals.
- **Integer:** A positive or negative whole number, or zero.
- **Whole number:** Counting or natural number, or zero. Whole numbers do not contain fractions, decimals, or percentages.
- **Fraction:** Any number that appears in the format $\frac{A}{B}$, where A represents a numerator and B represents a denominator. The denominator of any fraction can never be equal to zero.
- **Positive number:** Any number greater than zero.
- **Negative number:** Any number less than zero.
- **Even number:** All even numbers are integers and multiples of 2.
- **Odd number:** All odd numbers are integers that are not divisible by 2.
- **Prime number:** Any integer greater than 1 that has only 1 and itself as factors.
- **Consecutive numbers:** Numbers arranged in numerical order.

- **Factor:** A multiplier; one of two or more values whose product is the multiple.
- **Multiple:** Any number that a particular number will divide into without leaving a remainder.

If you feel that you need to, try reviewing some or all of these concepts before moving on to studying for the specific question types found on the civil service exam. A solid understanding of these underlying concepts will only help you with the more difficult ones you may encounter later.

A. Fractions and Decimals

Fractions and decimals are among the most commonly used mathematic structures. It's no surprise, then, that part of the Mathematics Ability test on the civil service exam is devoted to testing your ability to understand and work with both fractions and decimals.

1. Fractions

Before you begin solving any fraction or mixed number math problems, briefly review these simple concepts:

- **Proper fractions:** In a proper fraction, the numerator is less than the denominator. For example, in the fraction $\frac{1}{5}$, 1 is the numerator and 5 is the denominator. In all proper fractions, the numerator is always being divided by the denominator. This means that the numerator tells you how many of the division of the unit are being considered. For example, in the proper fraction above, 1 is being divided by 5.
- **Mixed numbers:** A mixed number is made up of an integer and a fraction. $3\frac{1}{2}$ is a mixed number. The integer in a mixed number is known as the integral part, whereas the fraction is known as the fractional part.
- **Improper fractions:** In an improper fraction, the numerator is equal to or greater than the denominator. $\frac{7}{4}$, $\frac{21}{12}$, and $\frac{9}{9}$ are all improper fractions.

The following rules will provide you with an outline for performing different mathematical operations using fractions and mixed numbers.

Converting Mixed Numbers and Improper Fractions

In most cases, the fraction questions on the Mathematics Ability test focus on converting mixed numbers and improper fractions.

To convert a mixed number to a fraction:

1. **Multiply the fraction's denominator by the integer.**
2. **Add this product and the numerator together.**
3. **Place the sum over the denominator.**

To convert an improper fraction to a mixed number:

1. **Divide the numerator by the denominator.** The quotient you get will be the integral part of the final mixed number.

2. **If there is a remainder, place it over the denominator.** This constitutes the fractional part of the mixed number.

Reducing Fractions

Sometimes, you can change a fraction's numerator and denominator (without changing the value of the fraction) by dividing both by the same number. This procedure is known as reducing a fraction. When a fraction has been reduced as far as possible, it is said to have been reduced to its lowest possible terms.

For example, the fraction $\frac{2}{4}$ can be reduced to $\frac{1}{2}$ if you divide both the numerator and the denominator by 2. This reduction does not change the value of the fraction.

Adding Fractions

In order to add two or more fractions, their denominators must be the same. When you encounter fractions with different denominators, you must first find a common denominator before you can begin adding.

The least common denominator (LCD) is the lowest possible number that can be divided evenly by all the denominators in a given problem. In the event that no two denominators can be divided by the same number, the LCD is the product of all the given denominators.

To determine the LCD, follow these steps:

1. **List the multiples of the numbers in the denominators until you find a common number.**

   For example, if you're asked to find the LCD of $\frac{1}{4}$, $\frac{1}{5}$, and $\frac{1}{10}$, begin by listing the multiples of 4: 4, 8, 12, 16, 20, 24, 28. . . . Do the same for 5: 5, 10, 15, 20, 25, 30. . . . Do you see a common number yet? Find the multiples of 10: 10, 20, 30, 40. . . .

2. **Find a common number within the multiples.**

   You can see from the lists in the previous step that 20 is the lowest common multiple of 4, 5, and 10. This is your LCD.

3. **Multiply each numerator and denominator by numbers that will help you reach fractions with the LCD.**

   For example, you know that 4 multiplied by 5 equals 20. Because you would multiply the denominator of $\frac{1}{4}$ by 5 to get 20, you have to multiply the numerator by 5, as well. So, $\frac{1}{4}$ becomes $\frac{5}{20}$. Apply these steps to the other fractions. Multiply the numerator and denominator of $\frac{1}{5}$ by 4 to get $\frac{4}{20}$ and the numerator and denominator of $\frac{1}{10}$ by 2 to get $\frac{2}{20}$. Now, each of your fractions has a common denominator of 20.

After you've found the LCD, you can begin adding:

1. **Add the numerators and place the sum above the common denominator.**
2. **Reduce the resulting fraction to its lowest possible terms.**

Subtracting Fractions

As with adding fractions, you'll need to find the LCD before you can begin subtracting.

To subtract two or more fractions:

1. **Find the LCD.**
2. **Convert the given fractions to equivalent fractions using the LCD.**
3. **Subtract the second fraction's numerator from the first fraction's numerator.**
   Place the difference above the LCD.
4. **If possible, reduce the resulting fraction and change improper fractions into mixed numbers.**
5. **If you're subtracting mixed numbers, you may need to "borrow" in order to make the fractional part of the first term larger than that of the second term.**
   Aside from this, the fractions and integers should be subtracted separately.

Multiplying Fractions

To multiply fractions:

1. **Convert mixed numbers to fractions.**
2. **If needed, reduce the fractions.**
   This ensures that you're working with the smallest—and simplest—numbers, which will make solving the problem easier for you.
3. **Multiply the numerators.**
4. **Multiply the denominators.**
   In the resulting fraction, the product of the numerators should be the numerator and the product of the denominators should be the denominator.
5. **Again, reduce if necessary.**

Dividing Fractions

In order to divide fractions, you must simply multiply the first fraction by the reciprocal of the second fraction. A fraction's reciprocal is just an inversion of the same fraction. This means that the reciprocal of $\frac{3}{4}$ is $\frac{4}{3}$.

To divide fractions:

1. **Convert any mixed numbers into improper fractions.**
2. **Change the second fraction to its reciprocal.**
3. **Multiply the fractions.**
4. **If needed, reduce the fraction and convert improper fractions to mixed numbers.**

Fraction Problems

The majority of the fraction questions on the Mathematics Ability test are likely to ask, "What fraction of a number is another number?" There are three important elements to this question: the fractional part, the number after *of*, and the number after *is*.

To answer this type of question:

- **When you're given the fraction and the *of* number, multiply them and you'll get the *is* number.** For example, what is $\frac{1}{4}$ of 100? One quarter of 100 *is* 25.
- **When you're given the fraction and the *is* number, you can get the *of* number by dividing the *is* number by the fraction.** For example, 25 is $\frac{1}{4}$ of which number? $25 \div \frac{1}{4} = 100$. And 25 is $\frac{1}{4}$ *of* 100.
- **When you're given the *of* number and the *is* number, you can get the fraction by dividing the *is* number by the *of* number.** For example, what fraction of 100 is equal to 25? $25 \div 100 = \frac{25}{100}$. Reduced, $\frac{1}{4}$ of 100 is equal to 25.

2. Decimals

Though they're presented differently, decimals are really fractions. The unseen denominator of a decimal is assumed to be a power of ten. The number of digits that appear after the decimal point determines which power of ten the denominator is. When there is only a single digit after the decimal point, the denominator is said to be 10, when there are two digits, the denominator is said to be 100, and so on.

A mixed number with a decimal can be converted to a fraction if you divide the decimal (mixed number) without a decimal point (which includes digits on both sides of the decimal point) and divide by the power of 10 indicated by the digits on the right of the decimal point. Remember that the fraction is not one of the decimal places.

Adding and Subtracting Decimals

You can add and subtract decimals in the same fashion as you do whole numbers. However, you'll need to keep the decimal points in a vertical line to determine where the decimal point should be placed in the answer and add the like units.

Multiplying Decimals

Decimals can be multiplied the same way as whole numbers. Remember that the number of decimal places in the product should be equal to the sum of the number of places in both the *multiplicand* (the first number being multiplied) and the *multiplier* (the second number being multiplied). If you end up with a product with fewer digits than the sum indicates, you'll need to add a sufficient number of zeros in front of the digits in the product and place the decimal point in front of the added zeros.

Dividing Decimals

There are four types of decimal division:

- **When only the *dividend* (the number being divided) is a decimal:** You can divide the same way you would with whole numbers. Remember that the number of decimal places in the answer must be the same as that in the dividend.

- **When only the divisor is a decimal:** You must omit the decimal point and add as many zeros as there are decimal points to the right of the dividend.
- **When the dividend and divisor are both decimals:** You must omit the decimal point in the divisor and move the decimal point in the dividend to the right as many decimal places as there are in the divisor. When there aren't enough places in the dividend, you'll need to add zeros.
- **When neither the dividend nor the divisor is a decimal:** This happens (a) when the dividend is smaller than the divisor and (b) when you're required to work your division out to a specified decimal place. With either type of problem, you'll simply need to place a decimal point after the dividend, add any necessary zeros, and divide.

Converting Fractions to Decimals

You can convert a fraction to a decimal by dividing the numerator by the denominator and working the division out to the required number of decimal places.

Practice

Directions (1–10): Answer the following questions based solely on the information provided.

1. Convert $3\frac{2}{3}$ to an improper fraction.

   A. $\frac{9}{3}$

   B. $\frac{10}{3}$

   C. $\frac{11}{3}$

   D. $\frac{12}{3}$

2. Find the least common denominator of $\frac{1}{3}$, $\frac{1}{9}$, and $\frac{1}{18}$.

   A. 3
   B. 18
   C. 27
   D. 48

3. Add $4\frac{2}{4}$ and $11\frac{3}{4}$.

   A. $16\frac{1}{2}$

   B. $16\frac{1}{4}$

   C. $16\frac{1}{6}$

   D. $16\frac{1}{8}$

4. If a crate of oranges weighs $12\frac{1}{4}$ pounds, how many pounds would four crates weigh?

   A. 46
   B. 47
   C. 48
   D. 49

5. In his first week of training, a runner travels $1\frac{3}{4}$, $2\frac{1}{2}$, and $2\frac{3}{4}$ miles. In his second week, he travels $2\frac{1}{2}$, $2\frac{3}{4}$, and $3\frac{1}{4}$ miles. How many more miles does he travel in his second week than he did in his first?

   A. 1
   B. $1\frac{1}{2}$
   C. 2
   D. $2\frac{1}{2}$

6. Multiply 12.52 and 15.25.

   A. 188.82
   B. 190.50
   C. 190. 93
   D. 192.68

7. What is $\frac{6}{20}$ in decimal form (to the nearest hundredth)?

   A. 0.20
   B. 0.25
   C. 0.30
   D. 0.35

8. After taking his car to the garage for repairs, George is charged $243.35 for parts, $425.50 for labor, and $27.83 for taxes. What is the total cost of George's bill?

   A. $696.68
   B. $697.02
   C. $698.47
   D. $698.95

9. What is the total cost of $2\frac{1}{2}$ pounds of ham at $3.50 per pound and 24 rolls at $4.99 per dozen (rounded to the nearest cent)?

   A. $16.50
   B. $16.84
   C. $17.36
   D. $18.73

10. This month, the balance of Karen's checkbook began at $642.47. Over the course of the month, she writes one check for $97.65 and another for $272.50. She also makes a deposit of $450. What is her balance by the end of the month?

   A. $692.50
   B. $702.44
   C. $712.96
   D. $722.32

Answers

1. **C** The correct answer is $\frac{11}{3}$. To find this answer, multiply the integral part (3) and the denominator (3) and add the product (9) with the numerator (2). Finally, place the sum (11) over the original denominator (3). This leaves you with $\frac{11}{3}$.

2. **B** The least common denominator among $\frac{1}{3}$, $\frac{1}{9}$, and $\frac{1}{18}$ is 18. To find the least common denominator, list the multiples of each denominator until you find a common denominator. The first six multiples of 3 are 3, 6, 9, 12, 15, and 18. The first six multiples of 9 are 9, 18, 27, 36, 45, and 54. You should already notice that your third denominator (18) has appeared in both lists of multiples for 3 and 9. Both 3 and 9 can be multiplied (by 6 and 2, respectively) to produce 18. The least common denominator of $\frac{1}{3}$, $\frac{1}{9}$, and $\frac{1}{18}$ is 18.

3. **B** Since these numbers already have common denominators, you simply have to add them together: $4\frac{2}{4}+11\frac{3}{4}=15\frac{5}{4}$. You can't leave $\frac{5}{4}$ as an improper fraction; so, you must convert it to a whole number first: $\frac{5}{4}=1\frac{1}{4}$. Then add it to 15: $15+1\frac{1}{4}=16\frac{1}{4}$.

4. **D** To find the answer, you must multiply $12\frac{1}{4}$ by 4. Think of 4 as a fraction to make this easier: $4=\frac{4}{1}$. Next, convert your mixed number to an improper fraction: $12\frac{1}{4}=\frac{49}{4}$. Now, just multiply across: $\frac{49}{4}\cdot\frac{4}{1}=\frac{196}{4}$. Finally, reduce the fraction. Since 4 divides evenly into 196, your answer will be a whole number: $196\div4=49$.

5. **B** To find this answer, you must add the distances of the runner's first three runs. Because these numbers are mixed and also have differing denominators, you'll have to convert them to improper fractions and then find the common denominator so you can add. First, convert them by multiplying the denominator by the whole number and then adding the numerator. Place your answer in the numerator's place: $1\frac{3}{4}+2\frac{1}{2}+2\frac{3}{4}=\frac{7}{4}+\frac{5}{2}+\frac{11}{4}$. Next, multiply the middle fraction by 2 in the numerator and the denominator, because 4 is the common denominator: $\frac{5}{2}\cdot\frac{2}{2}=\frac{10}{4}$. Finally, add your fractions to find the number of miles the runner completed during the first week. . Reduce to find that the runner ran a total of 7 miles his first week. Repeat these steps to find the total number of miles the runner ran during his second week of training. Your work should look like this: $2\frac{1}{2}+2\frac{3}{4}+3\frac{1}{4}=\frac{5}{2}+\frac{11}{4}+\frac{13}{4}=\frac{10}{4}+\frac{11}{4}+\frac{13}{4}=\frac{34}{4}$. Since 34 is not divisible by 4, convert this improper fraction to a mixed number: $\frac{34}{4}=8\frac{2}{4}=8\frac{1}{2}$. To answer the question, subtract the number of miles the runner completed during the first week of training from the number of miles he completed during the second. $8\frac{1}{2}-7=1\frac{1}{2}$. The runner traveled $1\frac{1}{2}$ more miles in his second week than in his first week of training.

6. **C** To find the answer, multiply the way you would if decimals were not present in the numbers. Your multiplication should look similar to the following:

$$
\begin{array}{r}
12.52 \\
\times 15.25 \\
\hline
6260 \\
25040 \\
626000 \\
+1252000 \\
\hline
190.9300
\end{array}
$$

Because there are two decimal places in each factor (12.52 and 15.25), place the decimal in the answer four places to the left, as shown above. The answer is 190.9300. You can drop the last two zeros to get 190.93.

7. **C** To find the answer, you must divide the numerator by the denominator: $6 \div 20 = 0.30$.

8. **A** To find the answer, add the cost of the three charges:

$$
\begin{array}{r}
\$24\overset{1\,1}{3}.35 \\
\$425.50 \\
\$\ \ 27.83 \\
\hline
\$696.68
\end{array}
$$

9. **D** To determine this answer, you must multiply $2\frac{1}{2}$ by \$3.50. To do this, convert the mixed fraction to a decimal. You know that $\frac{1}{2}$ is equal to 0.50, so $2\frac{1}{2}$ equals 2.50. Now, multiply: $\$3.50 \times 2.50 = \$8.75$. Next, multiply \$4.99 by 2 because you need to find the cost of two dozen rolls of bread: $\$4.99 \times 2 = \$9.98$. Finally, add the cost of the ham by the cost of the bread to find the answer: $\$8.75 + \$9.98 = \$18.73$.

10. **D** To determine this answer, you have to add and subtract decimals. First, start with the amount Karen had in her checkbook at the beginning of the month: \$642.47. From this number, subtract the amounts of the two checks Karen wrote this month: $\$642.47 - \$97.65 = \$544.82$ and $\$544.82 - \$272.50 = \$272.32$. Karen also made a deposit this month, so you must add the amount of the deposit to the new total of the checking account: $\$272.32 + \$450 = \$722.32$.

B. Percents, Ratio, and Proportion

The Mathematics Ability test on the civil service exam also includes questions on percents, ratio, and proportions. Questions involving these three concepts often are grouped together on the test because of their similar nature.

1. Percents

The most important thing to remember when faced with a percent question is that all percents are seen as "parts of a hundred." For example, when you see 70% written on the test, it is meant to be interpreted as 70 out of 100.

Percent questions may ask you to perform one of several tasks. Some will ask you to convert a decimal, fraction, or mixed number to a percent. Others may require you to change a percent into a fraction or a decimal to complete a given calculation. With this in mind, it would be a good idea to become familiar with the rules for making these conversions.

Changing Decimals to Percents

To change a decimal to a percent:

1. **Multiply the number by 100.**
2. **Tag the resulting product with a percent sign (%).**

Changing Fractions to Percents

To change a fraction or mixed number to a percent:

1. **Multiply the given fraction or mixed number by 100.**
2. **If needed, reduce the fraction or change improper fractions to mixed numbers.**
3. **Tag the resulting number with a percent sign (%).**

Percent Problems

The majority of the percent problems you're likely to encounter on the civil service exam will include three quantities:

- The rate (R), which is a value followed by a percent sign.
- The base (B), which usually appears after the word *of*.
- The amount of percentage (P), which usually appears after the word *is*.

In a particular question, you'll be given two of these values and asked to find the third. There is a unique formula for finding each of these values:

- When you know the rate and base, use $P = RB$.
- When you know the rate and percentage, use $B = \dfrac{P}{R}$.
- When you know the percentage and base, use $R = \dfrac{P}{B}$.

Tip: If you're given a rate in the form of a percentage, be sure to convert the percentage to decimal form before solving the problem.

2. Ratios

A ratio serves to represent the relationship shared between two or more quantities in terms of numbers. The punctuation used to designate a ratio is the colon (:), which is read as the word *to*. For example, the ratio 4:1 would be read as "4 to 1."

Ratios also can be used to represent division. This means that any ratio with two terms can be written as a fraction and vice versa. For example, the ratio 2:3 can also be written as $\frac{2}{3}$.

To solve a ratio problem in which the ratio expresses a relationship between two or more quantities:

1. **Add all the terms in the ratio together.**
2. **Divide the total amount that is to be split into a ratio by the sum of the terms.**
3. **Multiply each of the terms in the ratio by the quotient you arrived at in Step 2.**

For example, if a total of $288 is to be split among three people at the ratio of 2:4:6, how much money would each person get? To find the answer, you must:

1. **Add the ratio terms: 2 + 4 + 6 = 12.**
2. **Divide the full $288 by this sum: 288 ÷ 12 = 24**
3. **Multiply each ratio term by the quotient: $24 × 2 = $48, $24 × 4 = $96, $24 × 6 = $144.**

As a result, the money is divided as such: $48, $96, $144.

Complex ratios that contain fractions, decimals, or percents can be simplified by dividing the first term by the second term. When you have arrived at a quotient for a fraction ratio, reduce it, if necessary, to its lowest terms and write the resulting fraction as a ratio.

3. Proportions

Proportions state the equality of two ratios. A typical proportion may look like this: 3:6 = 6:12. You would read this proportion as "3 is to 6 as 6 is to 12." The outer terms (3 and 12) are called the *extremes* and the inner terms (6 and 6) are called the *means.* Some proportions are written as fractions. In fractional form, the ratio above would look like this: $\frac{3}{6} = \frac{6}{12}$.

In all proportions, the product of the means is equal to the product of the extremes. In the example above, $3 \times 12 = 36$ and $6 \times 6 = 36$. You can find these products in fractional proportions through cross-multiplication.

In most problems that deal with proportions, you'll be give three terms and asked to find the fourth. To solve this sort of proportion problem:

1. **Construct a ratio based on the given information.**
   Be very careful to copy all information correctly.
2. **Examine the ratio you have made and determine whether you know the means or the extremes.**
   Find the product of the pair you're given.
3. **Divide the resulting product by the third given term to find the fourth term.**

Practice

Directions (1–10): Answer the following questions based solely on the information provided.

1. What percent is 3 of 36?

   A. $6\frac{1}{2}$

   B. $7\frac{1}{6}$

   C. $8\frac{1}{3}$

   D. $9\frac{1}{4}$

2. Tim buys a stereo for $95.25 during a 25% off sale. What was the original price of the stereo?

   A. $112
   B. $117
   C. $125
   D. $127

3. Molly goes to the donut shop for her office and buys 36 donuts and 6 cups of coffee. The donuts cost $6.50 per dozen and the coffees cost $1.25 each. She is also given a 10% business discount. How much did she pay for her order?

   A. $20.47
   B. $24.30
   C. $25.15
   D. $27.00

4. The ratio of 42:54 is

   A. 7:9
   B. 6:13
   C. 9:7
   D. 13:6

5. Michael is reading a map. According to the scale, 4 inches on the map represents 40 miles. How much actual distance would be covered over 10 inches of the map?

   A. 100 miles
   B. 140 miles
   C. 400 miles
   D. 440 miles

6. Lupe is looking for soup at the market. She finds her favorite brand on sale at a cost of $1.50 for two cans. She buys a dozen cans. How much will she pay for all the soup?

   A. $7.50
   B. $8.00
   C. $9.00
   D. $10.50

7. What is 150% of 700?

   A.   1,000
   B.   1,050
   C.   1,400
   D.   1,500

8. Jim pays a $2\frac{1}{2}$% interest rate on the total balance on his credit card. The interest payment amounts to $20. What is the total value of Jim's credit card balance?

   A. $320
   B. $600
   C. $620
   D. $800

9. 73% written as a decimal is

   A.   7.3
   B.   0.73
   C.   0.073
   D.   0.0073

10. If a prize of $3,288 is to be split among three winners at a ratio of 1:2:3, how much money would each person get?

   A. $400, $900, $1,200
   B. $448, $996, $1,444
   C. $548, $1,096, $1,644
   D. $600, $1,200, $1,800

Answers

1. **C** The correct answer is $8\frac{1}{3}$. To find this answer, use the equation $R = \frac{P}{B}$. First, plug the numbers into the equation and solve for R. You know that $P = 3$ and $B = 36$, so $R = \frac{3}{36} = \frac{1}{12}$. Next, divide 1 by 12 to get 0.083333 and then multiply by 100 to get 8.33, so the rate is $8\frac{1}{3}$.

2. **D** To solve this problem, first set up a proportion. Next, cross-multiply and divide each side of the equation by 75 to get $127:

$$\frac{75}{100} = \frac{95.25}{x}$$
$$75x = 95.25 \cdot 100$$
$$75x = 9,525$$
$$x = \frac{9,525}{75}$$
$$x = \$127$$

3. **B** Molly's total before the discount would come to $27. To find out how much she paid *after* the discount, you must first determine that 100% minus 10% is 90%. You can then complete the equation $27 × 0.90 = $24.30.

4. **A** To find this answer, first put the ratio 42:54 into fraction form: $\frac{42}{54}$. Next, reduce this fraction to $\frac{7}{9}$ and turn it back into a ratio, which leaves you with 7:9.

5. **A** To solve this problem, first set up the proportion. Then cross-multiply and divide each side of the equation by 4 to get 100 miles:

$$\frac{4 \text{ miles}}{10 \text{ inches}} = \frac{40 \text{ miles}}{x \text{ miles}}$$
$$4x = 40 \cdot 10$$
$$4x = 400$$
$$x = \frac{400}{4}$$
$$x = 100$$

6. **C** To solve this problem, first set up the proportion. Then cross-multiply and divide each side of the equation by 2 to get $9:

$$\frac{2}{12} = \frac{\$1.50}{x}$$
$$2x = 1.50 \cdot 12$$
$$2x = 18$$
$$x = \frac{18}{2}$$
$$x = 9$$

7. **B** To find this answer, use the equation $R = PB$. First, convert the percentage (150%) to a decimal: 1.5. Then plug the numbers into the equation for the percentage and the base and solve for R: $R = 1.5 \cdot 700 = 1,050$.

8. **D** To find Jim's credit card balance, first convert $2\frac{1}{2}\%$ to a decimal: 0.025. The best way to solve this problem is to use cross-multiplication. Before you begin, set up a proportion, multiply, and then reduce:

$$\frac{2.5}{100} = \frac{20}{x}$$
$$2.5x = 100 \cdot 20$$
$$2.5x = 2,000$$
$$x = \frac{2,000}{2.5}$$
$$x = 800$$

9. **B** To covert a percentage to a decimal, move the decimal point two places to the left: 73% = 0.73.

10. **C** To solve this problem, first add the ratio terms: 1 + 2 + 3 = 6. Next, divide this number by the total prize: $3,288 ÷ 6 = 548. Then, multiply each ratio by this number: 1 · 548 = $548; 2 · 548 = $1,096; and 3 · 548 = $1,644.

C. Reasoning

In addition to the word problems you'll encounter in other sections of the Mathematics Ability test, you'll also find some word problems that are based on reasoning. There are two types of reasoning questions: work problems and arithmetic reasoning problems.

1. Work Problems

All work problems are based on three specifics factors: the number of workers, the time it takes them to finish a job, and the amount of work completed. There are three rules that all work problems must follow:

- The number of workers is directly proportional to the amount of work completed.
- The number of workers is inversely proportional to the time it takes to finish a job. This means that the more people there are working on a job, the less time it will take to complete it and vice versa.
- The amount of time it takes to complete a job is directly proportional to the amount of work completed. In other words, the more time workers spend doing a job, the more work will be completed and vice versa.

The work problems you'll find on the civil service exam will ask you to solve for the rate, time, or number of workers. Based on the information included in the question, find the answer by using the formulas discussed in this section.

Work Problems with Equal Rates

A person's rate of work is the total amount of work that a given person can do in an allotted amount of time. When all workers are working at an equal rate, you can determine how long it will take one, several, or all of them to finish their job by following these guidelines:

1. **Multiply the number of workers by the time to compute the amount of time it will take a single worker to finish the job.**
2. **Divide this time by the number of workers needed to finish the job to solve for how long it will take for all of them to complete the job.**

In some work problems, you equalize unequal rates by comparison. To solve such problems:

1. **Read the question and determine how many equal rates exist in the scenario.**
2. **Multiply the number of equal rates by the time stated in the question.**
3. **Divide the time you have found by the number of equal rates.**

For example, imagine that it takes five workers ten days to complete a job. Three of the workers are slow and two are fast. If you know that each fast worker is the equivalent of two slow workers, you can determine that there are a total of seven (slow) workers. If you multiply the seven workers by the ten days stated in the scenario, you'll find that it will take one slow worker 70 days to finish the job. Remembering that one fast worker is the equivalent of two slow workers, if you divide those 70 days by 2, you'll find that it will take one fast worker only 35 days to finish the job.

Work Problems with Time

Some questions may provide you with the different times in which each person in a group can finish a job. With this information, you can determine how long it would take to finish the whole job if all the workers worked together. To solve this type of problem:

1. **Invert each worker's time to determine how much work each could do in a given unit of time.**
2. **Add all these reciprocals together.**
3. **Invert the resulting sum to determine how long it will take all the workers to complete the job together.**

For example, if Caroline can fix a car in two days, Andre could fix it in four days, and Jack could fix it in eight days, how many days would it take the three of them to finish it together? To find out, you must first invert each worker time. This means that Caroline, Andre, and Jack could finish $\frac{1}{2}$, $\frac{1}{4}$, and $\frac{1}{8}$ of the job in one day, respectively. The lowest common denominator of the three fractions is 8; using the LCD, the fractions would be $\frac{4}{8}$, $\frac{2}{8}$, and $\frac{1}{8}$. Next, add these reciprocals together to arrive at the sum of $\frac{4}{8}+\frac{2}{8}+\frac{1}{8}=\frac{7}{8}$. Invert this result into the improper fraction $\frac{8}{7}$. Finally, convert this to the mixed number $1\frac{1}{7}$. You now know that it would take the workers $1\frac{1}{7}$ days to complete the job working together.

If a question gives you the total time it would take a group of workers to complete a job and the times of all the workers except for one, you can find the unknown time by following these steps:

1. **Invert the provided times to determine how much of the job each of the workers could complete in a given unit of time.**
2. **Add all these reciprocals together.**
3. **Subtract the resulting sum from the reciprocal of the total time required to finish the job.**
4. **Invert the resulting reciprocal to determine the unknown time.**

Work Problems with All Factors

Some work problems take a different approach. In these unique problems, you'll be provided with given values for the number of workers, the amount of work they complete, and the time in which they do it. In most cases, you'll be asked to determine what changes would occur when one or more of the factors are given a different value.

In order to solve these problems, you may need to make cancellations, multiply, and/or divide. The exact requirements of each question will vary depending on the given data and what changes you're asked to implement.

Arithmetic Reasoning Problems

These questions require you to reason out an answer based on given information. There are no special formulas or approaches to answering these questions. Instead, arithmetic reasoning questions simply use some of the mathematical concepts previously covered in this chapter. To review for arithmetic reasoning questions, you need to remember the rules and methods used for fractions, decimals, percents, ratios, and proportions.

Practice

Directions (1–10): Answer the following questions based solely on the information provided.

1. A certain construction job can be completed by 24 workers in 30 days. How many workers would be needed to finish the job in 16 days?

    A.   30
    B.   35
    C.   40
    D.   45

2. A five-man team is working on a certain job. Working together, it will take the men 36 days to finish. If one man works only half-days, how long will it take them to complete the job?

    A.   38
    B.   40
    C.   42
    D.   44

3. If a group of 250 clerical workers can file 9,500 documents in 20 minutes, what is the average number of documents filed by each worker per minute?

    A. $1\frac{1}{3}$

    B. $1\frac{7}{10}$

    C. $1\frac{9}{10}$

    D. $1\frac{3}{4}$

4. Michelle, an office clerk, is asked to file 600 documents. If Michelle can file the documents at a rate of 60 per hour, how many will she have left after seven hours?

    A.   160
    B.   180
    C.   220
    D.   240

5. If it takes four machines to do a certain job in six days, how long will it take three machines to complete the same job?

    A.   7
    B.   8
    C.   9
    D.   10

6. A construction company rented a dump truck for three days and was charged $600. The rental company charged $60 per day and an additional 30¢ per mile driven. How many miles was the dump truck driven?

    A.   900
    B.   1,000
    C.   1,200
    D.   1,400

7. If it takes four workers three eight-hour work days to repair a car, how many workers would it take to repair two cars in one eight-hour work day?

    A.   12
    B.   24
    C.   36
    D.   48

8. A company car is driven 75 miles at a constant rate of 45 miles per hour. How many minutes will the trip take?

    A.   80
    B.   90
    C.   100
    D.   110

9. Two labor unions with the same number of employees are debating a new policy. In one union, $\frac{1}{3}$ of the members supports the policy. In the other, $\frac{1}{6}$ of the members supports it. What is the average of the fractions of union members who support the policy?

   A. $\frac{1}{4}$

   B. $\frac{1}{3}$

   C. $\frac{1}{2}$

   D. $\frac{1}{5}$

10. If it takes one clerical worker two and a half hours to finish filing 5 reports, how many hours would it take two workers to file 20 reports, if they're working at the same rate?

   A. 2
   B. 3
   C. 4
   D. 5

Answers

1. **D** To solve this problem, set up a proportion and use cross-multiplication:

$$\frac{24}{16} = \frac{x}{30}$$
$$16x = 24 \cdot 30$$
$$16x = 720$$
$$x = \frac{720}{16}$$
$$x = 45$$

It would take 45 workers to finish the job in 16 days.

2. **B** To solve this problem, set up a proportion and use cross-multiplication:

$$\frac{36}{4.5} = \frac{x}{5}$$
$$4.5x = 36 \cdot 5$$
$$4.5x = 180$$
$$x = \frac{180}{4.5}$$
$$x = 40$$

It would take the team of men 40 days to complete the job.

3. **C** To solve this problem, first, determine how many documents each person filed in 20 minutes: 9,500 documents ÷ 250 people = 38 documents per person. Next, set up a proportion and use cross-multiplication:

$$\frac{38 \text{ documents}}{20 \text{ minutes}} = \frac{x \text{ documents}}{1 \text{ minute}}$$

$$38 = 20x$$

$$\frac{38}{20} = x$$

$$1\frac{18}{20} = x$$

$$1\frac{9}{10} = x$$

4. **B** To solve this problem, first determine the number of documents Michelle can file in seven hours by multiplying the number of documents she files in one hour by the total number of hours: $60 \times 7 = 420$ documents. Next, subtract this number from the total number of documents she has to file: $600 - 420 = 180$. Michelle has 180 documents left to file.

5. **B** To solve this problem, first determine how many days it would take one machine to do the job by multiplying the number of machines by the number of days: $4 \times 6 = 24$ days for one machine to complete the job. Next, divide this number by the number of machines: $24 \div 3 = 8$. It would take three machines eight days to finish the job.

6. **D** To solve this problem, first multiply the number of days by the rate charged to rent the dump truck per day: $3 \times \$60 = \$180$. Next, subtract this number from the total cost to rent the dump truck: $\$600 - \$180 = \$420$. To determine the number of miles driven, divide this amount by the amount charged by mile: $\$420 \div \$0.30 = 1,400$ miles.

7. **B** To solve this problem, first find out how many hours it would take one worker to repair one car by multiplying the number of workers by the number of hours it takes to repair one car: $4 \times 24 = 96$ hours for one worker to repair one car. Next, multiply the number of hours by two cars: $96 \times 2 = 192$ hours. Last, divide this number by the number of hours: $192 \div 8 = 24$. It would take 24 workers to repair two cars in one eight-hour day.

8. **C** To solve this problem, first set up a proportion and then use cross-multiplication:

$$\frac{45 \text{ miles}}{60 \text{ minutes}} = \frac{75 \text{ miles}}{x \text{ minutes}}$$

$$45x = 75 \cdot 60$$

$$45x = 4,500$$

$$x = \frac{4,500}{45}$$

$$x = 100$$

It would take 100 minutes to complete this trip.

9. **A** To solve this problem, you must determine the average of two fractions. First add the fractions:

$$\frac{1}{3}+\frac{1}{6}=\frac{2}{6}+\frac{1}{6}=\frac{3}{6}=\frac{1}{2}$$

Then divide the total by the total number of fractions:

$$\frac{1}{2}\div 2=\frac{1}{4}$$

The average of the number of union members that support the new policy is $\frac{1}{4}$.

10. **D** To solve this problem, first convert two and a half hours to a decimal: 2.5 hours. Next, set up a proportion and use cross-multiplication:

$$\frac{2.5}{5}=\frac{x}{20}$$
$$5x=2.5\cdot 20$$
$$5x=50$$
$$x=\frac{50}{5}$$
$$x=10$$

It would take *one* worker ten hours to file 20 reports, so it would take *two* workers five hours to file the same number of reports.

D. Algebra

In addition to the types of questions covered earlier in this chapter, most versions of the Mathematics Ability test also include algebra questions. Algebra is a kind of math in which certain unknown values are represented by letters. Algebra problems may require you to use addition, subtraction, multiplication, division, roots, or some combination of these.

EXAMPLE:

> If you purchase two tomatoes at the farmer's market for a total of 80¢, how much would one tomato cost?

To find the answer, you would need to construct a simple equation. Algebra provides you the framework for writing such an equation.

The equation you would write should look like this:

$$2b = 80$$

In this equation, the 2 in $2b$ is called the coefficient. It is a constant number that never changes. The b is the variable, which represents the unknown value.

To solve the equation for b:

$$2b = 80$$
$$\frac{2b}{2} = \frac{80}{2}$$
$$b = 40$$

Thus, using the equation above, you have determined that each tomato costs 40¢.

1. Algebraic Expressions

An algebraic expression is collection of quantities composed of coefficients and variables connect by operations like the addition, subtraction, multiplication, or division signs.

For example, imagine you have four pencils and you give one to another student. You could write this as an algebraic expression that would look like this:

$$4p - p$$

In this algebraic expression, p = 1 pencil.

This particular expression is known as a binomial expression. A binomial is a type of expression that contains two terms. Terms are the products of a constant, and one or several variables are separated by addition or subtraction. An expression with only one term is called a monomial. An expression with three terms is called a trinomial. Expressions with more than two terms are also known as polynomials.

For example:

- $3x$ is a monomial.
- $3x + x$ is a binomial.
- $3 + x - y$ is a trinomial.
- $3 - x^3 + y$ is a polynomial.

Most questions on the Mathematics Ability test that deal with algebraic expressions will provide you with a particular expression and ask you to simplify it.

When solving these kinds of questions, there are two important rules to keep in mind:

- **Remember to solve using the order of operations (parentheses, exponents or roots, multiplication or division, addition or subtraction).** You can memorize the order of operations using the mnemonic device, Please Excuse My Dear Aunt Sally. When more than one of the same operation appears, perform the operations moving from left to right. (You can work on either roots or exponents first, multiplication or division first, or addition and subtraction first as long as you solve the problem using the correct order of operations.)
- **Remember that only like terms can be combined when adding and subtracting.**

When you encounter unlike terms, there are two ways you can proceed:

- **If you're adding or subtracting,** you can simplify the equation as much as possible.
- **If you're multiplying or dividing,** you can multiply or divide unlike terms to simplify the equation.

For example:

$$4n + 2n = 6n$$

$$(2x)(3y) = (2 \cdot 3)(x \cdot y) = 6xy$$

2. Simplifying

You can use a method called FOIL to multiply binomials. FOIL stands for first, outer, inner, and last. This means you multiply the first number or variable in each binomial, then the numbers or variables on the outside, then the inside, and then the last two numbers in each binomial.

EXAMPLE:

Simplify the binomial $(x + 4)(x + 3)$.

Using FOIL, you follow these steps:

- **FIRST:** Multiply x by x to get x^2.
- **OUTER:** Multiply x by 3 to get $3x$.
- **INNER:** Multiply 4 by x to get $4x$.
- **LAST:** Multiply 3 by 4 to get 12.

Now, add together the expressions to form an equivalent expression: $x^2 + 3x + 4x + 12 = x^2 + 7x + 12$.

3. Equations

Many of the algebra questions you'll likely find on the Mathematics Ability test will simply ask you to solve a given equation. If you have a firm understanding of the fundamentals of algebra discussed in this chapter, this task should be relatively simple. The most important thing you need to remember while solving an equation is to perform the same operation on both sides of the equation.

A typical equation you may find on the test might look like this:

$$6x + 3 = 23 - 4x$$

To start, subtract 3 from both sides of the equation. This will leave you with:

$$6x = 20 - 4x$$

Next, add $4x$ to both sides of the equation. This will leave you with:

$$10x = 20$$

Finally, divide both sides of the equation by 10 to solve for x.

$$x = 2$$

Remember: You may not be able to combine all the terms in an equation, so you may only have to simplify the given equation as much as possible to solve it.

4. Substitutions

Some questions may give you an equation and the values of the variables. In such a case, you'll have to plug in the given values and solve the equation.

EXAMPLE:

> If $a = 4$ and $b = 5$, what is the value of $6a(a + b)$?

To solve, you would first need to plug in the values of the variables and then solve:

$$6(4)(4 + 5) = 6(4)(9) = 216$$

5. Inequalities

Inequalities are another type of relationship you might find on the Mathematics Ability test. With inequalities, you're solving for a range of values for a variable, rather than a specific value. As such, these equations use the greater than (>) or less than (<) signs, as opposed to the equal (=) sign.

EXAMPLE:

> Solve for x: $4x + 4 > 2x + 12$.

To solve for x, you must first subtract 4 from both sides. This leaves you with:

$$4x > 2x + 8$$

Next, you must subtract $2x$ from both sides. This leaves you with:

$$2x > 8$$

Finally, divide each side by 2 to find:

$$x > 4$$

One important thing to remember when solving inequalities is that when you multiply or divide an inequality by a negative number, you have to reverse the direction of the sign.

EXAMPLE:

> Solve for n: $-4n > 8$.

When you divide each side of the equation by –4, you're left with:

$$n < -2$$

6. Word Problems

Some algebra questions also may be presented in the form of word problems. These questions will generally require you to solve a problem based on a specific formula. You'll be given the values for certain variables and asked to solve for the remaining variable.

For example, you may be asked to determine the distance a motorist has traveled based on his average rate of speed and time spent driving. To solve this problem, you would have to use the formula Distance = Rate · Time.

If the motorist's average rate of speed was 55 miles per hour and he traveled for four hours, the equation would look like this:

$$d = 55 \cdot 4$$

Thus,

$$d = 220 \text{ miles}$$

Some algebra word problems will not be based on formulas. These questions will include wording that will explain what you need to do with the given data.

Practice

Directions (1–10): Answer the following questions based solely on the information provided.

1. Solve for x: $4x + 8 = 2x + 18$.

   A. $x = 4$
   B. $x = 5$
   C. $x = 6$
   D. $x = 7$

2. If $n = 3$ and $m = 4$, what is the value of $6n(n + m)$?

   A. 103
   B. 108
   C. 115
   D. 126

3. Solve for y: $15y - 7 > 10y + 18$.

   A. $y > 3$
   B. $y > 4$
   C. $y > 5$
   D. $y > 6$

4. A motorist has traveled for 220 miles at an average speed of 55 miles per hour. How many hours has the motorist been driving?

    A. 2
    B. 3
    C. 4
    D. 5

5. Simplify: $(x + 2)(x + 3)$.

    A. $x^2 + 5x + 6$
    B. $x^2 + 4x + 5$
    C. $x^2 + 2x + 3$
    D. $x^2 + x + 6$

6. Solve for n: $6n + 7 = 4n + 21$.

    A. $n = 2$
    B. $n = 4$
    C. $n = 7$
    D. $n = 9$

7. Tom is making cupcakes. In three hours, Tom finishes 90 cupcakes. At this rate, how many minutes did Tom spend working on each cupcake?

    A. 1
    B. 2
    C. 3
    D. 4

8. If $x = 6$ and $y = 8$, what is the value of $2x(y + 4)$?

    A. 120
    B. 132
    C. 144
    D. 156

9. Solve for a: $-6a + 4 = 2a + 20$.

    A. $a = 2$
    B. $a = -2$
    C. $a = 6$
    D. $a = 8$

10. Solve for x: $12x + 6 < 7x + 36$.

    A. $x < 2$
    B. $x < 3$
    C. $x < 4$
    D. $x < 6$

Answers

1. B To solve the equation $4x + 8 = 2x + 18$ for x:

$$4x + 8 = 2x + 18$$
$$4x = 2x + 10$$
$$2x = 10$$
$$x = 5$$

2. D To evaluate the expression $6n(n + m)$, you must first substitute the variables with their given values. This leaves you with $6(3)(3 + 4)$. To solve this expression, you must follow the order of operations. First, add the integers within the parenthesis to get $6(3)(7)$. Now, just multiply: $6 \cdot 3 \cdot 7 = 126$.

3. C To solve the inequality $15y - 7 > 10y + 18$:

$$15y - 7 > 10y + 18$$
$$15y > 10y + 25$$
$$5y > 25$$
$$y > 5$$

4. C In this problem, you're given the distance (220 miles) and the rate (55 miles an hour), so you must solve for time:

$$\text{Time} = \frac{\text{Distance}}{\text{Rate}}$$
$$\text{Time} = \frac{220}{55}$$
$$\text{Time} = 4$$

5. A To simplify this expression, use the FOIL method. Multiply the first number or variable in each binomial, then the numbers or variables on the outside, then the inside, and then the last two numbers in each binomial. First, multiply x by x to get x^2. Then, multiply x by 3 to get $3x$. Then, 2 multiplied by x is $2x$. Finally, multiply 2 by 3 to get 6. Now, add them together to simplify the original expression: $x^2 + 3x + 2x + 6 = x^2 + 5x + 6$.

6. C To solve the equation $6n + 7 = 4n + 21$:

$$6n + 7 = 4n + 21$$
$$2n = 14$$
$$n = 7$$

7. **B** To solve this problem, you must first convert hours to minutes, because the question asks you for the number of minutes Tom spent working on each cupcake. One hour is 60 minutes, and three hours are $3 \times 60 = 180$ minutes. Now, divide the number of cupcakes Tom baked by the amount of time he spent baking them to find how many cupcakes Tom baked each minute: 180 minutes ÷ 90 cupcakes = 2. So, Tom spent 2 minutes working on each cupcake.

8. **C** To evaluate the expression $2x(y + 4)$, first substitute the variables with their given values. You know that $x = 6$ and $y = 8$; so, the expression will look like this: $2(6)(8 + 4)$. To solve, follow the order of operations. First, work with what is within the parentheses; this gives you $2(6)(12)$. Now, multiply: $2 \cdot 6 \cdot 12 = 144$.

9. **B** To solve the equation $-6a + 4 = 2a + 20$:

$$-6a + 4 = 2a + 20$$
$$-8a = 16$$
$$-a = 2$$
$$a = -2$$

10. **D** To solve the inequality $12x + 6 < 7x + 36$:

$$12x + 6 < 7x + 36$$
$$5x < 30$$
$$x < 6$$

E. Geometry

Many civil service employees must use geometry in their jobs. Geometry is the branch of math that focuses on the measurements of lines, angles, triangles, circles, and other shapes. Some civil service employees use geometry to find area, volume, perimeter, and angle sizes. Understanding these concepts in geometry will help you ace the civil service exam.

When answering geometry questions on the civil service exam, you may be asked to find the measurement of an angle, the perimeter of a quadrilateral, the circumference of a circle, the location of a coordinate in a quadrant, or the length of a triangle's hypotenuse. Understanding certain concepts, equations, and rules will help you answer these questions easily.

1. Lines and Angles

Lines and angles are important parts of geometry. Sometimes you'll have to use line segments and angles to find the measures of other line segments and angles. Other times the shape or size of angle or line will give you important information about problem.

In geometry, straight lines go on forever, rays have a stopping point at one end but continue infinitely in the other direction, and line segments have a starting point and a stopping point (so they have a measurable length).

Angles are formed by two rays or by two line segments. The angle of a straight line is 180°. Right angles are angles that are exactly 90°, or exactly half the angle of a straight line. Obtuse angles are angles larger than 90° and less than 180°, and acute angles are angles smaller than 90°.

2. Triangles

Triangles are three-sided shapes whose interior angles always add together to be 180°.

- **Right triangles** include a right angle, or a 90° angle.
- **Obtuse triangles** have one angle that is larger than 90°.
- **Acute triangles** include three angles that are smaller than 90°.
- **Equilateral triangles** have three equal angles, each 60°.
- **Isosceles triangles** have two equal angles and two equal sides.
- **Scalene triangles** have three different side lengths.

Review the following equations that help determine a triangle's area and perimeter:

$A = \frac{1}{2}bh$, where b is the base and h is the height perpendicular to the base

$P = s_1 + s_2 + s_3$, where s is a side

EXAMPLE:

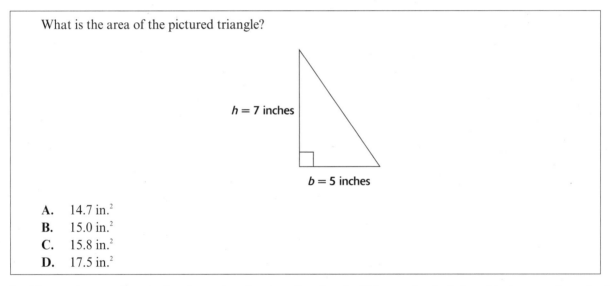

What is the area of the pictured triangle?

$h = 7$ inches

$b = 5$ inches

A.   14.7 in.^{2}
B.   15.0 in.^{2}
C.   15.8 in.^{2}
D.   17.5 in.^{2}

In this question, you're asked to determine the area of a triangle. This question is designed to test your knowledge of geometry facts and formulas. To solve this problem, you need to know that the area of a triangle can be found using this formula: $A = \frac{1}{2}bh$. The image indicates that the triangle's height (h) is 7 inches and its base (b) is 5 inches. You can answer the problem by substituting these values for the variables in the equation: $A = \frac{1}{2}(5)(7) = \frac{1}{2}(35) = 17.5$.

> **Remember: Geometry questions, like many different math questions, can be seen as puzzles that need solving. Sometimes a puzzle can seem overwhelming when all the pieces are mixed up. When you take your time and think about what the question is asking you, however, you can begin to put the puzzle pieces together.**

3. Quadrilaterals

Quadrilaterals are four-sided shapes.

- A **square** is a quadrilateral whose sides are all the same length and whose angles are all 90°.
- A **rectangle** is a quadrilateral that has two sets of equal sides and four 90° angles.
- A **rhombus** is a quadrilateral that has four equal sides and two sets of equal angles.

Review the following equations that help determine a quadrilateral's area and perimeter:

Square:

$A = s^2$, where s is a side

$P = 4s$, where s is a side

Rectangle:

$A = lw$, where l is the length and w is the width

$P = 2(l + w)$, where s is a side

Rhombus:

$A = bh$, where b is the base and h is the height perpendicular to the base

$P = s_1 + s_2 + s_3 + s_4$

4. Circles

A circle consists of all the points that are the same distance from its center. Finding the measurements of circles is different from finding measurements of other shapes. The length of the outside of the circle is called the circumference (C), rather than the perimeter. The diameter (d) is the segment that goes through the center of the circle and has endpoints on the circle, and half the diameter is a radius (r). Many equations dealing with circles use the Greek letter π, which represents a number that roughly equals 3.14.

Review the following equations that help determine a circle's area and circumference:

$A = \pi r^2$

$C = 2\pi r$

5. Coordinate Planes

In geometry, a coordinate plane is two-dimensional plane that includes an x-axis (horizontal axis) and a y-axis (vertical axis). The plane is broken into four quadrants, and points on the plane are identified by their positions in relation to the x-axis and the y-axis. Coordinates are pairs of numbers written inside parentheses. The first number in the parentheses indicates the point's position in relation to the x-axis, and the second number in the parentheses indicates the point's position in relation to the y-axis.

Practice

Directions (1–10): Answer the following questions based on the information provided.

1. Determine the value of x.

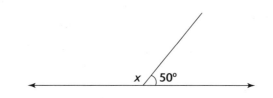

   A. 100°
   B. 130°
   C. 210°
   D. 250°

2. What is the length the triangle's hypotenuse, y?

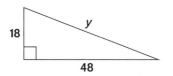

   A. 24.63
   B. 36.48
   C. 42.79
   D. 51.26

3. If triangles ABC and DEF are similar, what is the length of x?

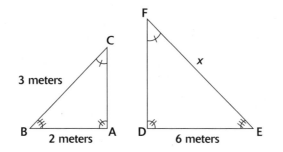

   A. 3 meters
   B. 6 meters
   C. 9 meters
   D. 12 meters

4. The circumference of a circle is 20 inches. What is the circle's diameter?

    A. 6.37
    B. 7.89
    C. 8.21
    D. 9.63

5. In which quadrant would a point with the coordinates (3, −12) appear?

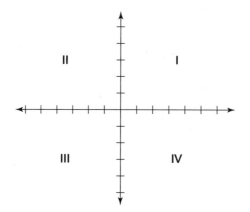

    A. I
    B. II
    C. III
    D. IV

6. A worker is installing a fence around a square yard. How many feet of fencing will the worker need to surround the yard?

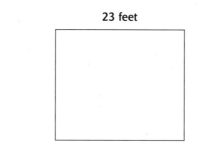

23 feet

    A. 46
    B. 92
    C. 133
    D. 529

7. What is the area of the pictured rhombus?

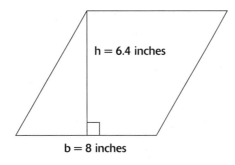

h = 6.4 inches

b = 8 inches

    A.   25.6 in.^{2}
    B.   28.8 in.^{2}
    C.   51.2 in.^{2}
    D.   57.6 in.^{2}

8. Which coordinate correctly corresponds with the following graph?

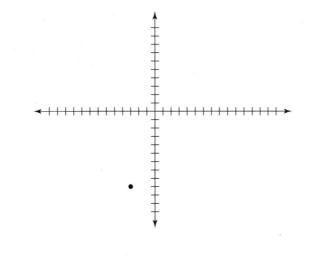

    A.   (−9, 3)
    B.   (−9, −3)
    C.   (9, 3)
    D.   (–3, –9)

9. Determine the area of the triangle pictured below.

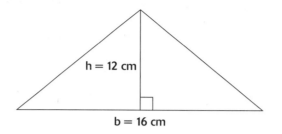

A.   96 cm²
B.   192 cm²
C.   259 cm²
D.   384 cm²

10. The perimeter of the quadrilateral is 92 units. What is the value of x in the image?

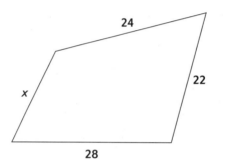

A.   18 units
B.   22 units
C.   25 units
D.   32 units

Answers

1. **B** The image shows a 180° line being divided by another line, which creates a 50° angle and an unknown angle (x). To find the value of the other angle, (x), subtract 50° from 180°: 180° − 50° = 130°.

2. **D** To find the length of the hypotenuse (y), use the equation $a^2 + b^2 = c^2$, where c is the hypotenuse and a and b are the other sides of the sides of the triangle. So,

$$a^2 + b^2 = c^2$$
$$18^2 + 48^2 = c^2$$
$$324 + 2{,}304 = c^2$$
$$2{,}628 = c^2$$
$$\sqrt{2{,}628} = \sqrt{c^2}$$
$$c \approx 51.26$$

3. **C** Similar triangles are triangles in which two triangles have corresponding angle sizes. Also, the lengths of the triangle's sides are proportional to one another. Sides AB and DE and sides BC and EF are proportional to one another. Since side DE is three times as large as side AB, side EF must also be three times as large as BC. BC is 3 meters, so EF is 9 meters.

4. **A** To find the circle's diameter, use the equation $C = d\pi$, so $20 = d\pi$. Then you should solve the equation for d by dividing both sides by π:

$$\frac{20}{\pi} = \frac{d\pi}{\pi}$$
$$\frac{20}{\pi} = d$$
$$\frac{20}{3.14} = d$$
$$d \approx 6.37$$

5. **D** The coordinates in the question ask you to first follow the x-axis (the horizontal axis) and then follow the y-axis (the vertical axis). You would follow the x-axis to the right because 3 is a positive number and then you would follow the y-axis down because -12 is a negative number. Quadrant IV is the correct answer.

6. **B** To find the amount of fencing that will surround the yard, you should find the yard's perimeter. The question states that the yard is a square, so you know that all the lengths of the sides are equal. To find the perimeter of a square, you add together all its sides: 23 feet + 23 feet + 23 feet +23 feet = 92 feet.

7. **C** A rhombus is special type of quadrilateral whose sides are all equal in length. To find the area of a rhombus, you can use this equation: $A = bh$. The image shows the height of the rhombus is 6.4 inches and its base is 8 inches. So, $A = (6.4)(8) = 51.2$.

8. **D** To the find the correct coordinates, first find where the point lies in relation to the x-axis (the horizontal axis); then find where the point lies in relation to the y-axis (the vertical axis). Then, you know the point has the coordinates of $(-3, -9)$.

9. **A** To find the area of a triangle, you should use the equation $A = \frac{1}{2}bh$. So,

$$A = \frac{1}{2}(16)(12)$$
$$= \frac{1}{2}(192)$$
$$= 96$$

10. **A** To find the value of the variable x, add together all the sides of the shape: $P = s_1 + s_2 + s_3 + s_4$. So, $92 = 22 + 24 + 28 + x = 74 + x$. Now, you should solve for x: $x = 92 - 74 = 18$.

F. Graphs and Tables

On the civil service exam, you may encounter mathematics questions involving graphs or tables. In most cases, answering these questions will involve simple addition and subtraction as well as reading comprehension skills. It's important for you to read all the information presented in each graph or table before attempting to answer the question.

1. Graphs

A graph is an illustration that depicts the relationship between certain quantities. *Remember:* You must read all the information in a graph carefully to answer the questions correctly. This includes any keys or legends presented in the graph.

There are four types of graphs that you may see on the civil service exam.

Bar graphs

A bar graph uses horizontal or vertical bars to represent specific quantities. Each bar may represent one quantity or may be sectioned to represent different quantities.

EXAMPLE:

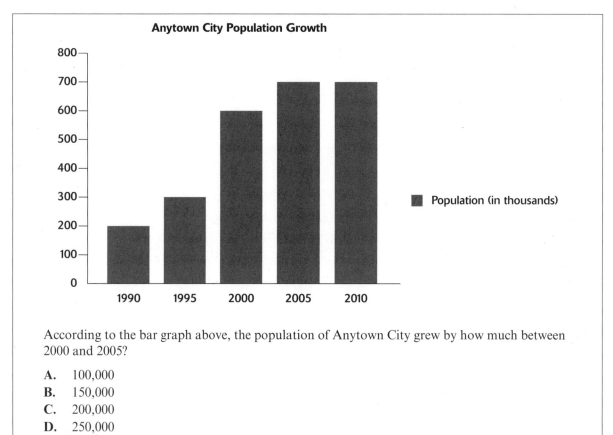

According to the bar graph above, the population of Anytown City grew by how much between 2000 and 2005?

A. 100,000
B. 150,000
C. 200,000
D. 250,000

The correct answer is choice A. If you read the chart correctly, you see that the population of Anytown City was 600,000 in 2000 and 700,000 in 2005. This indicates that, between 2000 and 2005, the population of Anytown City grew by 100,000.

Line graphs

Line graphs often represent changes in quantities over a period of time. Line graphs may contain more than one line and each line may represent a different object.

EXAMPLE:

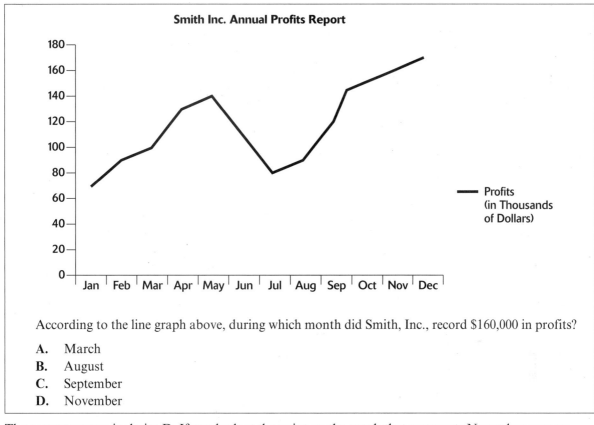

According to the line graph above, during which month did Smith, Inc., record $160,000 in profits?

A.   March
B.   August
C.   September
D.   November

The correct answer is choice D. If you look at the point on the graph that represents November, you see that it is the only month in which profits are at the $160,000 mark.

Circle graphs

Circle graphs (also known as pie graphs) illustrate the relationship between different parts of a whole quantity.

EXAMPLE:

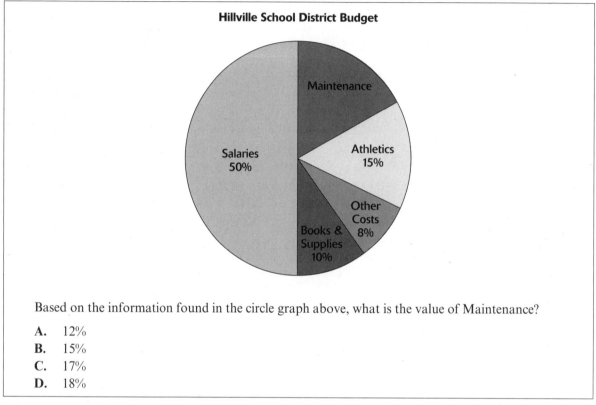

Hillville School District Budget

Based on the information found in the circle graph above, what is the value of Maintenance?

A. 12%
B. 15%
C. 17%
D. 18%

The correct answer is choice C. Logically, all the values in the chart must add up to 100%, so if you all the given values and subtract the sum from 100%, the difference will be the unknown value.

Pictographs

Pictographs use symbols to represent a give number of a particular quantity.

EXAMPLE:

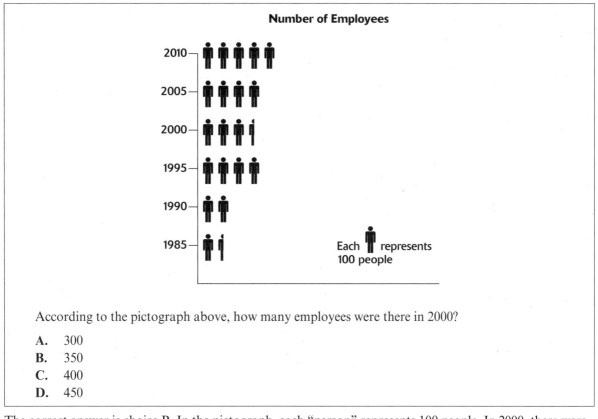

According to the pictograph above, how many employees were there in 2000?

A. 300
B. 350
C. 400
D. 450

The correct answer is choice B. In the pictograph, each "person" represents 100 people. In 2000, there were three and a half "people" or 350 employees.

2. Tables

Some questions on the Mathematics Ability test will be based on information found in a table. In many of these questions, you'll be presented with a table in which certain data is missing. You'll be asked to determine the value of the unknown data. To do this, you'll need to either add or subtract the given data according to what information you're looking for.

In other cases, you may also be given a complete table and asked to answer questions about the data found within the table.

EXAMPLE:

Greenville City Budget Expenditures, 2008–2010			
Item	**2008**	**2009**	**2010**
Utilities	$30,000	$40,000	III
Transportation	$25,500	II	$27,000
Emergency Departments	$62,000	$65,000	$66,000
Total Expenditures	**I**	**$131,000**	**$136,000**

In the above table, what is the value of I?

A. $115,500
B. $116,500
C. $117,500
D. $118,500

The correct answer would be choice C. To find this answer, you simply add the three given values for 2008 to find their sum. If you were asked to find the value of either II or III, you would have to subtract the given values from the Total Expenditures value to find the unknown value.

Practice

Directions (1–2): Answer the following questions based solely on the information provided.

Questions 1 and 2 refer to the following figure.

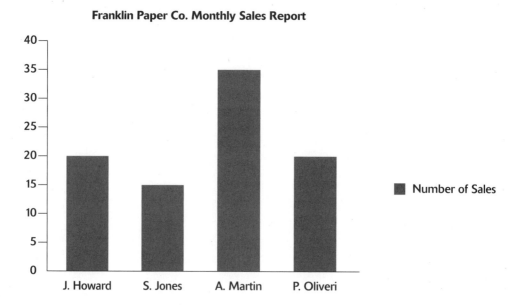

Franklin Paper Co. Monthly Sales Report

1. Which salesperson had the lowest number of sales?

   A. J. Howard
   B. S. Jones
   C. A. Martin
   D. P. Oliveri

2. What was the average number of sales among all the salespeople?

   A. 20
   B. 20.5
   C. 22
   D. 22.5

Questions 3 through 5 refer to the following figure.

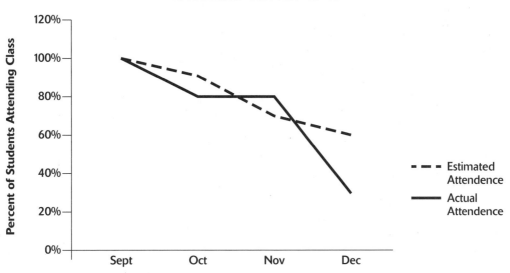

3. Which month saw the biggest difference between estimated attendance and actual attendance?

   A. September
   B. October
   C. November
   D. December

4. What was the estimated percentage of students attending class for October?

   A. 90
   B. 80
   C. 70
   D. 60

5. In which month did the actual percentage of students attending class exceed the estimated percentage?

    A.   September
    B.   October
    C.   November
    D.   December

Questions 6 and 7 refer to the following figure.

How the 2009 $800,000 Landsfield Paper Co. Budget Was Spent

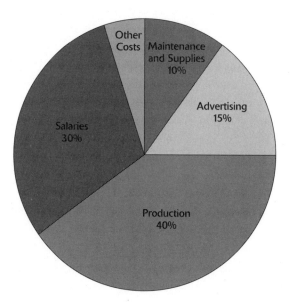

6. Based on the information in the circle graph, what is the value of Other Costs?

    A.   1%
    B.   5%
    C.   10%
    D.   15%

7. Based on the information in the circle graph, how much did Landsfield Paper Co. spend on advertising?

    A. $80,000
    B. $100,000
    C. $115,000
    D. $120,000

Questions 8 through 10 refer to the following table.

Midvale Propane Annual Expense Report, 2008–2010			
Item	**2008**	**2009**	**2010**
Employee Salaries	$798,436	$786,839	$799,589
Employee Benefits	$342,894	$340,355	III
Pensions	$416,563	$418,621	$419,823
Supplier Costs	$894,877	$895,398	$896,903
Transportation	$75,432	II	$78,490
Television Advertising	$30,502	$28,974	$30,557
Radio Advertising	$20,567	$18,430	$20,631
Print Advertising	$15,930	$13,737	$17,449
Other Costs	$25,877	$23,539	$24,777
Total Expenditures	**I**	**$2,603,296**	**$2,636,156**

8. Based on the information in the table above, what is the value of I?

    A. $2,354,899
    B. $2,436,273
    C. $2,621,078
    D. $2,787,510

9. Based on the information in the table above, what is the value of II?

    A. $76, 040
    B. $77,403
    C. $78,832
    D. $79,151

10. Based on the information in the table above, what is the value of III?

    A. $344,823
    B. $345,339
    C. $346,584
    D. $347,937

Answers

1. **B** According to the bar graph, S. Jones has the lowest number of recorded sales. S. Jones has only 15 sales for the month represented by the graph. Choices A and D are incorrect because J. Howard and P. Oliveri each had 20 sales for the month. Choice C is incorrect because A. Martin had 35 sales for the month.

2. **D** The average number of sales among all the salespeople is 22.5. To reach this number, add all the recorded sales and divide the sum by the number of salespeople: $15 + 20 + 20 + 35 = 90$ and $90 \div 4 = 22.5$

3. **D** December saw the biggest difference between estimated attendance and actual attendance. According to the graph, the estimated attendance was 60%, while the actual attendance was only 30%. You can determine this answer by looking at the line graph. The largest gap between estimated attendance and actual attendance fell in December, so this is the correct answer.

4. **A** According to the graph, the estimated percentage of students attending class in October was between 80% and 100%, so 90% is the correct answer.

5. **C** In November, the estimated percentage of students attending class was 70%, but the actual number was 80%. You can determine this answer by looking at the line graph. The actual attendance line is above the estimated attendance line only in November.

6. **B** According to the circle graph, the value of Other Costs is 5%. To determine this answer, add the percentages of the other values and subtract from the total percentage value: $40\% + 30\% + 15\% + 10\% = 95\%$ and $100\% - 95\% = 5\%$.

7. **D** According to the circle graph, Landsfield Paper Co. spent 15% of $800,000 on advertising. To find the answer, multiply 15% by $800,000: $0.15 \cdot \$800,000 = \$120,000$.

8. **C** According to the chart, I represents the total number of all expenditures for 2008. To find this answer, add all the expenditures for 2008: $\$798,436 + \$342,894 + \$416,563 + \$894,877 + \$75,432 + \$30,502 + \$20,567 + \$15,930 + \$25,877 = \$2,621,078$.

9. **B** According to the chart, II represents the 2009 Transportation costs. To find the answer, add all the expenditures for 2009, and subtract the sum from the total expenditures: $\$786,839 + \$340,355 + \$418,621 + \$895,398 + \$28,974 + \$18,430 + \$13,737 + \$23,539 = \$2,525,893$ and $\$2,603,296 - \$2,525,893 = \$77,403$.

10. **D** According to the chart, III represents the 2010 Employee Benefits costs. To find the answer, add all the expenditures for 2010, and subtract the sum from the total expenditures: $\$799,589 + \$419,823 + \$896,903 + \$78,490 + \$30,557 + \$20,631 + \$17,449 + \$24,777 = \$2,288,219$ and $\$2,636,156 - \$2,288,219 = \$347,937$.

VII. Clerical Ability

Many government jobs require excellent clerical skills. Secretaries, clerks, and information specialists must know how to alphabetize files, type memos, and code important documents and reports. For this reason, most civil service exams have a section that tests candidates' clerical abilities.

Questions in this portion of the exam are designed to test your ability to interpret and use various office coding systems, cleanly and efficiently reproduce text, take dictation, and file documents in alphabetical or numerical order.

The Clerical Ability section of most civil service exams contains four separate parts:

- Typing and stenography
- Filing and alphabetizing
- Coding
- Speed and accuracy

Practicing these skills is the best way to prepare for this portion of the exam. In some parts of the test, the time it takes you to complete a task is just as important as the accuracy of your answers. Regular practice will ensure that you have the necessary skills to do well on the exam, so take time to complete all the practice exercises in this chapter.

A. Typing and Stenography

The typing and stenography portion of the civil service exam is divided into two separate tests: the typing test and the stenography test. Various civil service exams may include one or both of these tests.

1. The Typing Test

The typing test is used on almost all the civil service exams. In many instances, the typing test serves as a qualifying test that all candidates must pass to be considered for a specific position. As such, this test is designed to demonstrate your ability to meet a minimum standard of speed and accuracy. When used as a qualifying test, your score on the typing test does not usually impact your score on the rest of the exam. However, some institutions score the typing test competitively, meaning that it counts toward the candidate's final score.

The format of the typing test is simple. You must replicate a brief passage exactly as it is written in a specific amount of time. These tests usually last about five minutes. Your score is based on the number of words per minute you type and the total number of errors you make.

In most cases, you have the chance to practice before taking the actual test. These practice exercises will help you warm up at the keyboard and acclimate yourself to the test format. The practice exercises will not affect your final score.

In order to prepare for the typing test, it's important to understand the factors that will affect your grade. As mentioned earlier, scoring on the typing test is divided into two basic categories:

- **Speed:** Your speed score is based on the number of words per minute you type. The minimum speed requirement may vary, but the most common standard is 30 words per minute. Some tests may require a higher minimum speed. *Remember:* A faster speed will most likely lead to a higher score.
- **Accuracy:** Speed alone does not guarantee a passing score on the typing test. You must also type with accuracy. Just as the minimum typing speed varies from test to test, so does the number of errors allowed. The following errors will count against your overall score on the typing test:
  - Incorrectly typed words or punctuation
  - Omission, repetition, insertion, or transposition of any series of consecutive words
  - Full or partial lines typed over other material, typed using all capital letters, or typed with fingers on the incorrect keys
  - Changes in the margin where the typist begins most lines or in the paragraph indentation most often used by the typist
  - Erasures of any kind

Be sure that you're familiar with the basic principles of typing and that you can type fluidly using the traditional typing method. Even if you're sure of your typing abilities, practice, practice, practice! Find printed material that you enjoy and practice replicating it exactly as it's presented. Always use the correct spelling, punctuation, and capitalization. Time yourself or have someone else time your progress to help increase your speed.

2. The Stenography Test

The stenography test is required only for those candidates who are applying for positions as stenographers. Stenographers are skilled typists who take dictation in shorthand during meetings, conferences, and legal proceedings. They later transcribe their notes using a computer. Many stenographers work in legal settings, recording the communication between lawyers, judges, defendants, and witnesses. Others work for government agencies or businesses that require accurate records of verbal communication. Some stenographers take dictation of awards ceremonies, sporting events, movies, and TV series for closed-captioning companies, which provide transcripts of broadcasted programs for people who have difficulty hearing.

For this test, you'll be expected to take dictation of a passage and use your notes to fill in the blanks of a portion of the original passage. You'll be tested on your ability to successfully use your notes to complete the selected portion of the dictated passage.

The passage will be dictated to you at a rate of about 80 words per minute, and you'll be responsible for taking the appropriate notes. Then you'll be given a section of the dictation in which a number of the original words have been removed. You must fill in the blanks with the correct words using your notes and an alphabetic word list that will be provided with the test.

The questions on the stenography test are, in effect, multiple-choice questions. The alphabetic list consists of a sizable group of words, one of which will be appropriate for a given blank space in the passage. Each question corresponds to a blank space. Each word on the alphabetic word list will be classified as A, B, C, or D. Although there will be multiple words represented by each letter, only one of the words will be appropriate for a given blank. For example, a certain blank might require the word *training*. Looking at the word list, you may find the word *training* classified as a D. If you look at the other words classified by the letter D, you'll find that none of them would make sense in the same blank as *training*. As a result, all you have to do is list your answer as D and it will be understood that you're referring to the word *training*.

As with the typing test, the best way to prepare for the stenography test is to practice. Set aside a little time each day to study the proper methods of stenography and practice taking dictation. Have a friend or family member dictate a text passage and record the appropriate notes. Make sure that the person giving the dictation reads the text slowly and accurately. This person should read the passage at a rate of 80 words per minute. All periods should be dictated, but all other punctuation should be indicated only through the appropriate verbal expression (for example, a pause for a comma or a questioning tone of voice for a question).

Now that you understand the basic requirements for the typing and stenography tests, try the following practice exercises. These practice questions will strengthen your skills and build confidence in your ability to do well on this portion of the exam.

Practice

Directions (1): Retype this passage in its entirety. Continue typing for five minutes. If you come to the end of the passage before time is up, double-space once, and start again from the beginning.

Office secretarial and clerical workers have many responsibilities pertaining to the daily operations of a business office. One of their most important responsibilities is communicating with clients and customers over the telephone. Secretaries and clerical workers are required to answer phones, interact with callers, and take and deliver messages. As a result, it's very important that employees have strong interpersonal communication skills and always communicate with callers in a professional and friendly manner. Proper telephone etiquette begins with the first telephone ring. Always try to answer the telephone in a timely manner so that the caller is not waiting on the line. A prompt response indicates that your company cares about their clients and customers. You should always identify your company and yourself to the caller when answering the telephone. This keeps the caller informed and promptly ends wrong-number calls.

In some cases, the caller may be asking a general question for which you may be able to provide an answer. Other callers may need to be directed to another department. If you must transfer a call to another department, inform the caller that you are putting her on hold before transferring the call. Some callers may ask to speak with your superiors. Ask for the caller's name and company affiliation. If your boss is expecting this call, place the caller on hold and inform your boss of the call. You will want to screen any unexpected calls for your superiors. Inform the caller that your superior is unavailable at the moment but that you'd be happy to take a message. Ask for the caller's name, company affiliation, and telephone number. Next, you should find out what the call is in reference to. You will also want to ask the caller when it would be best for your superior to call back. When taking specific messages, you should have pen and paper readily available and be prepared to quickly write down any important information the caller would like to relate to your superior. Be sure to record this information carefully and accurately. When you have finished taking the message, assure the caller that you will deliver it right away and politely end the call. Following these basic guidelines will help you hone your telephone skills and improve your company's quality of communication.

Directions (2–15): Ask a friend or study partner to dictate the following passage while you take notes. Then, using your notes and the alphabetic word list that follows, fill in the blanks of the following transcript of the passage. Do not look at the passage itself. Finally, find the corresponding answer choice for each word and fill in the answer sheet with the correct letter.

In today's fast-paced society, speedy communication is essential to the success of any business. (Period) Companies need to complete tasks in a timely manner if they have any hope of surviving in this competitive economy. (Period) Although speed is an important part of communication, accuracy is often overlooked. (Period) In our efforts to get things done as quickly as possible, many of us forget the importance of proper spelling, grammar, and punctuation in our written communications. (Period) Mistakes in these areas are not only embarrassing to the writer, but also, in some cases, quite costly to the company. (Period) In 2006, a simple comma error cost a Canadian telecommunications company millions of dollars during a contract dispute. (Period) The court ruled that the company's ignorance of proper punctuation nullified a lucrative long-term contract. (Period) The best way to avoid such egregious errors is to proofread your memos, e-mails, and reports. (Period)

Most people believe that spell-checking programs will catch any and all errors in their documents. (Period) While spell-checkers can catch glaring errors in written communication, they often miss subtle mistakes. (Period) For example, your spell-checker won't indicate that you're using *its* (an adjective relating to it or itself as a possessor) when you should be using *it's* (meaning "it is"). (Period) In addition, spell-checkers won't clear up confusing wording or help you figure out when a comma is necessary. (Period) This is why you must spell-check and proofread all of your documents. (Period) One of the best ways to proofread is to read what you have written aloud. (Period) This often can help you catch errors that you might otherwise overlook when reading silently to yourself. (Period) If you're unsure about the spelling of a word or the punctuation of a sentence, the best thing to do is to consult a dictionary or your company's preferred style manual. (Period) *Remember:* Don't hit the send button until you've read through your document several times. (Period)

Alphabetic Word List			
Word	**Answer Choice**	**Word**	**Answer Choice**
accuracy	C	quantity	B
avoid	D	rebuke	C
company	B	regularly	A
competitive	D	release	B
discipline	C	remove	C
dismiss	A	reprimand	D
dispute	A	requirements	C
embarrassing	D	society	B
error	D	surviving	A
essential	B	talents	D
ignorance	B	tolerate	C
lucrative	D	values	D
possible	B	watching	C
punctuation	A	withstand	A

Transcript

In today's fast-paced _____, speedy communication is _____ to the success of any business.
                          2   3

Companies need to complete tasks in a timely manner if they have any hope of _____ in this _____
                                                                              4   5

economy. Although speed is an important part of communication, _____ is often overlooked. In our
                                                               6

efforts to get things done as quickly as _____, many of us forget the importance of proper spelling,
                                          7

grammar, and _____ in our written communications. Mistakes in these areas are not only _____
             8   9

to the writer, but also, in some cases, quite costly to the _____. In 2006, a simple comma _____
                                                           10   11

cost a Canadian telecommunications company millions of dollars during a contract _____. The court
                                                                                 12

ruled that the company's _____ of proper punctuation nullified a _____ long-term contract. The
                         13   14

best way to _____ such egregious errors is to proofread your memos, e-mails, and reports.
            15

Answers

1. The minimum speed for the typing test will vary from state to state. The number of errors allowed
   will also vary. Contact your local testing facility for more information on the requirements for the
   typing test.

2. **B** The correct answer is choice B, society.

3. **B** The correct answer is choice B, essential.

4. **A** The correct answer is choice A, surviving.

5. **D** The correct answer is choice D, competitive.

6. **C** The correct answer is choice C, accuracy.

7. **B** The correct answer is choice B, possible.

8. **A** The correct answer is choice A, punctuation.

9. **D** The correct answer is choice D, embarrassing.

10. **B** The correct answer is choice B, company.

11. **D** The correct answer is choice D, error.

12. **A** The correct answer is choice A, dispute.

13. **B** The correct answer is choice B, ignorance.

14. **D** The correct answer is choice D, lucrative.

15. **D** The correct answer is choice D, avoid.

B. Filing and Alphabetizing

The filing and alphabetizing portion of the Clerical Ability section of the civil service exam is designed to test your ability to file the names of various people or businesses in alphabetical order. In order to answer filing and alphabetizing questions correctly, you'll need to understand the basic principles of filing and some specific rules for special circumstances.

1. Rules for Filing and Alphabetizing

The basic rule for filing names in alphabetical order is to carefully examine each letter in the full name. Remember that when filing the names of individuals, you must start with the last name first. Outside of this, there are some additional rules that apply to filing names of individuals and businesses.

a. Filing Names of Individuals

Remember the following rules when alphabetizing the names of individuals:

- Names of individuals are filed by the last name first. After the last name, the name is then filed by first name or initial. Following this, the name is filed according to middle name or initial. If you follow this rule, *Joseph Ayers* would come before *Steven Carter,* and *Matthew A. Jones* would come before *Matthew S. Jones.*

- In cases where two or more individuals share the same last name and first initial, the name with the initial is placed before the name in which the person's full name is spelled out. For example, *P. Kelly* would come before *Peter Kelly.*

- When two or more individuals share the same first and last name, the name that does not include a middle name or initial is placed before the ones with a middle name or initial. Following this rule, *Frank Smith* would come before *Frank T. Smith* and *Frank Thomas Smith.*

- When two or more individuals share the same first and last names, the name with the middle initial would come before the name with a spelled-out middle name that starts with the same initial. If you were filing names in alphabetical order, *John J. Miller* would come before *John Joseph Miller.*

- Names that include prefixes such as *Mc, Mac, De, O',* or *Van* are filed precisely as they are written and are considered part of the names they precede. Apostrophes do not affect filing order. For example, *Edward DeGeorge* would come before *David Duggan.*

- Foreign names with prefixes or articles are filed precisely as they are written, meaning that *Charlotte La Presto* would come before *Francois L'Perant.*

- Hyphenated surnames are filed as though the hyphen is joining the two last names. This means that *Isaac Thomason* would come before *Theresa Thomas-Riley.*

- Names that have been abbreviated are filed as though they are fully spelled out. For example, *Jos.* is alphabetized as *Joseph* and *Will.* is alphabetized as *William.*

- Titles such as *Dr., Fr., Mr., Jr., Prof.,* and *III* are given the very last consideration when filing.

b. Filing Names of Businesses

Note the following rules when alphabetizing the names of businesses:

- Business, organization, and building names are all filed based on the order of each word in the name. The only exception to this is when the name contains the full name of an individual.

- Business names that include the full name of an individual are filed according to the normal rules for filing individual names. This means that *Cyril Johnson Landscaping Co.* would be filed as *Johnson, Cyril Landscaping Co.*

- Words such as *the, and,* and *of,* and punctuation marks like apostrophes are ignored for filing purposes.

- Numerals in business names should be spelled out. For example, *5th Avenue Shoes* would be filed as *Fifth Avenue Shoes.*

- Sometimes, business names will be written along with their addresses. If two or more businesses names written in this fashion are identical, they should be filed alphabetically according to their city or town. If the city or town is also the same, they then should be filed alphabetically according to their state. The following provides an example of this rule: *Chester Realty Co., Baltimore, MD; Chester Realty Co., Eastland, NY; Chester Realty Co., Eastland, PA.*

- Abbreviated business names are filed as though the names are spelled out. If you came across the business name *Reiter Mfg.,* it would be filed as *Reiter Manufacturing.*

- Business names that are hyphenated are treated as separated words. Following this rule, *Cold-Westin, Inc.,* would be filed before *Coldtrent Systems, Inc.*

- Compound geographic names that appear as separated words are filed as though they are separate words. For example, *North Brook Institute* would be filed before *Northbrook Institute.*

- The names of government departments, bureaus, offices, and boards are filed according to the names of the chief governing body. This means that *Department of the Interior* would be filed as *Interior, Department of the.*

2. Types of Filing and Alphabetizing Questions

There are four possible types of filing and alphabetizing questions on the civil service exam. The questions vary from state to state, so it's important to prepare for all four.

The first type of question is designed to test your basic alphabetizing skills. Each of these questions will have a given word and four answer choice words. You must select the answer choice that would follow the given word in an alphabetical list.

EXAMPLE:

METEOR

- **A.** metal
- **B.** maple
- **C.** metric
- **D.** model

The correct answer is choice C, metric. *Meteor* would be followed by *metric.* You might have noticed that choice D, model, also would come after *meteor* in an alphabetic list, but *metric* would come before *model,* so choice C is correct.

The second type of filing and alphabetizing question is based on your understanding of the rules regarding the filing of names of individuals. In each of these questions, you'll be given a name and a list of four names in alphabetical order. Each of the spaces between the four names represents an answer choice. You will be asked to choose the space where the given name would fit in the list.

EXAMPLE:

Nelson, Florence

A. _____

Napier, Charles

B. _____

Neely, Rachel

C. _____

Netter, Stephanie

D. _____

Noone, Timothy

The correct answer is choice C. Alphabetically, *Nelson, Florence* would be filed between *Neely, Rachel* and *Netter, Stephanie.*

The third possible kind of filing and alphabetizing question is designed to test your ability to alphabetize individual and business names. In each of these questions, you'll find a list of four names in no particular order. One of the names will be bolded. You must determine where the name would be filed if all the names were put in alphabetical order. The answer choices give you the option to decide if the bolded named should be filed first, second, third, or fourth.

EXAMPLE:

Kelly, Thomas

Kent, Leslie

Keller, Max

Kelsey, Robert

A. First
B. Second
C. Third
D. Fourth

The correct answer is choice A. *Keller, Max* would come first in an alphabetical list of these four names.

The final type of filing and alphabetizing question is also based on your ability to file both individual and business names. In these questions, you're presented with a list four names. You must determine which name would be *third* if the list were alphabetized.

EXAMPLE:

---

1. **A.** Earl Wilson & Sons Auto
   B. William's Market
   C. Wilson-Masters, Inc.
   D. Wilhelm Bros. Audio

The correct answer would be choice A, *Earl Wilson & Sons Auto,* which would be filed as *Wilson, Earl & Sons Auto,* making it third in the alphabetized list.

Remember that various civil service exams may use any combination of these question types. Be sure to familiarize yourself with all four as you prepare for the exam.

Practice

Directions (1–2): Choose the word that should follow the given word in alphabetical order.

1. RESULT

   A. resale
   B. respite
   C. resolve
   D. resume

2. INSOLENT

   A. indecision
   B. intelligence
   C. instigate
   D. incomplete

Directions (3–4): Choose the space where the given name would appear in the alphabetical list.

3. Jones, Marvin

   A. _____
   Johnson, Peter

   B. _____
   Johnston, James

   C. _____
   Jolly, Kevin

   D. _____
   Joseph, Christopher

4. Wells, George E.

   A. _____
     Weathers, Edwin J.

   B. _____
     Westin, Calvin, S.

   C. _____
     Wetter, Simon R.

   D. _____
     White, Eugene L.

Directions (5–7): Using the list of names provided, determine which position the bolded name would be in if the list were alphabetized.

5. Langley, Rita

Lawrence, Andrew

Lambert, Sheldon

Lacey, Russell

   A. First
   B. Second
   C. Third
   D. Fourth

6. Snider Diner

Snyder Financial Corp.

John Snider & Sons Glass

Snyder-Freedman, Inc.

   A. First
   B. Second
   C. Third
   D. Fourth

7. Drake, Henry

Drake, David M.

Drake, Dr. Robert

Drake, Mrs. Martin

   A. First
   B. Second
   C. Third
   D. Fourth

Directions (8–10): Of the four names listed, choose the one that would be *third* if the list were alphabetical.

8. **A.** Davidson, Timothy
   B. Davis, William
   C. Davids, Paul
   D. David, Harold

9. **A.** Ashford Street Cafe
   B. Ashland & Morris, Inc.
   C. Ashley Thomas Co.
   D. Ashton Community Trust

10. **A.** Jeffery Lucas
    B. Michael Lombardi
    C. Samuel Lewis
    D. Patrick Loudon

Answers and Explanations

1. **D** *Resume* should follow *result.*

2. **C** *Instigate* should follow *insolent.*

3. **D** *Jones, Marvin* should be filed between *Jolly, Kevin* and *Joseph, Christopher.*

4. **B** *Wells, George E.* should be filed between *Weathers, Edwin J.* and *Westin, Calvin, S.*

5. **D** *Lawrence, Andrew* would be fourth in an alphabetical list.

6. **A** *Snider Diner* would be first in an alphabetical list.

7. **C** *Drake, Mrs. Martin* would be third in an alphabetical list.

8. **A** *Davidson, Timothy* would be third in an alphabetical list.

9. **C** *Ashley Thomas Co.* would be third in an alphabetical list.

10. **D** *Patrick Loudon* would be third in an alphabetical list.

C. Coding

Some civil service jobs require the use of coding systems. These systems are designed to be an efficient means of organizing or categorizing files, documents, cases, or other pieces of information. The codes themselves may be composed of letters, numbers, names, or some arrangement of the three. When understood and used properly, coding significantly increases office efficiency by simplifying the methods for filing and locating various types of information.

Clerical workers may be responsible for hundreds or even thousands of files or documents. These workers use various coding systems on a daily basis and need strong coding skills. For this reason, many civil service exams contain a section of questions designed to test your ability to correctly interpret and utilize coding systems.

The type of coding system you'll be tested on may vary, but there are two main types of coding systems commonly covered on the civil service exam: postal coding and standard coding.

1. Postal Coding Questions

As you can probably tell from the name, postal coding refers to the coding system used by the U.S. Postal Service. Questions based on postal coding are most commonly found on the postal worker exam and will not likely appear on other tests. However, other individuals may find these questions useful as they prepare for the exam.

Postal coding questions are usually presented as a short series of questions based on a provided coding guide. You can determine the correct answer by consulting the coding guide. A typical postal coding guide might look like the following.

Postal Coding Guide	
Address Range	**Delivery Route**
101–600 Broad Street 61–200 Maple Street 21–90 Chestnut Street	A
31–150 Lester Avenue 71–300 Adams Avenue 201–400 Miller Street	B
11–80 Cartwright Road 75–100 Turner Hill Road	C
Any mail that is not deliverable to one of the above address ranges	D

A typical question will ask you to determine the correct delivery route for the given address.

EXAMPLE:

> 167 Adams Avenue
>
> A. A
> B. B
> C. C
> D. D

The correct answer is choice B. To determine the correct answer, you should read the given address. You can then look at the coding guide and quickly find the code The address 167 Adams Avenue fits into the address range of 71–300 Adams Avenue, which is part of delivery route B.

When answering postal coding questions, remember to keep up your pace and don't spend too long on one question. On the postal worker exam, you'll have to answer 36 of these questions in only six minutes. Although you probably won't be able to answer every question in that period of time, you should try to answer as many questions as possible. Working quickly and carefully will be critical to your success. The following are some helpful hints for using your time wisely:

- **Memorize the answer choices.** In postal coding questions, the answer choices will always be the same. This makes it easy for candidates to memorize the routes. For example, in the sample question, the delivery routes are labeled A, B, C, and D, which corresponds to the answer choices. All the other questions using the same coding guide will have the same options. If you keep this in mind, you can save time when answering each question.

- **Don't spend too much time reviewing the coding guide.** You can save time by ignoring the information concerning route D since it has no listed addresses. Memorize the address ranges for the other routes and remember that any address that doesn't fall within those ranges will be part of route D.

- **Remember the three factors that indicate that an address will be classified as route D: address number, street name, or street type.** When you see an address in which one of these factors differs from the address ranges in routes A, B, and C, you should automatically know that it must be coded as route D. You can save time by choosing route D as soon as you recognize that one of these factors is different.

2. Standard Coding Questions

Standard coding questions are much more common and can be found on a wide variety of civil service tests. These questions cover the various forms of coding used in business offices on a daily basis. These questions are often more complex and challenging than the types of questions found on the postal worker exam.

Standard coding questions generally follow a format similar to postal coding questions. You'll be provided with a coding guide or a list of codes from which you must determine the correct code for a particular document. In some cases, you also may find a short paragraph that briefly explains the code and provides your instructions.

EXAMPLE:

Filing Code		
Year	**Originator**	**Department**
AB – 2007	1 – Paul Grady	BB – Billing
AC – 2008	2 – Dan Clemson	HR – Human Resources
AD – 2009	3 – Sharon Davis	SA – Sales
AE – 2010	4 – Marshall Sanders	SH – Shipping

Document Report Filing Form		
Year	**Originator**	**Department**

What code would be used for a 2008 file created for the Sales Department by Marshall Sanders?

- A. AB2SH
- B. AC4SA
- C. AD3BB
- D. AE1HR

The correct answer is choice B. When answering this question, you must use the information in the Filing Code table to determine which of the given codes accurately reflects the information provided in the question. After you've read the details of the file, you can use the Document Report Filing Form to learn how the code should be constructed. According to this form, the code should begin with the year the document was created. Since the file in the question was created in 2008, the proper year code would be AC. Next, you must find the right code for the originator of the document, Marshall Sanders. His originator code is 4. Finally, you must find the correct department code. The document was created for the Sales Department, so the appropriate department code is SA. Putting all three elements together, the correct code is AC4SA.

> **Tip:** You can save time by looking at the answer choices as you figure out the correct code. In the preceding example, as soon as you figured out that the first two letters were AC, you could've determined that the correct answer was choice B, since none of the other choices begin with AC.

Some standard coding questions may be presented in an expanded format.

EXAMPLE:

Document Report Filing Form				
Year	**Department**	**Document Type**	**Classification**	**Status**

Codes for this form are developed using the following keys:

Year	Department	Document Type	Classification	Status
A. 2005	A. Administrative	A. Administrative document	A. Confidential	A. Active
B. 2006	B. Finance		B. Restricted	B. Inactive
C. 2007	C. Sales	B. Financial report	C. Internal	C. Under review
D. 2008	D. Customer Service	C. Interdepartmental document	D. Public	D. Incomplete
E. 2008		D. Legal document		E. Destroyed
F. 2010				

Code the information found in each question using the keys above. Be sure to use only the given information to determine the code. The code should be ordered in the same format as the Document Report Filing Form shown above, from left to right.

An inactive 2006 financial report for the Sales Department that was classified as internal would have the code:

A. BCBCB
B. CBBCB
C. BBCCB
D. CCBCB

The correct answer is choice A. Since the file was created in 2006, the correct year code for the file would be B. Because it was created for the Sales Department, the correct department code is C. The document type code would be B because it is a financial report, and the correct classification code is C because the document is internal. Finally, since the file is considered inactive, the correct status code is B. This makes the final code BCBCB.

As with postal coding questions, you'll most likely have a limited amount of time to answer standard coding questions. You must answer the questions carefully and quickly. Although speed is important, it's very easy to confuse the codes.

One way to save time is to skim any additional information and focus your attention on the coding guide. Introductory or other explanatory paragraphs usually repeat information that you can find in the coding guide, so don't spend time focusing on these directions. Instead, concentrate on studying the information in the coding guide.

You also can reduce your answer time by remembering the correct coding order. Some questions may present you with data in an order other than the one established by the coding guide. If you remember to order the code according to the coding guide, you can eliminate some of the answer choices that don't follow the coding guide.

Finally, you should avoid rechecking your answers. When you're working under a strict time limit, you may not even have enough time to answer all the questions. Going back and rechecking your answers will only reduce the total number of questions you can answer. Your best option is to choose the best possible answer and immediately move on to the next question.

Practice

Directions (1–5): Use the following coding chart to determine the correct delivery route for the addresses given in each question.

Postal Route Guide	
Address Range	**Delivery Route**
1001–4000 South Street 501–1800 Broad Street 901–1300 Patterson Avenue	A
4001–8000 South Street 401–1200 Carter Avenue 101–400 Beachwood Drive	B
21–100 Commerce Boulevard 1–31 Sawmill Road	C
All mail that cannot be delivered to any of the above address ranges	D

1. 974 Carter Street

   A. A
   B. B
   C. C
   D. D

2. 1775 Broad Street

   A. A
   B. B
   C. C
   D. D

3. 5612 South Street

    A. A

    B. B

    C. C

    D. D

4. 423 Beachwood Drive

    A. A

    B. B

    C. C

    D. D

5. 9 Commerce Boulevard

    A. A

    B. B

    C. C

    D. D

Directions (6–10): Use the following table to determine the correct code for the file described in each question. Each code consists of a two-letter code, followed by a one-number code, followed by a two-letter code.

Filing Code		
Year	**Originator**	**Department**
AA – 2003	1 – David Henderson	AD – Administrative
AB – 2004	2 – Thomas Daley	HR – Human Resources
AC – 2005	3 – Charles Vincent	SA – Sales
AD – 2006	4 – Barry Simms	FI – Finance

Document Report Filing Form		
Year	**Originator**	**Department**

6. What code would be used for a 2005 file for the Sales Department created by Charles Vincent?

    A. AD3SA

    B. AA2FI

    C. AB1AD

    D. AC3SA

7. What code would be used for a file for the Finance Department created by David Henderson in 2004?

   A. AD3SA
   B. AB1FI
   C. AC2HR
   D. FI1AB

8. What code would be used for a file created in 2003 by Barry Simms for the Administrative Department?

   A. AA4AD
   B. AC1AD
   C. AB3AD
   D. AA2AD

9. What would be the correct code for a 2005 file for the Human Resources Department created by Thomas Daley?

   A. AB2HR
   B. AD3FI
   C. AA3SA
   D. AC2HR

10. What would be the correct code for Charles Vincent's 2003 Finance Department file?

   A. AC1FI
   B. AD4SA
   C. AA3FI
   D. AB2AD

Directions (11–12): Use the following Document Report Filing Form and coding instructions to answer the questions.

Document Report Filing Form

Year	Department	Document Type	Classification	Status

Codes for this form are developed using the following keys:

Year	Department	Document Type	Classification	Status
A. 2000	A. Legal	A. Business report	A. Confidential	A. Active
B. 2001	B. Accounting	B. Financial report	B. Restricted	B. Inactive
C. 2002	C. Billing	C. Customer Inquiry	C. Interdepartmental	C. Under review
D. 2003	D. Customer Service	D. Legal document	D. Public	D. Complete
E. 2004	E. Human Resources	E. Personnel document		E. Destroyed
F. 2005	F. Public Relations			
G. 2006				
H. 2007				
I. 2008				
J. 2009				
K. 2010				

Code the information found in each question using the keys above. Be sure to use only the given information to determine the code. The code should be ordered in the same format as the Document Report Filing Form shown above, from left to right.

11. What would be the correct code for a confidential 2000 financial report created for the Public Relations Department that has been destroyed?

   A. AFCAD
   B. AFBAE
   C. ABAEC
   D. ABACE

12. What would be the correct code for a restricted 2003 legal document created for the Accounting Department that is currently under review?

   A. DBDBC
   B. DBDBA
   C. DBBDC
   D. DABDB

Answers

1. **B** The address 974 Carter Street is part of route B.

2. **A** The address 1775 Broad Street is part of route A.

3. **B** The address 5612 South Street is part of route B.

4. **D** The address 423 Beachwood Drive is not included in the assigned delivery routes and would be classified as route D.

5. **D** The address 9 Commerce Boulevard is not included in the assigned delivery routes and would be classified as route D.

6. **D** The correct code for this document is AC3SA.

7. **B** The correct code for this document is AB1FI.

8. **A** The correct code for this document is AA4AD.

9. **D** The correct code for this document is AC2HR.

10. **C** The correct code for this document is AA3FI.

11. **B** The correct code for this document is AFBAE.

12. **A** The correct code for this document is DBDBC.

D. Speed and Accuracy

Most of the Clerical Ability questions on the civil service exam require you to select your answers with great speed and accuracy. Some questions test your speed and accuracy skills indirectly while analyzing your other clerical skills, but the questions in this section are specially designed to provide a direct assessment of this important skill set.

Speed and accuracy may not always seem to go hand-in-hand. Speeding through your work to get as much done as possible can lead to many errors. On the other hand, working very carefully to avoid any errors can be very time-consuming. Ideally, you should strive to work quickly and with a minimum of errors. It takes a great deal of time to hone these skills, but with some patience, and a lot of practice, you can learn to work as quickly and accurately as possible.

Although the exact format of speed and accuracy questions can vary from test to test, the basic principle of the questions is always the same. You'll be presented with a series of items and asked to determine how many of them are alike. On most tests, these items will be a series of names or numbers. You must examine the names or numbers quickly and carefully to determine if any, all, or none of them are identical. Although this sounds simple, these questions are quite challenging and will require careful attention.

With each question, you should immediately examine the list of names or numbers and look for any differences. Differences in line lengths, middle initials, the number of digits, or the size of words will help you determine which items are different.

Sometimes, you may find it helpful to use a special system of reading the items to make spotting differences easier. You can try reading words exactly as you see them and sounding them out according to their syllables. For example, if you find the abbreviated word *Rd.,* try reading it as "ar-de," rather than "road." This system can also be applied to numbers. If you find the number 1389, read it as "one-three-eight-nine" rather than "one thousand three hundred eighty-nine." This approach can help you spot differences quickly.

For the following question you must determine how many names are the same.

EXAMPLE:

Patrick L. Welles
Patrick I. Welles
Patricia L. Wells
Patrick L. Welles
A. 0
B. 2
C. 3
D. 4

Looking carefully at the four names in the list, you can see that only the first and last names, written as "Patrick L. Welles," are the same. The second name, Patrick I. Welles, includes a different middle initial. The third name, Patricia L. Wells, includes a different first and last name. As a result, the correct answer would be choice B.

The following is an example of a numerical speed and accuracy question.

EXAMPLE:

10911384
10911304
10911384
10911384
A. 0
B. 2
C. 3
D. 4

When you examine the numbers in this question, you can easily find that only one of them is not like the others. Three of the numbers are written as "10911384." The second number is written as "10911304." In this case, the correct answer would be choice C.

Like other Clerical Ability questions on the civil service exam, the speed and accuracy section contains a large number of questions and a very strict time limit. You won't be expected to answer every question, but you will be penalized for incorrect answers.

When answering speed and accuracy questions, the best approach is to work at a steady pace until your time is up. You won't be penalized for unanswered questions.

You should not attempt to guess on any question. Since there is a penalty for incorrect answers, guessing could negatively affect your final score.

Try not to rush through the questions. Remember to examine each question carefully and choose the correct answer. For this section of the test, quality is more important than quantity.

Practice

Directions (1–10): Each question contains a list of four names or numbers that may or may not be exactly alike. Compare the items and determine how many items are the same.

1. Francis M. DeVito

   Francis M. DeVito

   Francis N. DeVito

   Francis M. DeVito

   A.   0
   B.   2
   C.   3
   D.   4

2. Harvey F. Greene

   Harvey E. Green

   Harvey E. Greene

   Harvey F. Green

   A.   0
   B.   2
   C.   3
   D.   4

3. Brian A. Connors, Jr.

   Bryan A. Connors, Jr.

   Brian A. Connors, Sr.

   Brian A. Connors, Jr.

   A. 0
   B. 2
   C. 3
   D. 4

4. 28424149

   28421419

   28442149

   28424149

   A. 0
   B. 2
   C. 3
   D. 4

5. Maximilian R. Harrison

   Maximilian R. Harrison

   Maximilian R. Harrison

   Maximilian R. Harrison

   A. 0
   B. 2
   C. 3
   D. 4

6. Cristina S. Kelley

   Christina S. Kelly

   Cristina S. Kelley

   Cristina S. Kelley

   A. 0
   B. 2
   C. 3
   D. 4

7. Thomas B. Jameson

   Thomas B. Jamison

   Thomas P. Jamison

   Thomas B. Jameson

   A. 0
   B. 2
   C. 3
   D. 4

8. Allison R. Newman

   Alison R. Newman

   Allison R. Neuman

   Allison P. Newman

   A. 0
   B. 2
   C. 3
   D. 4

9. Reese M. Howell

   Reese M. Howell

   Reese M. Howell

   Reece M. Howell

   A. 0
   B. 2
   C. 3
   D. 4

10. 48201532

    48201532

    48201532

    48201532

    A. 0
    B. 2
    C. 3
    D. 4

Answers

1. **C** Three of the names are written as "Francis M. DeVito," while one name is written as "Francis N. DeVito."

2. **A** None of the choices is the same.

3. **B** Two of the names are written as "Brian A. Connors, Jr." The other two names are written as "Bryan A. Connors, Jr." and "Brian A. Connors, Sr."

4. **B** Two of the numbers are written as "28424149." The other two numbers are written as "28421419" and "28442149."

5. **D** All four are the same.

6. **C** Three of the names are written as "Cristina S. Kelley," while one name is written as "Christina S. Kelly."

7. **B** Two of the names are written as "Thomas B. Jameson." The other two names are written as "Thomas B. Jamison" and "Thomas P. Jamison."

8. **A** None of the choices is the same.

9. **C** Three of the names are written as "Reese M. Howell," while one name is written as "Reece M. Howell."

10. **D** All four are the same.

VIII. Other Abilities

In addition to verbal, mathematical, and clerical abilities, the civil service exam tests a number of other abilities. It's important to remember that the questions on the civil service exam will differ according to the type of job you're applying for and the guidelines set forth by the state or municipality where you take the exam.

Although this chapter can't cover every type of question that you might encounter on the civil service exam, it's designed to introduce you to some of the most common questions—the ones that you'll most likely see.

On the other abilities portion of the civil service exam, you'll likely encounter questions in the following categories:

- Memory and following directions
- Judgment and decision-making
- Mechanical aptitude
- Personal experience

It may seem like these types of questions have little to do with the type of job you hope to secure, but many of these questions test skills that are crucial to a number of civil service jobs. Read each section carefully and then complete the practice questions. Review the answer explanations to identify any sections that present difficulties for you.

A. Memory and Following Directions

Having a sharp memory is critical to many civil service jobs and having the ability to accurately follow directions will help you complete almost any task. This section introduces you to the types of memory and following directions questions that you'll most likely see on the civil service exam.

1. Memory

Imagine that you're working as a building inspector for a local municipality. Building inspectors examine new construction and remodeling projects to determine if they're safe to use. Although building inspectors take many notes on the job, they also need to recall important details about building codes as they record information about the structure. For example, a building inspector would need to remember if changes to the local building code prevent a homeowner from installing a fire pit in his backyard. Police officers, firefighters, and clerical workers must also have sharp memories in order to complete their jobs quickly and effectively.

In general, there are two types of memory questions used on the civil service exam:

- Image-based questions
- Text-based questions

Image-Based Questions

Image-based questions usually include a photograph that you'll be asked to study for a specified time, usually between five and ten minutes. Typically, these photographs are printed on a separate page or book that must be returned to the exam proctor before you begin answering the questions.

Try to commit as many details as you can to memory. For most tests, you won't be able to take notes about what you see in the photograph. When the time limit has expired, you won't have an opportunity to refer back to the photograph as you answer the questions.

This might seem like an overwhelming task, but there are several questions you can ask yourself as you study the photograph to help you recall the most significant details in the photograph:

- What does the photograph show?
- Are there people in the photograph? If so, how many?
- Are there any distinguishing characteristics about the people?
- What are the people doing?
- What are the people wearing or holding?
- Is there any text in the photograph? If so, what does the text say?
- Are there any animals in the photograph? If so, what kind?
- What objects appear in the photograph?
- Are there any vehicles or buildings in the photograph? If so, how many of each?
- What are some distinguishing characteristics of the vehicles or buildings?

These questions will help you locate the most important details in each photograph.

Remember: Even insignificant details might show up in the questions, so it's important to try to take in as much as possible as you study the photograph.

Of course, the best way to understand image-based memory questions is to take a look at a few examples. Study the photograph for ten minutes; then cover the photograph and answer the questions based on your memory.

EXAMPLES:

Photo credit: National Park Service

---

1. How many picture frames hang above the fireplace?

    A. 2
    B. 3
    C. 6
    D. 7

Choice D is correct. There are two large picture frames hanging above five smaller picture frames. In total, there are seven picture frames hanging above the fireplace.

---

2. How many rugs are on the floor?

    A. 1
    B. 2
    C. 3
    D. 4

Choice B is correct. There are two rugs on the floor in this picture.

Text-Based Questions

Text-based questions ask you to study a passage for several minutes before answering questions about what you've read. These texts may look like memos or e-mail messages. It may seem like an impossible task to memorize an entire passage in just a few short minutes, but you can look for the most important details in the passage.

Think about the following questions as you read each passage:

- What is the passage about?
- Who is involved in the passage?
- What dates are mentioned in the passage?
- What places does the passage discuss?
- What events are mentioned in the passage?
- What is the passage trying to communicate to the reader?

Now that you've read some tips, try the following example question. Study the passage for five minutes; then cover the passage and answer the questions based on your memory.

EXAMPLES:

> Date: March 20, 2011
> To: All Employees
> From: James Rodan, Human Resources Manager
> Subject: Company Events
>
> This is a reminder to all employees about the upcoming company events for the month of April. Representatives from the California office will be sitting in on meetings from Monday, April 4, to Friday, April 8. General Manager Austin Collins will be holding a seminar on global diversity on April 7. On April 12, the company softball tournament will be held at McCade State Park; those wishing to participate in the tournament should contact Caitlyn Dawes before April 4. The company's annual Friends and Family Day will be held on Saturday, April 23, at Jenkins Amusement Park; tickets to the event will go on sale April 1. Please contact me for more information on this event. The office will be closed on Monday, April 25. Finally, all employees should submit vacation requests for the months of June, July, and August to Joanne Garcia by April 29.
>
> Sincerely,
> James Rodan
> Human Resources Manager

---

1. When was the memo sent?

   A. March 20
   B. April 4
   C. April 12
   D. April 25

Choice A is correct. The memo was sent on March 20. In the memo, the author discusses other important dates for the month of April.

2. Who should employees contact if they're interested in participating in the company softball tournament?

    A. James Rodan
    B. Austin Collins
    C. Caitlyn Dawes
    D. Joanne Garcia

Choice C is correct. Employees should contact Caitlyn Dawes for more information on the company softball tournament.

3. When will the company's annual Friends and Family Day be held?

    A. April 7
    B. April 12
    C. April 23
    D. April 29

Choice C is correct. According to the memo, the Friends and Family Day will be held on April 23.

2. Following Directions

Supervisors and managers provide employees with directions to improve efficiency and ensure that projects are completed in a particular manner. That's why following directions questions are included on the civil service exam. Officials are looking for candidates who have the ability to follow directions carefully.

There are two types of following directions questions on the civil service exam:

- Oral direction questions
- Written direction questions

Oral Direction Questions

For oral direction questions, you'll need to listen carefully to the exam proctor as he or she reads a question aloud. The proctor will ask you to select the correct answer in your test booklet. No part of the question will actually appear in your test booklet. However, in this book, you'll be able to see the question as well as the answer choices.

To achieve the full testing experience, you should ask a friend or family member to read the question to you aloud, and then you should cover the question and, looking only at the answers, select the best one. The person reading the question will need to pause to give you some time to answer the question.

EXAMPLES:

---

1. In your test booklet, you'll see four answer choices marked A through D. For question 1, select the answer choice that shows the earliest time of day.

   A. 12:45 a.m.
   B. 1:13 p.m.
   C. 2:22 a.m.
   D. 3:54 p.m.

Choice A is correct. The earliest time of day listed in the answer choices is 12:45 a.m.

---

2. In your test booklet, you'll see four answer choices marked A through D. For question 2, select the answer choice that shows the proper abbreviation for the Northwest Lumber Company.

   A. NCL
   B. NWLC
   C. NLC
   D. NWCL

Choice C is correct. The proper abbreviation for the Northwest Lumber Company would be NLC. It's important to remember that *northwest* is one word.

Written Direction Questions

Written direction questions are similar to reading comprehension passages in a lot of ways. You'll be asked to read a paragraph or a set of directions. You'll need to use what you've learned from reading the paragraph to answer the questions. These paragraphs may discuss a number of different topics. Remember to read each paragraph carefully. Occasionally, you might find that it's a good idea to read the question and then reread the paragraph to find the answer.

EXAMPLES:

The National Park Service (NPS) employs thousands of park rangers. The responsibilities of the park rangers differ depending on their classification. The following provides a description of the different classification of park rangers employed by the NPS.

- **Law enforcement rangers** are responsible for the safety of the people who visit the park. These rangers have the authority to enforce both federal and state laws within the park. In the park, these rangers serve as the primary law enforcement officials. In addition to commissioned law enforcement agents, the NPS also employs some special agents who handle complicated criminal investigations.

- **Interpretation rangers** provide visitors with information. Interpretation rangers may provide visitors with directions, weather forecasts, or general information about park hours. These rangers are responsible for making the guests' stay a safe and comfortable experience.

- **Educational rangers** offer educational programs based on the history of the park or the cultural significance of the region. Programs may include information on indigenous animals or plants or significant historical events. Educational rangers will often create new programs and present their work to visitors.

■ **Emergency response rangers** are responsible for the safety of the park and its visitors. Many of these rangers are trained emergency medical technicians or firefighters. These rangers are prepared to handle any emergency that might arise in the wilderness.

---

1. Which type of park ranger would most likely provide visitors with information on hiking trails?

   A.   Law enforcement ranger
   B.   Interpretation ranger
   C.   Education ranger
   D.   Emergency response ranger

Choice B is correct. From what you've read, you can tell that interpretation rangers often deal with guests and would be best equipped to provide information about hiking trails.

---

2. Which type of ranger would be most helpful if a park guest's car were broken into?

   A.   Law enforcement ranger
   B.   Interpretation ranger
   C.   Education ranger
   D.   Emergency response ranger

Choice A is correct. A law enforcement ranger would be best equipped to handle a car break-in.

Practice

Directions (1–3): Study the photograph for ten minutes; then cover the photograph and answer the questions based on your memory.

Photo credit: National Park Service

1. How many wood poles are positioned over the fence on the left-hand side of the photograph?

   A. 2
   B. 3
   C. 5
   D. 6

2. What is directly under the archway?

   A. A gate
   B. A bush
   C. Stairs
   D. Signs

3. How many steps are on the right-hand side of the gate?

    A. 3
    B. 4
    C. 5
    D. 6

Directions (4–5): Study the passage for five minutes; then cover the passage and answer the questions based on your memory.

Date: September 15, 2011
To: All Employees
From: Allison Hernandez, General Manager
Subject: Vacation Requests

This is a reminder to all employees that vacation requests for the months of October, November, and December are due by September 30, 2011. All requests should be forwarded to your immediate supervisor and Paul Berke, the head of human resources. Questions about vacation schedules can be addressed to Paul or his two assistants, Janice Field and Brian Jones. The office will be closed on the following days in October, November, and December:

- October 10 (Columbus Day)
- November 11 (Veterans Day)
- November 24 and 25 (Thanksgiving holiday)
- December 23 and 26 (Christmas holiday)
- December 31 (New Year's Eve)

Sincerely,
Allison Hernandez
General Manager

4. Who is the head of human resources?

    A. Allison Hernandez
    B. Paul Berke
    C. Janice Field
    D. Brian Jones

5. When are vacation requests due?

    A. September 15
    B. September 30
    C. October 10
    D. November 11

Directions (6–8): To achieve the full testing experience, don't simply read the following questions and select an answer. Instead, ask a friend to read these questions aloud to you, and then select the best answer based on what you hear. Have your friend pause before moving on to the next question to give you time to select the answer.

6. In your test booklet, you'll see four answer choices marked A through D. For question 6, select the answer choice that shows the latest calendar date.

   A. May 31
   B. March 7
   C. June 2
   D. January 25

7. In your test booklet, you'll see four answer choices marked A through D. For question 7, select the answer choice that shows the correct initials for Amanda Mary Lewis.

   A. AML
   B. MAL
   C. ALM
   D. MLA

8. In the town of Kingston, garbage is picked up on Mondays, glass bottles are picked up on Tuesdays, plastic is picked up on Wednesdays, and paper and cardboard are picked up on Thursdays. In your test booklet, you'll see four answer choices marked A through D. For question 8, select the answer choice that shows which day glass bottles are picked up in the town of Kingston.

   A. Monday
   B. Tuesday
   C. Wednesday
   D. Thursday

Directions (9–10): Answer the following questions based solely on the information provided.

The Department of Motor Vehicles employs many people who perform a variety of tasks for citizens in their state. Here are some of the responsibilities that various employees perform:

- **Customer service representatives** are responsible for answering questions about licenses and titles. Customer service representatives also help drivers with a number of tasks, such as changing an address or renewing a license.

- **Licensing agents** conduct a variety of tests to assess a driver's abilities. These agents notify candidates of testing results and keep records of all testing. Licensing agents also review all official documents of those individuals who are applying for a license.

- **Motor vehicle inspectors** examine vehicles to ensure that they are safe to drive. These employees must make sure that all vehicles pass various tests required by the state.

- **Motor vehicle emissions agents** are responsible for waiver processing and contractor monitoring within the emissions department, which ensures that all vehicles meet the minimum emissions standards. These agents also keep records of emissions reports.

9. Which employee would most likely assist a customer in changing the name on a license?

   A. Customer service representative
   B. Licensing agent
   C. Motor vehicle inspector
   D. Motor vehicle emissions agent

10. Which employee would most likely need to be familiar with the working parts of most motor vehicles?

   A. Customer service representative
   B. Licensing agent
   C. Motor vehicle inspector
   D. Motor vehicle emissions agent

Answers

1. **D** There are a total of six wood poles positioned over the fence. The six poles form three triangles.

2. **A** There is a gate directly under the archway.

3. **D** There are a total of six steps on the right-hand side of the gate.

4. **B** The head of human resources is Paul Berke.

5. **B** Vacation requests are due by September 30.

6. **C** June 2 is the latest calendar date.

7. **A** The correct initials for the name Amanda Mary Lewis are AML.

8. **B** According to the passage, glass bottles are picked up on Tuesday.

9. **A** A customer service representative would assist a customer in changing the name on a license.

10. **C** A motor vehicle inspector would most likely need to be familiar with the working parts of most motor vehicles.

B. Judgment and Decision-Making

Employers are always looking for employees who have excellent judgment and decision-making skills. Although most of us don't think of these abilities as marketable job skills, judgment and decision-making skills help employees complete a variety of tasks every day. Supervisors and managers provide employees with policies for many important tasks, but there are many instances when employees must rely on their own reasoning to make decisions. These skills are especially important in the fields of law enforcement and firefighting, but they're also used in office environments. Some civil service exams don't include questions on judgment and decision-making; however, it's a good idea to study these questions to improve your skills.

1. Judgment

There are two types of judgment questions that you may encounter on the civil service exam. Both types require you to use prior knowledge, or the skills and experiences you already possess, to make a judgment about a particular situation.

Most Important Information Questions

The first type of question presents information about a scenario and then asks you to choose the answer that most clearly and accurately rephrases the most important information.

These types of questions may ask you about a crime or incident. Your task is to use your judgment to choose the answer that clearly restates the most important information. The passage will most likely contain a lot of details, but it's your job to sort through these details to find the crucial facts.

The best way to handle these types of questions is to imagine that you're reporting this information to the police. You must use your judgment to provide the police with the best information to help them apprehend the criminal.

Ask yourself the following questions as you search for the best answer:

- Who was involved in the incident?
- When did the incident take place?
- Where did the incident occur?
- What happened?
- What other important details should be mentioned?

EXAMPLE:

> You're working as an assistant on the ground floor of an office building. There are many other offices in your building. At 11 a.m., a young man comes into the building. He says that his car was broken into in the parking lot. The windows have been smashed and the air has been let out of all the tires. The man says that his GPS and CD player have been stolen. He believes that he is also missing some CDs. The man asks you to call the police. Which of the following expresses the information most clearly and accurately?
>
> A. You work as a secretary at an office building where a young man claims that his car has been broken into.
> B. At 11 a.m., a young man came into your office to report that his car had been broken into in the parking lot and that several personal items had been stolen.
> C. A young man's car has been broken into. His windows were smashed, all the air was let out of his tires, and he believes that his CDs were stolen.
> D. You were working at 11 a.m. when a young man came into your office building. His car has been broken into in the parking lot.

Choice B is correct. This choice explains what happened, who it happened to, and when it happened. This is the most clear and accurate restatement of the information in the passage.

Inference Questions

The other type of judgment question will ask you to use your judgment to make an inference about a situation. An *inference* is an educated guess that is based on what you've read and what you already know. For example, if you were walking down the street and noticed a lot of people carrying umbrellas, you could infer that the weather forecast calls for rain. You can make this inference because most people don't carry umbrellas unless it's supposed to rain.

EXAMPLES:

1. You're working as a police officer in a small town. You're called to the scene of a home break-in. When you arrive, you notice several plastic shopping bags and a container of milk scattered on the front porch. You find the distraught homeowner sitting on the front steps. She tells you that she was only at the store for 30 minutes and returned home to find her front door open. The house has been torn apart and several high-priced items are missing. What can you infer from this situation?

   A. The homeowner was grocery shopping before discovering the break-in.
   B. The homeowner knew the person responsible for the crime.
   C. The criminal left the shopping bags scattered on the front porch.
   D. The criminal knew that the front door would be unlocked.

Choice A is correct. From the information above, you can't infer that the homeowner knew the person responsible for the crime. You also can't assume that the criminal left the shopping bags or knew that the front door was unlocked. The shopping bags and milk led you to believe that the homeowner must have been grocery shopping before discovering the break-in. This is further confirmed by the fact that the homeowner tells you that she was at the store.

2. On a Saturday afternoon, you see several women in matching dresses headed into a church. The women are followed by several men dressed in tuxedoes. Flowers and ribbons that match the color of the women's dresses decorate the steps of the church. What can you infer from this situation?

   A. The church is hosting a funeral.
   B. The church is hosting a concert.
   C. The church is hosting a wedding.
   D. The church is hosting a play.

Choice C is correct. You can infer that the church is hosting a wedding based on a number of clues. The women wearing matching dresses are most likely bridesmaids. The men in tuxedoes are probably groomsmen. The flowers and ribbons are the same color as the bridesmaids' dresses, which must be the colors the engaged couple picked out for their wedding. This judgment is further supported by the fact that many weddings are held on Saturdays.

2. Decision-Making

Decision-making questions are pretty straightforward. You'll be presented with a scenario and then asked to make a decision based on what you've read. In most cases, you can use common sense to eliminate some of the answer choices. Remember that the question will most likely involve a situation that you could encounter in a work environment. Bearing this in mind, you should choose the answer that reflects the way that a professional would behave while on the job.

For example, suppose that a question asks you how you should handle a co-worker who is playing his music too loudly. You know that the correct response would most likely involve politely asking your co-worker to turn down the music. It would be unprofessional to yell at your co-worker or immediately report him to your supervisor. You want to select the decision that will help resolve the issue in a civilized manner.

EXAMPLES:

1. You're trying to finish a report that is due by the end of the day. You find it difficult to concentrate because two of your co-workers are talking loudly in the cubicle next to yours. How should you respond to this situation?

   A. E-mail your supervisor about the disturbance.
   B. Ask your co-workers if they can speak quietly.
   C. Tell your co-workers to take their conversation to the break room.
   D. Ask your supervisor if you can move your desk to another area.

Choice B is correct. The first thing you should do is ask your co-workers if they can speak quietly. If they continue to speak loudly, you might ask if they can speak to each other in the break room. You should only e-mail your supervisor if repeated attempts to ask your co-workers to be quiet go ignored. Moving your desk would be time-consuming and would not resolve the problem.

2. Your supervisor asks you to manage a large project. As you review the files, you realize that the project requires more work than you originally expected. To complete the project on time, you'll need the assistance of two co-workers. You're uncertain if your supervisor will allow your co-workers to help you. How should you proceed?

   A. Tell your supervisor that you no longer want to manage the project.
   B. Ask your co-workers to help you on their breaks.
   C. Work overtime to complete the project on time.
   D. Inform your supervisor of your concerns and ask for assistance.

Choice D is correct. The first thing you should do is inform your supervisor of your concerns and ask for assistance. There is no need to work overtime or tell your supervisor that you don't want to manage the project before you ask for assistance.

Practice

Directions (1–10): Answer the following questions based solely on the information provided.

1. At 1:05 p.m., Janet Anderson enters the police department to report her elderly father missing. She last saw him at 9 a.m. in her kitchen. He was eating a muffin for breakfast. Janet usually does chores around the house as her father reads the paper, exercises, or watches television. She went to check on her father after finishing some laundry at 11 a.m. He was not in the house. Janet searched the surrounding neighborhood and could not find her father. She reports that he was wearing tan slacks, a blue shirt, and a striped vest. The clerk at the police department must report this information to the Missing Persons Department. Which of the following expresses the information most clearly and accurately?

   A. Janet Anderson realized that her elderly father was missing at around 11 a.m.
   B. At 1:05 p.m., Janet Anderson reported her elderly father missing. He was last seen in her kitchen at 9 a.m., and he was wearing tan slacks, a blue shirt, and a striped vest.
   C. Janet Anderson thought her father was reading the paper or watching television while she did the laundry. She discovered that he was missing around 11 a.m.
   D. After discovering that her elderly father was missing, Janet Anderson searched her house and her neighborhood.

2. You're managing a project at work. Anne, Leslie, and Ron are assisting you with this project. Leslie is not putting as much effort into the project as Anne and Ron are. As everyone else works, Leslie is usually talking with friends or answering e-mails. This has caused some tension in the group. How should you proceed?

   A. Remove Leslie from the project immediately.
   B. Ask Anne and Ron to ignore Leslie's behavior.
   C. Tell Leslie that she needs to focus on her work.
   D. Have Anne and Ron complete Leslie's work.

3. You're walking around your neighborhood early on a Monday morning. As you walk, you notice a man frantically knocking on the front door of a house. The man is holding a coffee mug in his other hand. His briefcase sits on the front porch. As you pass by, you hear the man call "Honey" through the door. What can you infer from this situation?

   A. The man has locked himself out of his house.
   B. The man has an appointment at the house.
   C. The man is trying to break into the house.
   D. The man is waiting to pick up a co-worker.

4. Police respond to a report of a break-in at a local business. When you arrive on the scene, you're greeted by a woman who is wearing a tall, white hat and an apron. She identifies herself as the business owner. What can you infer from this situation?

   A. The business owner is a doctor.
   B. The business owner is a teacher.
   C. The business owner is a dentist.
   D. The business owner is a chef.

5. At 2:30 a.m., you're awakened by the doorbell ringing. You find your neighbor, Alice Saunders, standing on your front porch. She says that her house is on fire. She escaped the home without injury, but her husband, Gerald, has broken his leg. Gerald is sitting in your front yard. They tell you that they think the fire is contained to the first floor because they did not see any flames as they climbed out their bedroom window. Alice asks you to call 911. Which of the following expresses the information most clearly and accurately?

    A.   Your neighbor's home is on fire and her husband has broken his leg.

    B.   Your neighbor's home is on fire, but the fire is contained to the first floor.

    C.   At 2:30 a.m., your neighbor awakened you to tell you that her house is on fire.

    D.   At 2:30 a.m., you found your neighbor sitting in your front yard with a broken leg.

6. At 4:55 p.m., Tom Guster entered an appliance store to ask the owner to call a tow truck. Tom was driving down Wyoming Avenue when he realized that he had a flat tire. He parked his car across from the library, next to the appliance store. He told the appliance store owner that he hit a pothole when he was turning onto Wyoming Avenue. He's worried that he has damaged the axle. Which of the following expresses the information most clearly and accurately?

    A.   At 4:55 p.m., Tom Guster entered the appliance store. He asked the owner to call a tow truck because he has a flat tire.

    B.   At 4:55 p.m., Tom Guster realized that he had a flat tire and parked on Wyoming Avenue next to the appliance store, across from the library.

    C.   Tom Guster has a flat tire and is worried that his axle is damaged. He is parked on Wyoming Avenue next to the appliance store, across from the library.

    D.   Tom Guster was driving down Wyoming Avenue when he realized that he had a flat tire. He thinks that he damaged his tire by hitting a pothole.

7. Your co-worker receives a bouquet of flowers at work. You are highly allergic to pollen and begin sneezing as soon as the flowers arrive. Your eyes start to water and itch. It's difficult for you to concentrate on your work. How should you respond to this situation?

    A.   Move the flowers into the break room.

    B.   Ask your co-worker to place the flowers in another location.

    C.   E-mail your supervisor that you need to change your desk.

    D.   Tell your supervisor that you are sick and need to go home.

8. Your supervisor asks your team to stay late on Thursday evening. This is the same night as your daughter's piano recital. It's important to your daughter that you attend. How should you proceed?

    A.   Tell your supervisor about the recital and ask for the evening off.

    B.   Ask one of your co-workers to cover for you on Thursday evening.

    C.   Leave work on Thursday night without telling anyone where you're going.

    D.   Call in sick to work on Thursday morning and attend the recital that evening.

9. You look out your window and notice a woman walking hurriedly up and down the street. She is looking at all the houses and peering into yards. She keeps calling a name and holds a leash in one hand. What can you infer from this situation?

   A. The woman is looking for a missing child.
   B. The woman is trying to break into a house.
   C. The woman is trying to find a parking space.
   D. The woman is looking for a lost dog.

10. You turn onto your street only to find it blocked off by police. You notice that the street is wet, even though it hasn't rained in days. You also can see several large trucks farther down the street. You spot workers digging in the middle of the road. What can you infer from this situation?

    A. A power line is down.
    B. A house is on fire.
    C. A water main has broken.
    D. A house has been broken into.

Answers

1. **B** This answer choice explains what happened, who was involved, and when it happened. The other choices do not provide all the necessary information.

2. **C** As the manager of the project, you should tell Leslie that she needs to focus on her work. Leslie must be informed that her behavior is unacceptable before you can remove her from the project. You may decide to remove Leslie later if her behavior doesn't improve. You can't ask Anne and Ron to ignore Leslie's behavior or to do her work.

3. **A** From the information in the paragraph, you can infer that the man has locked himself out of his house. The man calls "Honey" through the door, which supports the idea that the man lives there and is trying to get his significant other to open the door.

4. **D** From the information in the paragraph, you can infer that the business owner is a chef. Chefs usually wear tall, white hats and aprons or chefs' jackets.

5. **A** The most important information that you must communicate to the 911 operator is that your neighbor's house is on fire and her husband has broken his leg. This information tells the 911 operator that he or she needs to send firefighters and EMTs to the residence.

6. **C** This response provides the tow truck operator with all the necessary information in a clear and accurate manner.

7. **B** The first thing you should do is ask your co-worker to move the flowers to another location. This is the most professional way to handle the matter.

8. **A** You should tell your supervisor about the recital and ask for the evening off. Your supervisor may be able to work with you so you can have the evening off to see your daughter perform.

9. **D** From the information, you can infer that the woman is looking for a lost dog. Because she is calling a name and is holding a leash, you can assume that her dog has gone missing.

10. **C** From the information, you can infer that a water main is broken. The fact that the street is wet even though it hasn't rained in days tells you that water is leaking from somewhere. In this situation, it's safe to assume that the street is blocked off so that workers can repair the damage.

C. Mechanical Aptitude

Not every civil service exam will include mechanical aptitude questions. These types of questions generally are used to assess how well a candidate will do in a job involving the use or maintenance of machinery. Oftentimes, these questions focus on knowledge that you have acquired through education or job experience.

Mechanical knowledge questions involve knowledge of tools, electronics, automotives, and other machinery. The questions also ask you to use your knowledge of machines to solve problems. For some questions, you may see an image of a tool or mechanical part. Other questions will ask you about the best way to perform a task, such as changing a car's oil or putting a structure together. Some of these questions may require you to use particular formulas, such as the formula for mechanical advantage.

EXAMPLES:

---

1. What is the first step in changing a flat tire?

   A. Jack up the car.
   B. Locate the spare tire.
   C. Set the emergency brake.
   D. Remove the old tire.

Choice C is correct. The first thing you should do when changing a flat tire is set the emergency brake. This will ensure that the car doesn't roll as you're working on the tire. After that, you should locate the spare tire, jack up the car, and remove the old tire.

---

2. The best method to employ when putting out a grease fire is

   A. Smothering the fire with a dry cloth
   B. Using a dry chemical fire extinguisher
   C. Dousing the fire with a bucket of water
   D. Covering the fire with dirt from outside

Choice B is correct. You never should use water to put out a grease fire. Water will only cause the grease to splash, potentially spreading the fire. The best way to put out the fire is by using a dry chemical fire extinguisher.

3. What is the name of the saw shown below?

A. Continuous band saw
B. Reciprocating blade saw
C. Crosscut saw
D. Miter saw

Choice D is correct. The saw shown in the picture is a miter saw. Miter saws can be electric or manual. They're used to make crosscuts and miter cuts.

Now that you've seen what mechanical aptitude questions look like, try the practice questions.

Practice

Directions (1–10): Answer the following questions based solely on the information provided.

1. In which situation would you most likely use a pinch bar?

A. To pry open a stuck door
B. To tighten a bolt on a car
C. To ensure that a beam is level
D. To connect two pieces of metal

2. What is one use for pliers?

A. Tightening bolts
B. Bending wire
C. Cutting through wood
D. Holding two objects together

Question 3 refers to the following illustration.

3. Box 1 and Box 2 are the same size and made of the same material. Based on the illustration, which box will require more effort to slide up the ramp?

    A. Box 1 will require more effort to slide up the ramp.
    B. Box 2 will require more effort to slide up the ramp.
    C. The boxes will require the same amount of effort to slide up the ramp.
    D. Neither box will require any effort to slide up the ramp.

4. If the radius of a wheel is 24 inches and the radius of the wheel's axle is 8 inches, what is the mechanical advantage?

    A. 1
    B. 2
    C. 3
    D. 4

Question 5 refers to the following illustration.

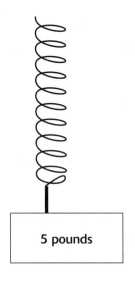

5 pounds

5. Based on the illustration, a spring bearing 5 pounds has stretched $\frac{1}{4}$ inch. If you increased the weight to 20 pounds, how far would the spring stretch?

   A. $\frac{1}{2}$ inch

   B. $\frac{3}{4}$ inch

   C.   1 inch

   D. $1\frac{1}{4}$ inches

6. What do a crow bar, a hydraulic spreader, and a Kelly tool have in common?

   A.   They are all pushing tools.
   B.   They are all striking tools.
   C.   They are all cutting tools.
   D.   They are all prying tools.

Question 7 refers to the following illustration.

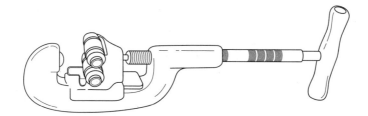

7. What is the tool shown?

   A.   A pipe cutter
   B.   A bolt cutter
   C.   A Kelly tool
   D.   A claw tool

8. Which pushing/pulling tool also can be used for leverage?

   A.   A drywall hook
   B.   A Clemens hook
   C.   A San Francisco hook
   D.   A roofman's hook

9. What is the nominal voltage of a C-size battery?

   A.   0.5 volt
   B.   1 volt
   C.   1.5 volts
   D.   2 volts

10. Which of the following could cause a car to overheat?

    A. A bad fuel pump

    B. A damaged head gasket

    C. A dead car battery

    D. A damaged ignition

Answers

1. **A** Pinch bars are used to pry. The most likely situation in which you would use a pinch bar is to pry open a stuck door.

2. **B** One use for pliers is to bend wire. Pliers also are used to grip objects.

3. **B** Box 2 will require more effort to slide up the ramp because this box is set at a steeper angle than Box 1.

4. **C** The mechanical advantage is 3. Mechanical advantage is calculated by dividing the radius of the wheel by the radius of the wheel's axle: $24 \div 8 = 3$.

5. **C** The spring stretches $\frac{1}{4}$ inch for every 5 pounds. You can easily figure, then, that the spring stretches $\frac{1}{2}$ inch for 10 pounds, $\frac{3}{4}$ inch for 15 pounds, and 1 inch for 20 pounds. If you'd rather set up an equation, you can figure it out like this:

$$\frac{\frac{1}{4}}{5} = \frac{x}{20}$$
$$5x = \frac{1}{4} \cdot 20$$
$$5x = 5$$
$$x = 1$$

6. **D** Crow bars, hydraulic spreaders, and Kelly tools are used to force open objects, so they are all prying tools.

7. **A** The tool shown in this picture is a pipe cutter. A bolt cutter has long handles and short blades and is used to cut through metal objects such as chains, padlocks, and wires. A Kelly tool is mostly used by firefighters in forcible entry situations, such as prying open windows or doors. A claw tool is mostly used by firefighters to pry up objects such as floorboards or baseboards.

8. **D** The only pushing/pulling tool that also can be used for leverage is the roofman's hook. The other tools are all pushing/pulling tools. A drywall hook is used by firefighters to remove drywall, ceiling, or plaster in emergency situations. A Clemens hook is similar to a drywall hook and also can be used to pry the siding off structures. A San Francisco hook is similar to a drywall hook and Clemens hook and also has a built-in gas shut-off and directional slot used for ventilation.

9. **C** The voltage for most household batteries, including C-size batteries, is 1.5 volts.

10. **B** A damaged head gasket could cause a coolant leak, which would increase the heat around the engine and cause the car to overheat.

D. Personal Experience

Potential employers don't just want to know how you would perform on a job; they also want to know what type of employee you'll be. Will you be able to handle a stressful work environment? Do you prefer to work alone? Do you take directions well?

Most employers learn this information during an interview, but the civil service exam often includes some personal experience questions to help determine a candidate's personality traits. Keep in mind that certain civil service jobs, including police officers and firefighters, require candidates to take an additional psychological exam.

Although there are no correct or incorrect answers on personal experience questions, your answers to these questions will be assessed by potential employers to determine if you're the right candidate for a particular job. This is why it's important to answer these questions as carefully and truthfully as possible.

For example, imagine that one of the questions asks how you handle stress. You say that stress doesn't bother you, even though you don't work well in stressful environments. You've chosen an answer that you believe potential employers will respond to favorably. However, this response could backfire if you're chosen for a particularly stressful position. You won't be able to do the job to the best of your ability.

There are three types of personal experience questions that you may encounter on the civil service exam:

- **Agree/disagree questions** ask candidates how strongly they agree or disagree with a statement.
- **Frequency questions** ask candidates how often they perform certain work-related tasks.
- **Experience questions** ask candidates to respond to a certain statement based on their previous work experience.

All these questions are multiple choice. If none of the answer choices matches your response to a particular statement, choose the answer that most closely resembles the way you would respond.

EXAMPLES:

---

1. You have no problem working quietly by yourself.

   A. Strongly agree
   B. Agree
   C. Disagree
   D. Strongly disagree

Remember: There is no correct or incorrect answer to this question. This type of question is designed to identify your personality traits. It shows employers if you work well with others.

2. How often do you create to-do lists?

    A. Very often
    B. Often
    C. Sometimes
    D. Rarely

This type of question is designed to assess your organizational skills. Again, there is no right or wrong answer. Some jobs require more organizational skills than others, so employers will use this question to determine which type of job might suit you best.

3. What kind of work do you prefer?

    A. Doing the same task every day
    B. Managing the work of others
    C. Juggling multiple tasks
    D. Dealing with clients

This type of question is designed to determine which type of work might suit you best. Employers may use this question to decide whether you're suited to working with customers or handling other employees.

Now that you've reviewed these examples, answer the following practice questions. Although there are no incorrect answers, completing the practice section will help you determine how you'll answer similar questions on the actual exam.

Practice

Directions (1–10): Answer the following questions based solely on the information provided.

1. You prefer working on long-term projects.

    A. Strongly agree
    B. Agree
    C. Disagree
    D. Strongly disagree

2. You have trouble getting along with co-workers.

    A. Very often
    B. Often
    C. Sometimes
    D. Rarely

3. Your supervisors often acknowledge you for your

    A. Creative suggestions
    B. Strong work ethic
    C. Leadership skills
    D. Excellent attitude

4. How would you describe your current job?

    A. Challenging
    B. Repetitive
    C. Creative
    D. Demanding

5. You talk with co-workers while you work.

    A. Very often
    B. Often
    C. Sometimes
    D. Rarely

6. You tend to get more work accomplished in the afternoon.

    A. Very often
    B. Often
    C. Sometimes
    D. Rarely

7. You prefer that a supervisor oversees your work.

    A. Strongly agree
    B. Agree
    C. Disagree
    D. Strongly disagree

8. You always follow company policies.

    A. Strongly agree
    B. Agree
    C. Disagree
    D. Strongly disagree

9. How would your co-workers describe you?

    A. Friendly

    B. Helpful

    C. Talented

    D. Positive

10. You take lengthy breaks during work.

    A. Very often

    B. Often

    C. Sometimes

    D. Rarely

Answers

1. This type of question is designed to determine what type of work environment would suit you best.

2. This type of question is designed to identify your personality traits.

3. This type of question is designed to determine which talents you possess.

4. This type of question is designed to identify your personality traits.

5. This type of question is designed to identify your interaction with co-workers as you complete your tasks.

6. This type of question is designed to determine what time of day you're most efficient.

7. This type of question is designed to determine how you prefer to work.

8. This type of question is designed to assess how you follow rules and policies.

9. This type of question is designed to assess how others view you.

10. This type of question is designed to assess your work ethic.

IX. Practice Test

Answer Sheet

Section 1

1 Ⓐ Ⓑ Ⓒ Ⓓ	26 Ⓐ Ⓑ Ⓒ Ⓓ
2 Ⓐ Ⓑ Ⓒ Ⓓ	27 Ⓐ Ⓑ Ⓒ Ⓓ
3 Ⓐ Ⓑ Ⓒ Ⓓ	28 Ⓐ Ⓑ Ⓒ Ⓓ
4 Ⓐ Ⓑ Ⓒ Ⓓ	29 Ⓐ Ⓑ Ⓒ Ⓓ
5 Ⓐ Ⓑ Ⓒ Ⓓ	30 Ⓐ Ⓑ Ⓒ Ⓓ
6 Ⓐ Ⓑ Ⓒ Ⓓ	31 Ⓐ Ⓑ Ⓒ Ⓓ
7 Ⓐ Ⓑ Ⓒ Ⓓ	32 Ⓐ Ⓑ Ⓒ Ⓓ
8 Ⓐ Ⓑ Ⓒ Ⓓ	33 Ⓐ Ⓑ Ⓒ Ⓓ
9 Ⓐ Ⓑ Ⓒ Ⓓ	34 Ⓐ Ⓑ Ⓒ Ⓓ
10 Ⓐ Ⓑ Ⓒ Ⓓ	35 Ⓐ Ⓑ Ⓒ Ⓓ
11 Ⓐ Ⓑ Ⓒ Ⓓ	36 Ⓐ Ⓑ Ⓒ Ⓓ
12 Ⓐ Ⓑ Ⓒ Ⓓ	37 Ⓐ Ⓑ Ⓒ Ⓓ
13 Ⓐ Ⓑ Ⓒ Ⓓ	38 Ⓐ Ⓑ Ⓒ Ⓓ
14 Ⓐ Ⓑ Ⓒ Ⓓ	39 Ⓐ Ⓑ Ⓒ Ⓓ
15 Ⓐ Ⓑ Ⓒ Ⓓ	40 Ⓐ Ⓑ Ⓒ Ⓓ
16 Ⓐ Ⓑ Ⓒ Ⓓ	41 Ⓐ Ⓑ Ⓒ Ⓓ
17 Ⓐ Ⓑ Ⓒ Ⓓ	42 Ⓐ Ⓑ Ⓒ Ⓓ
18 Ⓐ Ⓑ Ⓒ Ⓓ	43 Ⓐ Ⓑ Ⓒ Ⓓ
19 Ⓐ Ⓑ Ⓒ Ⓓ	44 Ⓐ Ⓑ Ⓒ Ⓓ
20 Ⓐ Ⓑ Ⓒ Ⓓ	45 Ⓐ Ⓑ Ⓒ Ⓓ
21 Ⓐ Ⓑ Ⓒ Ⓓ	46 Ⓐ Ⓑ Ⓒ Ⓓ
22 Ⓐ Ⓑ Ⓒ Ⓓ	47 Ⓐ Ⓑ Ⓒ Ⓓ
23 Ⓐ Ⓑ Ⓒ Ⓓ	48 Ⓐ Ⓑ Ⓒ Ⓓ
24 Ⓐ Ⓑ Ⓒ Ⓓ	49 Ⓐ Ⓑ Ⓒ Ⓓ
25 Ⓐ Ⓑ Ⓒ Ⓓ	50 Ⓐ Ⓑ Ⓒ Ⓓ

Section 2

1 Ⓐ Ⓑ Ⓒ Ⓓ	26 Ⓐ Ⓑ Ⓒ Ⓓ
2 Ⓐ Ⓑ Ⓒ Ⓓ	27 Ⓐ Ⓑ Ⓒ Ⓓ
3 Ⓐ Ⓑ Ⓒ Ⓓ	28 Ⓐ Ⓑ Ⓒ Ⓓ
4 Ⓐ Ⓑ Ⓒ Ⓓ	29 Ⓐ Ⓑ Ⓒ Ⓓ
5 Ⓐ Ⓑ Ⓒ Ⓓ	30 Ⓐ Ⓑ Ⓒ Ⓓ
6 Ⓐ Ⓑ Ⓒ Ⓓ	31 Ⓐ Ⓑ Ⓒ Ⓓ
7 Ⓐ Ⓑ Ⓒ Ⓓ	32 Ⓐ Ⓑ Ⓒ Ⓓ
8 Ⓐ Ⓑ Ⓒ Ⓓ	33 Ⓐ Ⓑ Ⓒ Ⓓ
9 Ⓐ Ⓑ Ⓒ Ⓓ	34 Ⓐ Ⓑ Ⓒ Ⓓ
10 Ⓐ Ⓑ Ⓒ Ⓓ	35 Ⓐ Ⓑ Ⓒ Ⓓ
11 Ⓐ Ⓑ Ⓒ Ⓓ	36 Ⓐ Ⓑ Ⓒ Ⓓ
12 Ⓐ Ⓑ Ⓒ Ⓓ	37 Ⓐ Ⓑ Ⓒ Ⓓ
13 Ⓐ Ⓑ Ⓒ Ⓓ	38 Ⓐ Ⓑ Ⓒ Ⓓ
14 Ⓐ Ⓑ Ⓒ Ⓓ	39 Ⓐ Ⓑ Ⓒ Ⓓ
15 Ⓐ Ⓑ Ⓒ Ⓓ	40 Ⓐ Ⓑ Ⓒ Ⓓ
16 Ⓐ Ⓑ Ⓒ Ⓓ	41 Ⓐ Ⓑ Ⓒ Ⓓ
17 Ⓐ Ⓑ Ⓒ Ⓓ	42 Ⓐ Ⓑ Ⓒ Ⓓ
18 Ⓐ Ⓑ Ⓒ Ⓓ	43 Ⓐ Ⓑ Ⓒ Ⓓ
19 Ⓐ Ⓑ Ⓒ Ⓓ	44 Ⓐ Ⓑ Ⓒ Ⓓ
20 Ⓐ Ⓑ Ⓒ Ⓓ	45 Ⓐ Ⓑ Ⓒ Ⓓ
21 Ⓐ Ⓑ Ⓒ Ⓓ	46 Ⓐ Ⓑ Ⓒ Ⓓ
22 Ⓐ Ⓑ Ⓒ Ⓓ	47 Ⓐ Ⓑ Ⓒ Ⓓ
23 Ⓐ Ⓑ Ⓒ Ⓓ	48 Ⓐ Ⓑ Ⓒ Ⓓ
24 Ⓐ Ⓑ Ⓒ Ⓓ	49 Ⓐ Ⓑ Ⓒ Ⓓ
25 Ⓐ Ⓑ Ⓒ Ⓓ	50 Ⓐ Ⓑ Ⓒ Ⓓ

CUT HERE

Section 3

1 Ⓐ Ⓑ Ⓒ Ⓓ	26 Ⓐ Ⓑ Ⓒ Ⓓ
2 Ⓐ Ⓑ Ⓒ Ⓓ	27 Ⓐ Ⓑ Ⓒ Ⓓ
3 Ⓐ Ⓑ Ⓒ Ⓓ	28 Ⓐ Ⓑ Ⓒ Ⓓ
4 Ⓐ Ⓑ Ⓒ Ⓓ	29 Ⓐ Ⓑ Ⓒ Ⓓ
5 Ⓐ Ⓑ Ⓒ Ⓓ	30 Ⓐ Ⓑ Ⓒ Ⓓ
6 Ⓐ Ⓑ Ⓒ Ⓓ	31 Ⓐ Ⓑ Ⓒ Ⓓ
7 Ⓐ Ⓑ Ⓒ Ⓓ	32 Ⓐ Ⓑ Ⓒ Ⓓ
8 Ⓐ Ⓑ Ⓒ Ⓓ	33 Ⓐ Ⓑ Ⓒ Ⓓ
9 Ⓐ Ⓑ Ⓒ Ⓓ	34 Ⓐ Ⓑ Ⓒ Ⓓ
10 Ⓐ Ⓑ Ⓒ Ⓓ	35 Ⓐ Ⓑ Ⓒ Ⓓ
11 Ⓐ Ⓑ Ⓒ Ⓓ	36 Ⓐ Ⓑ Ⓒ Ⓓ
12 Ⓐ Ⓑ Ⓒ Ⓓ	37
13 Ⓐ Ⓑ Ⓒ Ⓓ	38 Ⓐ Ⓑ Ⓒ Ⓓ
14 Ⓐ Ⓑ Ⓒ Ⓓ	39 Ⓐ Ⓑ Ⓒ Ⓓ
15 Ⓐ Ⓑ Ⓒ Ⓓ	40 Ⓐ Ⓑ Ⓒ Ⓓ
16 Ⓐ Ⓑ Ⓒ Ⓓ	41 Ⓐ Ⓑ Ⓒ Ⓓ
17 Ⓐ Ⓑ Ⓒ Ⓓ	42 Ⓐ Ⓑ Ⓒ Ⓓ
18 Ⓐ Ⓑ Ⓒ Ⓓ	43 Ⓐ Ⓑ Ⓒ Ⓓ
19 Ⓐ Ⓑ Ⓒ Ⓓ	44 Ⓐ Ⓑ Ⓒ Ⓓ
20 Ⓐ Ⓑ Ⓒ Ⓓ	45 Ⓐ Ⓑ Ⓒ Ⓓ
21 Ⓐ Ⓑ Ⓒ Ⓓ	46 Ⓐ Ⓑ Ⓒ Ⓓ
22 Ⓐ Ⓑ Ⓒ Ⓓ	47 Ⓐ Ⓑ Ⓒ Ⓓ
23 Ⓐ Ⓑ Ⓒ Ⓓ	48 Ⓐ Ⓑ Ⓒ Ⓓ
24 Ⓐ Ⓑ Ⓒ Ⓓ	49 Ⓐ Ⓑ Ⓒ Ⓓ
25 Ⓐ Ⓑ Ⓒ Ⓓ	50 Ⓐ Ⓑ Ⓒ Ⓓ

Section 4

1 Ⓐ Ⓑ Ⓒ Ⓓ	26 Ⓐ Ⓑ Ⓒ Ⓓ
2 Ⓐ Ⓑ Ⓒ Ⓓ	27 Ⓐ Ⓑ Ⓒ Ⓓ
3 Ⓐ Ⓑ Ⓒ Ⓓ	28 Ⓐ Ⓑ Ⓒ Ⓓ
4 Ⓐ Ⓑ Ⓒ Ⓓ	29 Ⓐ Ⓑ Ⓒ Ⓓ
5 Ⓐ Ⓑ Ⓒ Ⓓ	30 Ⓐ Ⓑ Ⓒ Ⓓ
6 Ⓐ Ⓑ Ⓒ Ⓓ	31 Ⓐ Ⓑ Ⓒ Ⓓ
7 Ⓐ Ⓑ Ⓒ Ⓓ	32 Ⓐ Ⓑ Ⓒ Ⓓ
8 Ⓐ Ⓑ Ⓒ Ⓓ	33 Ⓐ Ⓑ Ⓒ Ⓓ
9 Ⓐ Ⓑ Ⓒ Ⓓ	34 Ⓐ Ⓑ Ⓒ Ⓓ
10 Ⓐ Ⓑ Ⓒ Ⓓ	35 Ⓐ Ⓑ Ⓒ Ⓓ
11 Ⓐ Ⓑ Ⓒ Ⓓ	36 Ⓐ Ⓑ Ⓒ Ⓓ
12 Ⓐ Ⓑ Ⓒ Ⓓ	37 Ⓐ Ⓑ Ⓒ Ⓓ
13 Ⓐ Ⓑ Ⓒ Ⓓ	38 Ⓐ Ⓑ Ⓒ Ⓓ
14 Ⓐ Ⓑ Ⓒ Ⓓ	39 Ⓐ Ⓑ Ⓒ Ⓓ
15 Ⓐ Ⓑ Ⓒ Ⓓ	40 Ⓐ Ⓑ Ⓒ Ⓓ
16 Ⓐ Ⓑ Ⓒ Ⓓ	41 Ⓐ Ⓑ Ⓒ Ⓓ
17 Ⓐ Ⓑ Ⓒ Ⓓ	42 Ⓐ Ⓑ Ⓒ Ⓓ
18 Ⓐ Ⓑ Ⓒ Ⓓ	43 Ⓐ Ⓑ Ⓒ Ⓓ
19 Ⓐ Ⓑ Ⓒ Ⓓ	44 Ⓐ Ⓑ Ⓒ Ⓓ
20 Ⓐ Ⓑ Ⓒ Ⓓ	45 Ⓐ Ⓑ Ⓒ Ⓓ
21 Ⓐ Ⓑ Ⓒ Ⓓ	46 Ⓐ Ⓑ Ⓒ Ⓓ
22 Ⓐ Ⓑ Ⓒ Ⓓ	47 Ⓐ Ⓑ Ⓒ Ⓓ
23 Ⓐ Ⓑ Ⓒ Ⓓ	48 Ⓐ Ⓑ Ⓒ Ⓓ
24 Ⓐ Ⓑ Ⓒ Ⓓ	49 Ⓐ Ⓑ Ⓒ Ⓓ
25 Ⓐ Ⓑ Ⓒ Ⓓ	50 Ⓐ Ⓑ Ⓒ Ⓓ

CUT HERE

Section 1: Verbal Ability

Time: 45 minutes

50 questions

Directions (1–6): Choose the answer that best describes the meaning of the italicized word.

1. What is the meaning of *acquiesce?*

   A. To show interest in
   B. To give leave to
   C. To ponder
   D. To comply with

2. What is the meaning of *pacific?*

   A. Having a strange character
   B. Being lively or exciting
   C. Having a calming effect
   D. Being unbelievable

3. What is the meaning of *belligerent?*

   A. Combative
   B. Generous
   C. Forgiving
   D. Wealthy

4. What is the meaning of *inconsequential?*

   A. Irrelevant
   B. Very stubborn
   C. Unhappy
   D. Very similar

5. What is the meaning of *intangible?*

   A. Imaginary
   B. Unperceivable
   C. Unethical
   D. Motionless

6. What is the meaning of *pillage?*

   A. To steal
   B. To mend
   C. To risk
   D. To fake

Directions (7–12): Choose the correct answer solely on the basis of the corresponding passage.

Question 7 refers to the following passage.

The personal computer has emerged as one of the most significant technological inventions of the 20th century. From the early computer systems that filled entire rooms to today's tiny, handheld computer devices, computers have become an essential part of everyday life. Today, computers are so widely used and depended upon that it's hard to imagine the modern world functioning without them.

7. The passage best supports the statement that

    A. Computers have become a vital part of modern life.
    B. Computers are not a significant technological invention.
    C. Computers are not widely used in all parts of the world.
    D. Computers have not had a major impact on world culture.

Question 8 refers to the following passage.

Dr. Martin Luther King, Jr., is considered by many to be the greatest civil rights figure in U.S. history. Leading African Americans in their struggle for equality and civil liberties throughout the turbulent 1950s and 1960s, King established himself as the preeminent voice of victims of discrimination and racism across the country. His untimely and tragic death made him an icon of the civil rights movement and firmly cemented his place in American history.

8. Dr. Martin Luther King, Jr., is best known for his

    A. Military service
    B. Business acumen
    C. Political activism
    D. Religious doctrine

Question 9 refers to the following passage.

In today's innovative world, even something as simple as reading a book has been enhanced by technology. The emergence of electronic reading devices has changed the way the world reads by making it possible to purchase electronic books that can be read and stored on lightweight, handheld devices. Not only does this technology make it possible to download and read a book anywhere at any time, but it also allows readers to have a virtual library at their fingertips.

9. What is the main idea of this paragraph?

    A. Electronic reading devices are too costly for most people.
    B. Modern technology has changed the way many people read.
    C. The need for libraries is continually decreasing.
    D. Traditional books are quickly becoming obsolete.

Question 10 refers to the following passage.

   Prohibition was an ill-fated attempt to establish moral order in America by outlawing the sale and consumption of alcohol. The people who spearheaded the movement believed alcohol was the cause of what they saw as rampant immoral behavior throughout the country. Although it lasted for more than ten years, prohibition proved a failure, as public interest in alcohol never waned, and crime and violence only escalated due to bootlegging and the smuggling of alcohol.

10. Alcohol was outlawed during prohibition because it was

   A.   Believed to be an immoral vice
   B.   Not as profitable as it could have been
   C.   Produced by America's political enemies
   D.   A major source of income for organized crime

Question 11 refers to the following passage.

   With the proliferation of online commerce and the widespread popularity of online social networks, identity theft has become an increasingly serious problem. Now that so much of our personal information is accessible online, it has only become easier for criminals to use our private data for personal gain. For this reason, it has become critically important to protect our personal information online as much as possible.

11. What is the main idea of this paragraph?

   A.   Identity theft has become more common due to the Internet.
   B.   The Internet is an increasingly powerful business tool.
   C.   Criminals have become more creative in recent years.
   D.   States should pass legislation that restricts Internet use.

Question 12 refers to the following passage.

   Throughout the history of professional sports, athletes have been seen as heroes by many young admirers. Although many children still idolize sports stars, many modern professional athletes are not appropriate role models. Inflated egos, drug use, unprofessional conduct, and even criminal behavior have seriously jeopardized the professional athlete's status as a positive role model for children.

12. The paragraph best supports the statement that

   A.   Sports salaries have become outrageously high.
   B.   Many modern athletes make poor role models for kids.
   C.   There should be strict codes of conduct for sports stars.
   D.   Children should choose television stars for role models.

Directions (13–14): Choose the best revision for each underlined portion of the paragraph. If no change is required, select choice A.

One of the most significant scientific accomplishments of the 20th century was the moon landing. The sky and outer space have <u>peaked</u> human curiosity for thousands of years, and the moon landing was a major
13
accomplishment in the attempts to explore space. Just a few decades after the invention of the automobile, humans invented vehicles that were capable of leaving Earth's atmosphere. Almost immediately after the first explorers entered space, scientists quickly set a new <u>goal; the moon</u>. In little more than ten years, and with the
14
efforts of countless numbers of engineers, scientists, and astronauts, we had developed the technology and the ability to reach the moon. On July 20, 1969, that once lofty goal became reality when Neil Armstrong made history as the first person to set foot on the surface of the moon.

13. **A.** NO CHANGE
    B. peeked
    C. piqued
    D. picked

14. **A.** NO CHANGE
    B. goal the moon
    C. goal, the moon
    D. goal: the moon

Directions (15–16): Choose the best answer to complete the following sentences.

15. After singlehandedly apprehending the robbery suspect, the police officer was _____ by his chief for his good work.

    A. reprimanded
    B. commended
    C. matriculated
    D. immolated

16. Following his arrest on corruption charges, the congressman's reputation was _____ damaged, so he had to resign from office.

    A. irreparably
    B. vicariously
    C. imperceptibly
    D. marginally

Directions (17–18): Choose the correct sentence order for the following paragraphs.

17. Just as Howard Davis began to close his corner drugstore for the night, he saw a man in a dark hooded sweatshirt step through the door.

    1.   Then Howard completely emptied the drawer and cautiously gave the man the money.

    2.   Pretending to fully cooperate, Howard tripped a silent alarm as he slowly opened the cash drawer.

    3.   The man quickly approached the counter, produced a pistol, and demanded that Howard give him all the money in the register.

    4.   Grabbing the money, the man fled the store, only to be apprehended by police one block away.

    A.   3, 1, 2, 4
    B.   2, 3, 4, 1
    C.   2, 1, 3, 4
    D.   3, 2, 1, 4

18. Baseball player Steve Lombardi is next in line to bat for his team.

    1.   Stepping to the plate, Steve takes a few practice swings and stands in position.

    2.   Reacting swiftly, Steve swings and cracks the bat, sending the ball soaring into the stands.

    3.   Snapping into action, the pitcher arches back and launches the pitch.

    4.   As Steve looks on, the pitcher signals the catcher and prepares for his throw.

    A.   1, 3, 4, 2
    B.   1, 4, 3, 2
    C.   1, 2, 3, 4
    D.   1, 2, 4, 3

Directions (19–21): Choose the answer choice that best completes each sentence.

19. The guards were ordered to _____ the intruders.

    A.   sees
    B.   seas
    C.   cees
    D.   seize

20. The great white shark often _____ on seals and similar aquatic animals.

    A.   praise
    B.   prase
    C.   prays
    D.   preys

21. Frustrated, Paul sarcastically asked the man if he had any common _____.

    A. cense

    B. cents

    C. sense

    D. scents

Directions (22–23): Choose the word that reflects an error in capitalization.

22. I have heard that President Munley is well versed in english and physics.

    A. President

    B. english

    C. Munley

    D. physics

23. Senator Dodson, Professor Clark, and Jim Freewell, owner of Freewell Suites, were all originally from the south.

    A. south

    B. owner

    C. Senator

    D. Professor

Directions (24–25): Choose the sentence that corrects the error in punctuation.

24. The other patrons were amused by Frank's antics, the police officer was not.

    A. The other patrons, were amused by Frank's antics, the police officer was not.

    B. The other patrons were amused by Frank's antics; the police officer was not.

    C. The other patrons were amused, by Frank's antics: the police officer was not.

    D. The other patrons were amused by Frank's antics; the police officer, was not.

25. The office manager put Tom in charge of: billing, filing reports, and accounting.

    A. The office manager put Tom in charge of: billing, filing reports and accounting.

    B. The office manager put Tom in charge of billing, filing reports, and accounting.

    C. The office manager put Tom in charge of: billing, filing, reports, and accounting.

    D. The office manager put Tom in charge of; billing, filing reports, and accounting.

Directions (26–32): Choose the word that is spelled incorrectly.

26. **A.** iradiate

    B. sedentary

    C. gregarious

    D. terrestrial

27. **A.** indefinitely
    B. lightning
    C. couragous
    D. enviable

28. **A.** defendent
    B. corporal
    C. laborious
    D. committee

29. **A.** reparation
    B. condemn
    C. ascertain
    D. resivoir

30. **A.** inadvertent
    B. unscrupulous
    C. maintainance
    D. congratulations

31. **A.** camradarie
    B. insubordination
    C. psychiatry
    D. troubadour

32. **A.** effagy
    B. correspondence
    C. improbable
    D. corps

Directions (33–38): Choose the answer that best demonstrates the relationship between the two capitalized words.

33. KNIFE : SHARP ::

    A. cut : dull
    B. club : blunt
    C. silver : shiny
    D. spoon : metal

34. HORSE : MARE ::

   A. cow : steer
   B. lion : feline
   C. chicken : hen
   D. gorilla : primate

35. TIMID : SHY ::

   A. wet : dry
   B. melancholy : joy
   C. volatile : unstable
   D. arid : lush

36. EGG : CAKE ::

   A. yeast : bread
   B. cake : birthday
   C. potatoes : steak
   D. milk : coffee

37. HUNTER : STEALTHY ::

   A. architect : chaotic
   B. philosopher : wise
   C. worker : friendly
   D. forest : green

38. DELUGE : DROUGHT ::

   A. incoherent : unresponsive
   B. storm : hurricane
   C. water : beverage
   D. desert : rain forest

Directions (39–44): Choose the synonym for each italicized word.

39. *Impurity* most nearly means

   A. Error
   B. Sentiment
   C. Pollutant
   D. Catastrophe

40. *Futile* most nearly means

    A. Effective
    B. Depressed
    C. Movable
    D. Useless

41. *Benevolent* most nearly means

    A. Compassionate
    B. Gritty
    C. Indifferent
    D. Desirable

42. *Paragon* most nearly means

    A. Clown
    B. Follower
    C. Model
    D. Wanderer

43. *Recompense* most nearly means

    A. Knowledge
    B. Compensation
    C. Jeopardy
    D. Condemnation

44. *Censure* most nearly means

    A. Block
    B. Feel
    C. Guarantee
    D. Denounce

Directions (45–50): The following questions will present a sentence, part or all of which is underlined. Beneath the sentence, you will find three ways of rephrasing the sentence. Select the answer that represents the most effective revision of the sentence, paying attention to grammar, word choice, and clarity. If the original sentence is correct and as effective as possible, select choice D.

45. Everyone should hand in their weekly reports by noon on Friday.

    A. Everyone should hand in his or her weekly reports by noon on Friday.
    B. Everyone should hand in them weekly reports by noon on Friday.
    C. Weekly reports, written by everyone, should be handed in by noon on Friday.
    D. NO ERROR

46. Incident <u>reports that must be sent to the supervisor's secretary are reviewed</u> on Monday morning.

    A.   reports to the supervisor's secretary are reviewed

    B.   reports, sent to the supervisor's secretary, are reviewed

    C.   reports, which must be sent to the supervisor's secretary, are reviewed

    D.   NO ERROR

47. <u>Because of poor road conditions, all county employees, that work at the courthouse, should report to work at noon.</u>

    A.   Because of poor road conditions, all county employees, which work at the courthouse, should report to work at noon.

    B.   Because of poor road conditions, all county employees who work at the courthouse should report to work at noon.

    C.   Because of poor road conditions, all county employees which work at the courthouse, should report to work at noon.

    D.   NO ERROR

48. <u>All concerns about the new vacation policy should be directed to Mr. Woodhouse and myself.</u>

    A.   All concerns about the new vacation policy should be directed to Mr. Woodhouse and I.

    B.   All concerns about the new vacation policy should be directed to Mr. Woodhouse, and myself.

    C.   All concerns about the new vacation policy should be directed to Mr. Woodhouse and me.

    D.   NO ERROR

49. <u>Employees should include their personal identification numbers on all reports.</u>

    A.   On all reports, employees should include their personal identification numbers.

    B.   Employees should include his or her personal identification numbers on all reports.

    C.   Employees should include, their personal identification numbers, on all reports.

    D.   NO ERROR

50. The manager <u>reminded the employees to submitting their vacation requests</u> by next Thursday.

    A.   reminded the employees to submitted their vacation requests

    B.   reminded the employees to submitting his or her vacation requests

    C.   reminded the employees to submit their vacation requests

    D.   NO ERROR

IF YOU FINISH BEFORE TIME IS CALLED, CHECK YOUR WORK ON THIS SECTION ONLY. DO NOT WORK ON ANY OTHER SECTION IN THE TEST.

Section 2: Mathematical Ability

Time: 45 minutes

50 questions

Directions (1–50): Answer the questions solely on the basis of the information provided.

1. Convert $\frac{216}{16}$ into a mixed number.

   A. $\frac{13}{1}$

   B. $\frac{54}{4}$

   C. $13\frac{1}{2}$

   D. $54\frac{1}{16}$

2. $\frac{16}{4} \cdot 5.485 - 3\frac{2}{8} - 0.875$. Round to the nearest hundredth.

   A. 5.44
   B. 7.11
   C. 9.82
   D. 17.82

3. If a police cruiser travels at an average speed of 80 miles per hour during a chase for nine minutes, how many miles will the police cruiser have traveled?

   A. 7.2 miles
   B. 12 miles
   C. 36.5 miles
   D. 80 miles

4. Josie can type 60 words per minute, Frank can type 45 words per minute, and Ellen can type 52 words per minute. How many words can the group collectively type in 30 minutes?

   A. 4,421
   B. 4,590
   C. 4,625
   D. 4,710

5. Solve for a: $12a - 6a = 67 + 4a + 5$.

   A. 26
   B. 33
   C. 36
   D. 41

Question 6 refers to the following chart.

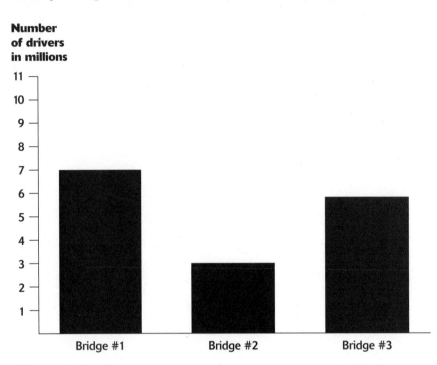

Number of drivers in millions

Bridge #1   Bridge #2   Bridge #3

6. The bar chart shows the number of drivers who travel over three particular bridges in the city of Maples. How many more drivers traveled over bridge 1 than over bridge 2?

    A.   1 million
    B.   3 million
    C.   4 million
    D.   7 million

Question 7 refers to the following table.

Business	Employees
Auto Plus	27
Design Center	17
Martin's Groceries	68
Sal's Tire Shop	11

7. The table shows the number of employees working for four different businesses. According to the table, how many more employees does Martin's Groceries have than Auto Plus?

    A.   11
    B.   17
    C.   39
    D.   41

Question 8 refers to the following chart.

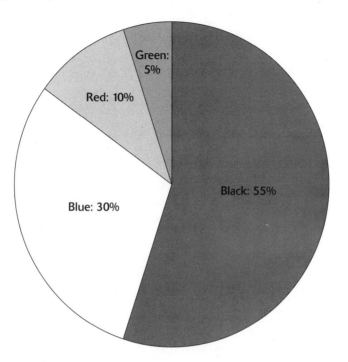

8. The chart shows the breakdown of the color of cars driven by 500 men. How many more men drive black cars than green cars?

    A. 250
    B. 275
    C. 300
    D. 325

9. The owner of a bakery has two ovens repaired at a cost of $500 each. When he originally researched the cost of repairs a few months ago, he found that it would only cost $420 each. By about what percentage has the cost of oven repairs increased since the baker did his research?

    A. 12
    B. 19
    C. 24
    D. 32

10. It takes four electricians nine hours to wire ten rooms in a new office building. If one electrician calls in sick, how many hours will it take the other electricians to complete the same job?

    A. 6
    B. 9
    C. 12
    D. 15

11. If it takes Ernie 9 hours to rebuild a car engine, Fiona 12 hours to rebuild the engine, and Michael 18 hours to rebuild the engine, how many hours would it take to rebuild a car engine if they worked together?

   A. 2

   B. $3\frac{1}{3}$

   C. 4

   D. $5\frac{3}{4}$

12. Reduce the fraction $\frac{18}{81}$ to the lowest terms.

   A. $\frac{2}{9}$

   B. $\frac{6}{27}$

   C. $\frac{3}{13.5}$

   D. $1\frac{4}{5}$

13. If three-fifths of the jobs that electrician Bill Michaels completes each week are nonemergency jobs, and he typically finishes 47 jobs per week. How many of Bill's jobs are emergencies? Round to the nearest tenth.

   A. 9.4
   B. 18.8
   C. 24.6
   D. 28.2

14. A plumber needs to buy a few pieces to fix a broken shower in a customer's home. The plumber knows the cost of the pieces will be $15.62, $80.45, and $55.03. If the customer pays for two-fifths of the pieces, how much will the plumber pay?

   A. $60.44
   B. $75.55
   C. $90.66
   D. $151.10

15. $6\frac{3}{4}\cdot\frac{2}{6}+\frac{8}{3}-\frac{1}{6}=$

   A. $4\frac{3}{4}$

   B. $6\frac{3}{4}$

   C. $12\frac{2}{4}$

   D. $20\frac{1}{4}$

16. 65% of 40 =

    A. 9
    B. 13
    C. 26
    D. 32

17. What is the ratio of 48 to 72?

    A. 2:3
    B. 4:8
    C. 5:6
    D. 9:12

18. Mary paid $42 for a sweater that was on sale for 15% off the original price. What was the original price of the sweater? Round your answer to the nearest hundredth.

    A. $42.75
    B. $49.41
    C. $52.83
    D. $57.50

19. If $900 is being divided among three students in a ratio of 2:3:4, how much money will each person receive, respectively?

    A. $150, $250, $500
    B. $200, $300, $400
    C. $250, $250, $400
    D. $300, $300, $300

20. If 64 rolls of paper towels were sold at a rate of 4 for $5, what is the total price for all 64 rolls?

    A. $25.60
    B. $40.00
    C. $65.20
    D. $80.00

21. If it takes five bakers eight hours to bake 300 loaves of bread, how many hours will it take to bake the same number of loaves of bread if one baker calls in sick?

    A. 8
    B. 10
    C. 12
    D. 16

22. A business owner replaces two fax machines at a cost of $350 each. If the business owner expected to pay $400 for each fax machine, what percentage of the expected cost was saved? Round to the nearest hundredth.

    A. 12.5
    B. 15
    C. 16.5
    D. 17

23. 45:15 =

    A. $\frac{1}{3}$

    B. $\frac{2}{3}$

    C. $\frac{3}{5}$

    D. $\frac{3}{1}$

24. 42% of 120 =

    A. 22.8
    B. 42
    C. 50.4
    D. 60

25. Desiree must earn at least 70% on her driving exam to pass. If the exam includes 50 questions, how many questions must she answer correctly to pass?

    A. 15
    B. 35
    C. 40
    D. 45

Question 26 refers to the following chart.

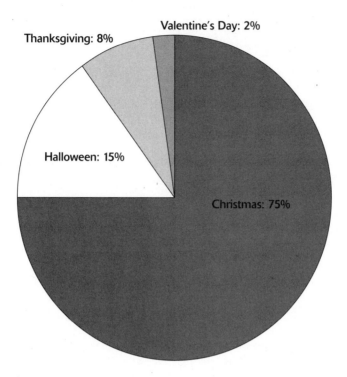

26. The chart shows a breakdown of 200 third-grade students' favorite holidays. How many students chose Halloween as their favorite holiday?

   A.   30
   B.   48
   C.   52
   D.   60

Question 27 refers to the following diagram.

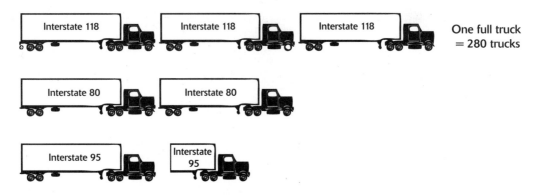

27. The diagram represents the number of trucks that traveled over three different interstates during the month of June. According to the diagram, how many trucks drove over Interstate 95?

    A.   140
    B.   280
    C.   320
    D.   420

28. It takes nine printing press machines six days to print 50,000 telephone books. If three printing press machines are unavailable, how many days will it take the other six machines to complete the same print job?

    A.   6
    B.   9
    C.   12
    D.   15

29. If it takes Anna three days to complete a job, Jorge four days to complete the job, and Miles six days to complete the job, how many days would it take the trio to finish the job working together?

    A. $1\frac{1}{3}$

    B.   2
    C.   3

    D. $3\frac{2}{3}$

30. If it takes a group of construction workers six hours to pave a driveway with an area of 252 square feet, how many hours would it take those same construction workers to pave a parking lot with an area of 714 square feet?

    A.   6
    B.   11
    C.   15
    D.   17

31. Solve for x: $9x + 6 = 50 - 2x$.

    A. 4
    B. 8
    C. 12
    D. 16

32. Martin has chopped down nine more trees than two times the number of trees Phillip has chopped down. If t represents the number of trees Phillip has chopped down, which of the following equations shows the total number of trees that both Martin and Phillip have chopped down?

    A. $2t - 9$
    B. $4t + 9$
    C. $3t + 9$
    D. $4t - 9$

Question 33 refers to the following figure.

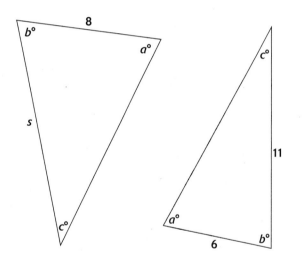

33. The triangles are similar. What is the value of s? Round to the nearest tenth.

    A. 14.7
    B. 15.0
    C. 15.8
    D. 16.3

Question 34 refers to the following graph.

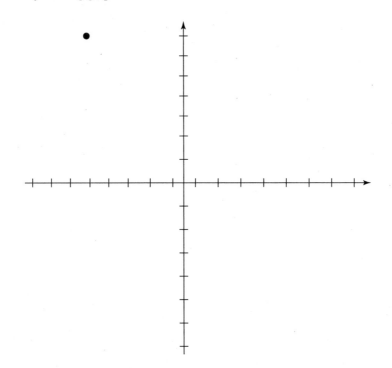

34. Which coordinate correctly corresponds with the graph?

    A. (5, 7)
    B. (5, –7)
    C. (–5, 7)
    D. (–5, –7)

35. In which quadrant would a point with the coordinates (–17, 4) appear?

    A. I
    B. II
    C. III
    D. IV

36. If $x = 15$ and $y = 25$, what is the value of $5x(2x + 4y)$?

    A. 3,790
    B. 5,970
    C. 7,950
    D. 9,750

37. If a dump truck travels at an average speed of 35 miles per hour for six hours, how many miles will the dump truck travel?

   A. 75
   B. 150
   C. 210
   D. 420

38. Virginia ran 2 miles less than three times the number of miles Stanley ran. If m represents the number of miles Stanley ran, which of the following equations shows the total number of miles that both Virginia and Stanley ran?

   A. $4m - 2$
   B. $2m - 3$
   C. $3m + 2$
   D. $2m + 2$

39. If $x = 9$ and $y = 7$, what is the value of $3x(9x - 5y)$?

   A. 1,131
   B. 1,242
   C. 1,313
   D. 1,424

Question 40 refers to the following figure.

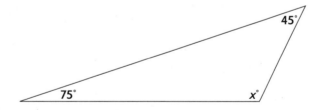

40. Determine the value of x in the triangle.

   A. 45°
   B. 60°
   C. 75°
   D. 80°

Question 41 refers to the following figure.

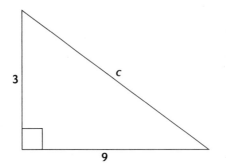

41. Determine the value of the hypotenuse in the triangle.

  A. $\sqrt{90}$
  B. $\sqrt{120}$
  C. $\sqrt{160}$
  D. $\sqrt{180}$

Question 42 refers to the following figure.

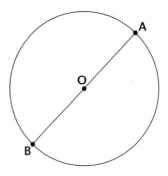

42. If $AO = 6$ and $\pi = 3.14$, what is the circumference of the circle?

  A. 19.45
  B. 23.14
  C. 31.84
  D. 37.68

Questions 43 and 44 refer to the following information.

As a mail clerk, Anne Ricardo often has to determine the total value of a group of packages that a customer wants to mail. Anne calculated the shipping costs of the following items for one of her customers earlier today.

Package 1: $5.65
Package 2: $3.82
Package 3: $10.95
Package 4: $7.14

43. What will it cost Anne's customer to ship packages 1, 2, and 4?

A. $5.65
B. $7.14
C. $16.61
D. $27.56

44. If package 3 weighs 2.5 pounds, what is the post office's shipping rate, assuming that there is a flat rate per pound and that there aren't separate rates for packages less than 1 pound?

A. $2.50 per pound
B. $4.38 per pound
C. $6.02 per pound
D. $8.54 per pound

Question 45 refers to the following chart.

	Jan	March	June	Sept	Nov
Mt. Pleasant	14°	38°	70°	60°	28°
Jonesville	19°	47°	76°	68°	32°
Williamsport	22°	45°	78°	74°	38°

45. The table shows the average temperature of three cities over five months. According to the table, what was the average temperature in Jonesville during the month of September?

A. 60°
B. 68°
C. 74°
D. 78°

Question 46 refers to the following graph.

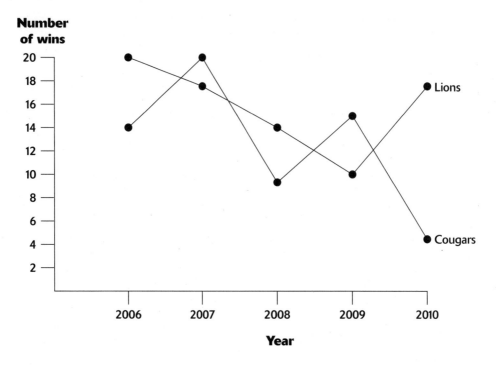

46. According to the graph, how many more wins did the Cougars have over the Lions in 2009?

    A.   2
    B.   3
    C.   5
    D.   7

Question 47 refers to the following chart.

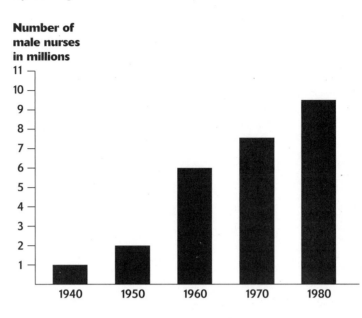

47. The chart shows the number of male nurses working in the United States from 1940 to 1980. Which decade experienced the greatest surge in males choosing nursing as a profession?

A.   1950
B.   1960
C.   1970
D.   1980

Question 48 refers to the following figure.

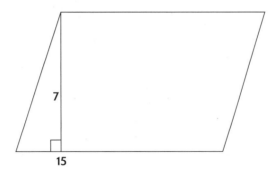

48. Determine the area of the parallelogram in the figure.

A.   90
B.   105
C.   120
D.   135

Question 49 refers to the following figure.

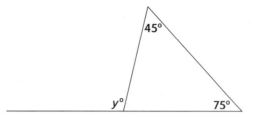

49. Determine the value of the exterior angle labeled *y* in the triangle.

   A.   55°
   B.   95°
   C.   120°
   D.   150°

Question 50 refers to the following figure.

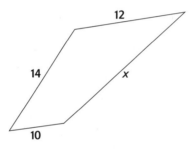

50. If the perimeter of the quadrilateral is 60, what is the value of *x*?

   A.   14
   B.   24
   C.   26
   D.   31

IF YOU FINISH BEFORE TIME IS CALLED, CHECK YOUR WORK ON THIS
SECTION ONLY. DO NOT WORK ON ANY OTHER SECTION IN THE TEST.

Section 3: Clerical Ability

Time: 45 minutes
50 questions

Directions (1–4): Each question contains a list of four names or numbers that may or may not be exactly alike. Compare the items and determine how many items are the same.

1. Steven E. Kelly

    Steven E. Kelley

    Steven F. Kelley

    Steven E. Kelley

    A. 0
    B. 2
    C. 3
    D. 4

2. 32864719

    32864719

    32864719

    32864719

    A. 0
    B. 2
    C. 3
    D. 4

3. Nicholas R. Davis

    Nicholas R. Davis

    Nicholas R. Davis

    Nicholas R. Davies

    A. 0
    B. 2
    C. 3
    D. 4

4. Kelsey MacCormick

Kelsey McCormick

Kelsey McCormack

Kellsay McCormick

A. 0
B. 2
C. 3
D. 4

Directions (5–15): Ask a friend or study partner to dictate the following passage while you take notes. Then, using your notes and the alphabetic word list that follows, fill in the blanks of the following transcript of the passage. Do not look at the passage itself. Finally, find the corresponding answer choice for each word and fill in the answer sheet with the correct letter.

In business, communication is vital. (Period) The very core of any business transaction is the exchange of information through various forms of communication. (Period) Because communication plays such a vital role in business, it is critical for a good employee to have a thorough understanding of the principles of communication and the ability to communicate effectively. (Period) At its most basic level, communication involves the sending and receiving of messages between two people. (Period) Simple, face-to-face interpersonal communication is an important part of any business. (Period) As such, a good employee should be able to communicate with others in a clear, professional manner that projects confidence and trust. (Period) This is especially true when interpersonal communication occurs between an employee and a customer. (Period) Employees represent not only themselves, but also their companies when they communicate with customers. (Period) As a result, employees should communicate as professionally and effectively as possible when dealing with customers. (Period) Face-to-face interpersonal communication is the cornerstone of many businesses, but it is not the only form of communication that is essential to business success. (Period) Employees also must be skilled at using other forms of communication such as letter writing, telephoning, and e-mailing. (Period) To communicate effectively through these forms, employees must possess strong writing and speaking skills and demonstrate a clear understanding of proper language and grammar. (Period) Furthermore, employees should be aware of business etiquette and professionalism when they communicate. (Period) Overall, the role of communication in business is extremely important, and the quality of one's communication skills can mean the difference between success and failure. (Period)

Alphabetic Word List			
Word	**Answer Choice**	**Word**	**Answer Choice**
aplomb	B	nexus	C
center	A	personal	B
communicate	B	principles	D
confidence	C	projects	A
converse	C	retrieving	D
core	C	self-esteem	D
data	A	sending	D
demonstrate	C	show	B
employee	A	speak	D
employer	B	talk	A
exchange	D	tenets	A
fundamentals	B	trade	C
individual	D	transfer	B
information	B	transmitting	A
interpersonal	A	vital	B
key	D	worker	C
messages	C		

Transcript

In business, communication is _____. The very _____ of any business transaction is the
               5   6

_____ of information through various forms of communication. Because communication plays
  7

such a vital role in business, it is critical for a good _____ to have a thorough understanding of
                                                    8

the _____ of communication and the ability to communicate effectively. At its most basic level,
     9

communication involves the _____ and receiving of _____ between two people. Simple,
                       10   11

face-to-face _____ communication is an important part of any business. As such, a good
             12

employee should be able to _____ with others in a clear, professional manner that _____
                          13   14

_____ and trust.
  15

Directions (16–18): Choose the word that should follow the given word in alphabetical order.

16. CORRELATE

    A. corner
    B. condition
    C. correction
    D. corridor

17. FACSIMLE

    A. facet
    B. facility
    C. factual
    D. fabricate

18. PRESENTATION

    A. prevalent
    B. prescience
    C. precedent
    D. perception

Directions (19–22): Use the following coding chart to determine the correct delivery route for the addresses given in each question.

Postal Route Guide	
Address Range	**Delivery Route**
51–800 Somerset Boulevard 100–600 Grange Street 125–500 Carson Avenue 200–900 Broad Street	A
501–800 Carson Avenue 25–100 Dearborn Street 1–75 Manchester Drive	B
160–300 Charleston Road 200–400 Hill Valley Road	C
All mail that cannot be delivered to any of the above address ranges	D

19. 225 Charleston Road

    A. A
    B. B
    C. C
    D. D

20. 462 Grange Street

    A. A
    B. B
    C. C
    D. D

21. 42 Manchester Drive

    A. A
    B. B
    C. C
    D. D

22. 475 Washington Avenue

    A. A
    B. B
    C. C
    D. D

Directions (23–26): Each question contains a list of four names or numbers that may or may not be exactly alike. Compare the items and determine how many items are the same.

23. 29583740

    29583748

    29583140

    29583740

    A. 0
    B. 2
    C. 3
    D. 4

24. Gregory M. Marshall

Gregory M. Marshall

Gregory N. Marshall

Gregory M. Marshall

   A.   0
   B.   2
   C.   3
   D.   4

25. Fredrick J. Meyer

Fredrick I. Meyer

Fredrick J. Meyer

Fredric J. Meyer

   A.   0
   B.   2
   C.   3
   D.   4

26. Rodger P. Clarke

Rodger P. Clarke

Roger P. Clarke

Rodger P. Clarke

   A.   0
   B.   2
   C.   3
   D.   4

Directions (27–29): Choose the space in which the given name would appear in the alphabetical list.

27. Fredrick, Nathaniel

    A. _____

        Foster, Charles

    B. _____

        Feeley, Robert

    C. _____

        Francis, Simon

    D. _____

        Fullerton, Peter

28. Lancaster, Maxwell J.

    A. _____

        La Bell, Marisa A.

    B. _____

        Lasher, Thomas F.

    C. _____

        Lawrence, Katharine P.

    D. _____

        Leary, Albert W.

29. Roberts, J. S.

    A. _____

        Reilly, A. J.

    B. _____

        Richards, M.

    C. _____

        Rodd, R. P.

    D. _____

        Rupert, M. J.

Directions (30–33): Use the following 2009 Report Filing Form and coding instructions to answer the questions.

2009 Report Filing Form				
Month	Department	Report Type	Reviewer	Restriction Level

Codes for this form are developed using the following keys:

Month	Department	Report Type	Reviewer	Restriction Level
A. January	A. Administrative	A. Financial	A. B. Kelly	A. R5
B. February	B. Accounts Receivable	B. Internal	B. D. Fitzsimmons	B. R4
C. March		C. Personnel	C. S. Mathers	C. R3
D. April	C. Accounts Payable	D. Sales	D. J. Thomson	D. R2
E. May	D. Human Resources		E. L. Richards	E. R1
F. June				
G. July	E. Marketing			
H. August	F. Sales			
I. September				
J. October				
K. November				
L. December				

Code the information found in each question using the keys above. Be sure to use only the given information to determine the code. The code should be ordered in the same format as the 2009 Report Filing Form shown above, from left to right.

30. What is the correct code for an August R2 financial report from the Sales Department that was reviewed by S. Mathers?

   A. HFACD
   B. HEACD
   C. HFADC
   D. HADAC

31. What is the correct code for an R4 internal report from the Marketing Department that was reviewed by B. Kelly after it was filed in May?

    A. BEEBA
    B. EBEAB
    C. EEBAB
    D. BEBBA

32. What is the correct code for a November R3 financial report from the Accounts Payable Department that was reviewed by L. Richards?

    A. CKECA
    B. KCAEC
    C. CKEAC
    D. KACEA

33. What is the correct code for an R5 personnel report from the Administrative Department that was reviewed in March by J. Thompson?

    A. GACDA
    B. ACADA
    C. CCADA
    D. CACDA

Directions (34–36): Using the list of names provided, determine which position the bolded name would be in if the list were alphabetized.

34. Peter Franklin

    Joseph Franchella

    Michael Francis

    Gary Frankford

    A. First
    B. Second
    C. Third
    D. Fourth

35. Daniel O'Brien, Jr.

    Fr. Peter O' Daniels

    John O'Malley, Sr.

    Dr. Joseph O'Kelly

    A. First
    B. Second
    C. Third
    D. Fourth

36. Connors, Elizabeth

Connolly, Adeline

Carroll, Mary

Connell, Denise

 A. First
 B. Second
 C. Third
 D. Fourth

Directions (37): Retype this passage in its entirety. Continue typing for five minutes. If you come to the end of the passage before time is up, double-space once and start again from the beginning.

Over the last 50 years, the tools of business have changed dramatically. Today's modern business offices utilize all sorts of technologies that have forever altered how we work and do business. Business offices are constantly changing and evolving to make use of the latest technologies. Although many pieces of technology have helped to drive productivity and innovation in the workplace, the piece of technology that most influenced the way people work is the computer. Since it first arrived in offices around the world, the computer has consistently driven the evolution of business and impacted virtually every aspect of the business office. Computers have drastically changed the way we work by simplifying difficult tasks, replacing inefficient filing systems, offering advanced means of communication, and more. No other advancement in office technology has had such a great influence.

Although computers eventually became a driving force in the modern workplace, these machines were not always welcome in the office. When personal computers first appeared in offices, many employees worried that these machines would make human capital less valuable and layoffs would skyrocket. People feared that business owners would attempt to increase profits by replacing costly human employees with computers. In the end, however, these fears proved to be unjustified. In fact, the computer has actually helped create more jobs over the years and helped businesses grow at astounding rates. Therefore, along with playing a vital role in the technological advancement of the modern business office, the computer has made significant contributions to the growth of the global business place. The changes the computer has brought to business and the business world make it one of the most important pieces of technology in the history of modern society.

Directions (38–41): Use the following table to determine the correct code for the file described in each question. Each code consists of a two-letter code, followed by a one-number code, followed by a two-letter code.

Filing Code		
File Type	**Originator**	**Department**
AA – Administrative	1 – Peter Franklin	AC - Accounting
AB – Financial	2 – Thomas Paulson	MA– Management
BB – Personnel	3 – Stephanie Quinn	HR – Human Resources
BC – Public Relations	4 – Rachel Travers	MK – Marketing

Document Filing Report Form		
File Type	**Originator**	**Department**

38. What is the correct code for a financial report from the Accounting Department created by Stephanie Quinn?

   A.   AC3AB
   B.   AB2AC
   C.   AA3AC
   D.   AB3AC

39. What is the correct code for a personnel report created by Thomas Paulson for the Marketing Department?

   A.   BB3MA
   B.   BB2MK
   C.   AB2MK
   D.   BB3MK

40. What is the correct code for an administrative file that Rachel Travers created for the Management Department?

   A.   AA4MA
   B.   MA4AA
   C.   AB4MA
   D.   AA4MK

41. What is the correct code for a personnel file created by Stephanie Quinn for the Human Resources Department?

   A.   AB3HR
   B.   BB3HR
   C.   BB2HR
   D.   AA2HR

Directions (42–45): Of the four names listed, choose the one that would be *third* if the list were alphabetical.

42. **A.** Stewart Leigh
    B. Richard Leah
    C. Patrick Lea
    D. Harold Lee

43. **A.** Leland Thomas
    B. Kevin Thomson
    C. Alexander Tomas
    D. Steven Thompson

44. **A.** Atherton & Morris, Inc.
    B. Atherton Insurance Co.
    C. Atherton Valley Bank
    D. Atherton Bistro

45. **A.** Douglas Carter, Sr.
    B. Edward Cartier
    C. Dr. Samuel Carter
    D. William F. Carder

Directions (46–50): Each question contains a list of four names or numbers that may or may not be exactly alike. Compare the items and determine how many items are the same.

46. Christina M. Paige

    Cristina M. Paige

    Cristine M. Paige

    Cristine M. Page

    A. 0
    B. 2
    C. 3
    D. 4

47. 3161138

    3161138

    3161130

    3191138

    A. 0
    B. 2
    C. 3
    D. 4

48. Gerald S. Daly

Gerard S. Daly

Gerald S. Daly

Gerald S. Daly

A. 0
B. 2
C. 3
D. 4

49. Roy T. Halle

Roy T. Halle

Roy T. Halle

Roy T. Halle

A. 0
B. 2
C. 3
D. 4

50. Dr. Anna Lane

Dr. Ana Lane

Dr. Anna Laine

Dr. Anne Lane

A. 0
B. 2
C. 3
D. 4

IF YOU FINISH BEFORE TIME IS CALLED, CHECK YOUR WORK ON THIS
SECTION ONLY. DO NOT WORK ON ANY OTHER SECTION IN THE TEST.

Section 4: Other Abilities

Time: 45 minutes

50 questions

Directions (1–5): Study the photograph for ten minutes; then cover the photograph and answer the questions based on your memory.

1. What is written on the awning on the left side of the photograph?

   A.   Seafood

   B.   Fish & Chips

   C.   Refreshments

   D.   Food & Drink

2. How many people are visible in the photograph?

   A.   1

   B.   2

   C.   3

   D.   4

3. What type of footwear is the man on the left wearing?

    A.   Sandals
    B.   Work boots
    C.   Sneakers
    D.   Dress shoes

4. What item is propped next to the door in the picture?

    A.   A fishing net
    B.   A shovel
    C.   A baseball bat
    D.   A broom

5. Which of the following is the man on the right wearing?

    A.   A scarf
    B.   Shorts
    C.   A hat
    D.   Boots

Directions (6-8): Answer the following question based solely on the information provided.

6. Which method is best for putting out a grease fire in a pan on your stove?

    A.   Throw water on it.
    B.   Use a fire extinguisher.
    C.   Pour baking soda on it.
    D.   Put on the pan's lid.

7. A miter saw is used to

    A.   Cut an irregular shape
    B.   Cut a very hard material
    C.   Make an accurate crosscut
    D.   Make an intricate curved cut

Question 8 refers to the following figure.

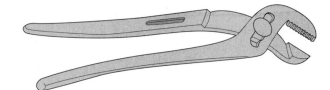

8. Which type of pliers is pictured?

   A. Channel-lock pliers
   B. Needle-nose pliers
   C. Stripper pliers
   D. Pincer pliers

Directions (9–11): To achieve the full testing experience, don't simply read the following questions and select an answer. Instead, ask a friend to read these questions aloud to you and select the best answer based on what you hear. Have your friend pause before moving on to the next question to give you time to select the answer.

9. For question 9, select the answer choice that contains the initials of federal worker Michelle Leonard Perry.

   A. M. I. P.
   B. L. M. P.
   C. N. L. P.
   D. M. L. P.

10. For question 10, select the answer choice that shows the most likely time that police officer Marty Jenkins started his nightshift patrol.

   A. 10:00 a.m.
   B. 12:15 p.m.
   C. 3:30 p.m.
   D. 11:15 p.m.

11. For question 11, select the answer choice that shows the number of letters that United States postal worker Deborah Kelly can deliver over the weekend if she delivers 64 letters per day.

   A. 64
   B. 128
   C. 192
   D. 320

Directions (12–17): Answer the following questions based solely on the information provided.

12. Bill is an accountant at a large accounting firm. While looking at document prepared by Maria, a fellow accountant who has recently been reprimanded for making too many mistakes, he finds many errors. What should Bill do?

    A. Correct the errors himself.
    B. Confront Maria about the errors.
    C. Report his discovery to their supervisor.
    D. Ignore the errors and continue working.

13. A police officer enters a corner grocery store to which he has been dispatched. Observing the scene, he sees a clerk lying on the ground behind the register, bleeding from a puncture wound to his chest. The register drawer is open and there is no money inside. What can the police officer infer happened from this situation?

    A. The clerk was stabbed in the course of an armed robbery at the store.
    B. The clerk cut himself with a large knife and stumbled to the front of the store.
    C. The clerk was injured when the cash register drawer swung open unexpectedly.
    D. The clerk fell and injured himself while attempting to do something with the register.

14. Mail carrier Rick Simpson is working on his normal Granger Street route at 3:45 p.m. when he witnesses two men in black sweatshirts approach a woman who is stepping into her vehicle, a silver Chevrolet Cavalier. One of the men strikes the woman with a small blunt object, knocking her unconscious. The two men then search the woman's purse, take her wallet and her keys, and drive off, heading south on Granger Street, leaving the woman lying in her driveway. Which of the following expresses the information most clearly and accurately?

    A. A woman was the victim of a carjacking on Granger Street. Two unidentified males wearing black sweatshirts approached the woman. One man hit the woman with a blunt object. The pair removed the victim's keys and wallet from her purse, stole her car, and fled in a southerly direction.
    B. At 3:45 p.m., a woman was the victim of a carjacking on Granger Street. Two unidentified males approached a woman entering her silver Chevrolet Cavalier. One man hit the woman with a blunt object. The pair removed the victim's keys and wallet from her purse, stole her car, and fled in a southerly direction.
    C. A woman was the victim of a carjacking at 3:45 p.m. Two unidentified males wearing black sweatshirts approached a woman entering her silver Chevrolet Cavalier. The pair removed the victim's keys and wallet from her purse, stole her car, and fled in a southerly direction.
    D. At 3:45 p.m., a woman was the victim of a carjacking on Granger Street. Two unidentified males wearing black sweatshirts approached a woman entering her silver Chevrolet Cavalier. One man hit the woman with a blunt object. The pair removed the victim's keys and wallet from her purse, stole her car, and fled in a southerly direction.

Questions 15 through 17 refer to the following information.

The federal, state, and local prison systems employ individuals in many different positions including correctional officers, probation officers, probation officer assistants, and correctional treatment specialists. The following are brief descriptions of the responsibilities of each of these positions:

- Correctional officers are responsible for enforcing federal regulations regarding the daily operation of prison facilities. These individuals aid in maintaining order, enforcing prison rules, and supervising inmates.
- Probation officers are responsible for conducting investigations and preparing reports concerning the activities of inmates within the prison system, including rehabilitation progress and internal criminal incidents.
- Probation officer assistants are responsible for carrying out duties designed to support the efforts of probation officers, including writing reports, aiding in investigations, and other clerical duties.
- Correctional treatment specialists who work in prisons assess inmates' progress toward rehabilitation. They can administer questionnaires and psychological tests to inmates.

15. Which of the following positions is responsible for investigating an inmate attack on a prison guard?

   A.   Correctional officer
   B.   Probation officer
   C.   Probation officer assistant
   D.   Correctional treatment specialist

16. Which of the following positions is responsible for monitoring inmates during their meal times?

   A.   Correctional officer
   B.   Probation officer
   C.   Probation officer assistant
   D.   Correctional treatment specialist

17. Which of the following positions may administer questionnaires or psychological tests to inmates?

   A.   Correctional officer
   B.   Probation officer
   C.   Probation officer assistant
   D.   Correctional treatment specialist

Directions (18–21): Answer the following questions honestly and completely. These questions do not have correct or incorrect answers. They are used to gauge aspects of your personality.

18. You are late for scheduled events.

   A.   Very often
   B.   Often
   C.   Sometimes
   D.   Rarely

19. You are capable of performing several tasks at once.

    A. Strongly agree
    B. Agree
    C. Disagree
    D. Strongly disagree

20. When working, which do you prefer?

    A. Performing repetitive tasks
    B. Making decisions
    C. Working with a team
    D. Working independently

21. You establish and maintain relationships easily.

    A. Strongly agree
    B. Agree
    C. Disagree
    D. Strongly disagree

Directions (22–32): Answer the following questions based solely on the information provided.

22. What is the full-charge voltage of an AA-size dry-cell alkaline battery?

    A. 1 volt
    B. 1.2 volts
    C. 1.5 volts
    D. 1.9 volts

23. In an internal combustion engine, which part converts the linear motion of the piston into rotational motion?

    A. Connecting rod
    B. Crankshaft
    C. Camshaft
    D. Cylinder

Question 24 refers to the following figure.

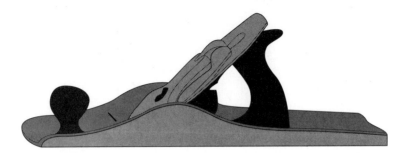

24. This tool would most likely be used for

    A. Scraping paint off a surface
    B. Shaping a piece of wood
    C. Sharpening a knife
    D. Sanding a surface

25. Which type of drill bit would you most likely use to drill a hole for a dowel?

    A. Twist
    B. Auger
    C. Spur point
    D. Countersink

Questions 26 through 28 refer to the following information.

Emergency medical technicians are divided into four levels of certification that determine their qualification to perform certain tasks in an emergency. The four levels are

- **First Responder:** May perform basic first aid, immobilize patients, and provide transport.
- **EMT-Basic:** May treat patients beyond first aid on the scene and during transport, use medical devices such as automated external defibrillators, administer some common medications with permission, and assess respiratory or cardiac problems.
- **EMT-Intermediate:** May use airway management devices, read electrocardiogram readings, administer drugs to control heart arrhythmia, and administer intravenous medication under supervision.
- **EMT-Paramedic:** May perform endotracheal intubation, administer a wide variety of drugs through intramuscular and subcutaneous routes, treat internal injuries, and monitor cardiac activity with an electrocardiogram machine.

26. Which of the following represents the minimum required certification level required for an EMT to administer the proper medications to a patient suffering from heart arrhythmia?

    A. First Responder
    B. EMT-Basic
    C. EMT-Intermediate
    D. EMT-Paramedic

27. Which of the following represents the minimum required certification level required for an EMT to use an automated external defibrillator on a patient in cardiac arrest?

    A. First Responder
    B. EMT-Basic
    C. EMT-Intermediate
    D. EMT-Paramedic

28. Which of the following represents the minimum required certification level required for an EMT to provide artificial respiration through endotracheal intubation?

    A. First Responder
    B. EMT-Basic
    C. EMT-Intermediate
    D. EMT-Paramedic

Questions 29 through 32 refer to the following information.

29. As a police officer, you're on patrol in Langley Park when a man approaches you and says he just witnessed a kidnapping. The man explains that he was sitting on a bench near the park's playground when he saw a white man—who was 5'10" tall, 200 pounds, and wearing a black coat—step out of a white delivery van parked on the street. The man approached a young boy on a swing, grabbed the child, and hurriedly placed the child in back of the van before driving off. Which of the following expresses the information most clearly and accurately?

    A. The witness reported that a tall, white man in a black coat abducted an unidentified male child from the playground, placed the child in the rear of a white delivery van, and fled the scene.
    B. A white male, approximately 5'10" tall, weighing about 200 pounds, and wearing a black trench coat abducted an unidentified male child in Langley Park. The suspect took the child from the park's playground and placed him in the rear of a white delivery van before driving off.
    C. A suspect described as a white male about 5'10" tall and 200 pounds was seen abducting an unidentified child from the playground in Langley Park. The man pulled the child off a swing and then fled in a white delivery van.
    D. The unidentified male child was abducted from the Langley Park playground by a white male suspect believed to be about 5'10" tall and 200 pounds. The suspect approached the child while he was on the swings, picked him up, placed him in the rear of a white delivery van, and drove off.

30. Clerical worker Carol has been distraught since Norma was transferred to her department several weeks ago. The two have not gotten along well, and Carol is becoming increasingly frustrated. She believes that Norma is trying to push her out of the department. Carol can't take it anymore, so she resolves to do something. What should Carol do?

    A. File a formal complaint against Norma.
    B. Report Norma's behavior to her supervisor.
    C. Talk to Norma and calmly discuss the situation.
    D. Ask her other co-workers to harass Norma until she quits.

31. Postal worker Steve is on duty at the post office's front desk when his friend approaches the desk. His friend tells him that he needs some stamps to send out his bills, but he has no money. He asks Steve to slip him a few stamps from the roll. What should Steve do?

    A. Ask his friend to leave and report the incident to his manager.
    B. Give his friend a few free stamps when no one is looking.
    C. Give his friend some stamps if he will agree to pay later.
    D. Tell his friend that he can't help because he could be fired.

32. At the end of the week, an office manager sends his secretary to the bank with the weekly deposit. This week's deposit totaled $1,800. When the manager visits the bank the following week, he discovers that only $1,600 was deposited on Friday. What can he infer from this situation?

    A. The secretary went to the wrong bank.
    B. The secretary kept some of the money.
    C. The bank charged a $200 processing fee.
    D. The bank misplaced some of the money.

Directions (33–34): Answer the following questions honestly and completely. These questions do not have correct or incorrect answers. They are used to gauge aspects of your personality.

33. You work efficiently and meet deadlines.

    A. Very often
    B. Often
    C. Sometimes
    D. Rarely

34. You enjoy being part of a team.

    A. Strongly agree
    B. Agree
    C. Disagree
    D. Strongly disagree

Directions (35–37): Study the passage for ten minutes; then cover the passage and answer the questions based on your memory.

Date: March 23, 2010
To: All Employees
From: Frank Barone, Paulson Sanitation General Manager
Subject: Procedural Violations

It has come to my attention that there have been numerous procedural violations in recent weeks. This letter is to be a reminder of the importance of observing all procedural regulations at all times. Failure to comply with any procedural regulation will result in a written warning for the first offense, a fine or suspension for the second offense, and immediate dismissal for the third offense. These procedural regulations include the following:

- Drivers should not exceed 15 miles per hour while on their pickup routes.
- Collectors must wear protective gear at all times.
- Collectors must use harnesses and handholds whenever the truck is in motion.
- Oversized metal objects should not be placed in compactor trucks.
- Collectors should remove only properly marked garbage bags.
- Garbage should be removed only from homes or apartments with properly displayed stickers.

These regulations are in place to guarantee the continued success of Paulson Sanitation and to ensure your personal safety. For these reasons, it is vitally important that you observe all procedural regulations while you are on the job. I simply ask that you do your part to keep our company as safe and successful as possible.

Thank you.

Sincerely,

Frank Barone
Paulson Sanitation General Manager

35. What is the name of the company in the memo?

    A.   P. Alson Sanitation
    B.   Paul and Sons Sanitation
    C.   Pallson Sanitation
    D.   Paulson Sanitation

36. What is the maximum allowed speed for a garbage truck on its route?

    A.   10 miles per hour
    B.   15 miles per hour
    C.   20 miles per hour
    D.   25 miles per hour

37. The letter writer's title is

   A.   General Manager
   B.   Safety Coordinator
   C.   Director of Operations
   D.   Chief Executive Officer

Directions (38–43): Answer the following questions based solely on the information provided.

38. Samantha is a telephone customer service representative for a national credit card company. One afternoon, she receives a call from an irate man who claims that he has been wrongly charged several fees on his account. He is yelling at Samantha and demanding that she remove the charges. How should Samantha respond in this situation?

   A.   Tell the man that she can remove all the charges just so that he will stop yelling.
   B.   Attempt to calm the caller and convince him to rationally discuss his problem.
   C.   Immediately connect the man with her supervisor so he or she can handle the problem.
   D.   Threaten to end the call if the man does not compose himself.

39. Firefighters arrive at the scene of a reported house fire. They find that a large portion of the rear of the home has been destroyed and most of the front of the home is engulfed in flames. The lawn has noticeable char marks on it, and debris is strewn around the back yard all the way to the property line. What can the firefighters infer has happened?

   A.   The fire was caused by an electrical short.
   B.   An arsonist was most likely responsible.
   C.   An exploding gas tank ignited the fire.
   D.   The homeowners were not injured.

40. At the end of his shift, factory worker Phil Miller heads to his locker to collect his things. When he approaches the door, he sees that his lock has been broken. Looking inside the locker, he finds that his wallet and several other items are missing. What can you infer has happened?

   A.   Phil misplaced his wallet earlier that day.
   B.   The maintenance person accidentally broke the lock.
   C.   Phil unintentionally opened the wrong locker.
   D.   Someone broke into the locker and stole Phil's things.

41. Which type of safety glove is most appropriate for use when handling caustic chemicals?

   A.   Leather
   B.   Fabric
   C.   Canvas
   D.   Rubber

42. A pulsating brake pedal is usually an indication of:

    A. A rusted or sticking shoe adjuster
    B. Air in the brake system
    C. A warped brake rotor
    D. Low engine vacuum

43. Which type of piping material is most often used for cold water systems?

    A. Cast iron
    B. Copper
    C. Brass
    D. Steel

Directions (44–46): Study the photograph for ten minutes; then cover the passage and answer the questions based on your memory.

44. What is the destination of the pictured train?

    A. Logan City
    B. Belmont City
    C. Perth City
    D. Hobart City

45. What are the daily departure times for the train?

    A. 8:00 a.m. to 6:35 p.m.
    B. 7:30 a.m. to 7:30 p.m.
    C. 6:15 a.m. to 10:45 p.m.
    D. 9:30 a.m. to 5:55 p.m.

46. What article of clothing are the three men in the far left of the photograph all wearing?

    A. Glasses
    B. Hats
    C. Neckties
    D. Windbreakers

Directions (47–50): Answer the following questions honestly and completely. These questions do not have correct or incorrect answers. They are used to gauge aspects of your personality.

47. Which do you prefer to do when working in a group?

    A. Assigning responsibilities
    B. Following orders
    C. Making decisions
    D. Carrying out tasks

48. Which of the following best describes your current job?

    A. Challenging
    B. Simple
    C. Stressful
    D. Repetitive

49. You are less productive in the afternoon than in morning.

    A. Very often
    B. Often
    C. Sometimes
    D. Rarely

50. You would like to have a flexible work schedule.

    A. Strongly agree
    B. Agree
    C. Disagree
    D. Strongly disagree

IF YOU FINISH BEFORE TIME IS CALLED, CHECK YOUR WORK ON THIS SECTION ONLY. DO NOT WORK ON ANY OTHER SECTION IN THE TEST.

Answer Key

Section 1: Verbal Ability

1. D	14. D	27. C	40. D
2. C	15. B	28. A	41. A
3. A	16. A	29. D	42. C
4. A	17. D	30. C	43. B
5. B	18. B	31. A	44. D
6. A	19. D	32. A	45. A
7. A	20. D	33. B	46. C
8. C	21. C	34. C	47. B
9. B	22. B	35. C	48. C
10. A	23. A	36. A	49. D
11. A	24. B	37. B	50. C
12. B	25. B	38. D	
13. C	26. A	39. C	

Section 2: Mathematical Ability

1. C	14. C	27. D	40. B
2. D	15. A	28. B	41. A
3. B	16. C	29. A	42. D
4. D	17. A	30. D	43. C
5. C	18. B	31. A	44. B
6. C	19. B	32. C	45. B
7. D	20. D	33. A	46. C
8. A	21. B	34. C	47. B
9. B	22. A	35. B	48. B
10. C	23. D	36. D	49. C
11. C	24. C	37. C	50. B
12. A	25. B	38. A	
13. B	26. A	39. B	

Section 3: Clerical Ability

1. B	14. A	27. D	39. B
2. D	15. C	28. B	40. A
3. C	16. D	29. C	41. B
4. A	17. C	30. A	42. D
5. B	18. A	31. C	43. B
6. C	19. C	32. B	44. A
7. D	20. A	33. D	45. C
8. A	21. B	34. B	46. A
9. D	22. D	35. B	47. B
10. D	23. B	36. C	48. C
11. C	24. C	37. Minimum speed requirements vary.	49. D
12. A	25. B		50. A
13. B	26. C	38. D	

Section 4: Other Abilities

1. B	15. B	27. B	40. D
2. B	16. A	28. D	41. D
3. C	17. D	29. B	42. C
4. A	18. See answer explanations.	30. C	43. D
5. B		31. D	44. C
6. D	19. See answer explanations.	32. B	45. D
7. C	20. See answer explanations.	33. See answer explanations.	46. B
8. A		34. See answer explanations.	47. See answer explanations.
9. D	21. See answer explanations.		
10. D	22. C	35. D	48. See answer explanations.
11. A	23. B	36. B	49. See answer explanations.
12. C	24. B	37. A	
13. A	25. C	38. B	50. See answer explanations.
14. D	26. C	39. C	

Answer Explanations

Section 1: Verbal Ability

1. **D** The word *acquiesce* means "to comply with." It does not mean "to show interest in," "to give leave to," or "to ponder." *(See Chapter V, Section A.)*

2. **C** The word *pacific* means "having a calming effect." It does not mean "having a strange character," "being lively or exciting," or "being unbelievable." *(See Chapter V, Section A.)*

3. **A** The word *belligerent* means "combative." It does not mean "generous," "forgiving," or "wealthy." *(See Chapter V, Section A.)*

4. **A** The word *inconsequential* means "irrelevant." It does not mean "very stubborn," "unhappy," or "very similar." *(See Chapter V, Section A.)*

5. **B** The word *intangible* means "unperceivable." It does not mean "imaginary," "unethical," or "motionless." *(See Chapter V, Section A.)*

6. **A** The word *pillage* means "steal." It does not mean "mend," "risk," or "fake." *(See Chapter V, Section A.)*

7. **A** The paragraph best supports the statement that computers have become a vital part of modern life. Nothing in the passage states that computers are an insignificant technological invention, that they are not widely used, or that they have not had an impact on culture. *(See Chapter V, Section B.)*

8. **C** According to the paragraph, Dr. Martin Luther King, Jr., is best known for his political activism. Nothing in the passage states that King was in the military, owned a business, or was religious, so choices A, B, and D are incorrect. *(See Chapter V, Section B.)*

9. **B** The main idea of this paragraph is that modern technology has changed the way many people read. Nothing in the passage refers to the cost of electronic reading devices or the need for libraries, so choices A and C are incorrect. It also does not mention anything about books becoming obsolete. *(See Chapter V, Section B.)*

10. **A** According to the paragraph, alcohol was outlawed during prohibition because it was believed to be an immoral vice. The passage does not have any information about profits or America's political enemies, so choices B and C are incorrect. It also doesn't state that alcohol was outlawed because it was a source of income for organized crime. *(See Chapter V, Section B.)*

11. **A** The main idea of this paragraph is that identity theft has become more common due to the Internet. Nothing in the passage supports that the Internet is an increasingly powerful business tool, criminals have become more creative, or states should restrict Internet use. *(See Chapter V, Section B.)*

12. **B** The paragraph best supports the statement that many modern athletes make poor role models for kids. The passage says nothing about sports salaries, codes of conduct for players, or television stars. *(See Chapter V, Section B.)*

13. **C** The author wants to convey the message that humans' curiosity has been stimulated by outer space for a long time. The word *piqued* properly conveys this idea. *(See Chapter V, Section C.)*

14. **D** This sentence requires a colon for correct punctuation. *(See Chapter V, Section D5.)*

15. **B** The word that best completes the sentence is *commended*, which means "praised." *Reprimanded*, *matriculated*, and *immolated* do not fit the context of this sentence. *(See Chapter V, Section C.)*

16. **A** The word that best completes the sentence is *irreparably,* which means "in a way that is not repairable." *Vicariously, imperceptibly,* and *marginally* do not fit the context of this sentence. *(See Chapter V, Section C.)*

17. **D** The correct sentence order is 3, 2, 1, 4: The man quickly approached the counter, produced a pistol, and demanded that Howard give him all the money in the register. Pretending to fully cooperate, Howard tripped a silent alarm as he slowly opened the cash drawer. Then Howard completely emptied the drawer and cautiously gave the man the money. Grabbing the money, the man fled the store, only to be apprehended by police one block away. *(See Chapter V, Section C.)*

18. **B** The correct sentence order is 1, 4, 3, 2: Stepping to the plate, Steve takes a few practice swings and stands in position. As Steve looks on, the pitcher signals the catcher and prepares for his throw. Snapping into action, the pitcher arches back and launches the pitch. Reacting swiftly, Steve swings and cracks the bat, sending the ball soaring into the stands. *(See Chapter V, Section C.)*

19. **D** The correct answer is *seize,* which is a verb that means "to take hold of." *Cees* is the plural form of word used to represent the letter *C. Seas* is a noun that refers to oceans or other large bodies of water. *Sees* is a form of *see,* which is a verb that means "to view." *(See Chapter V, Section D6c.)*

20. **D** The correct answer is *preys,* which is verb that means "to hunt." *Praise* as a verb means "to laud." *Prase,* a noun, is a type of translucent quartz. *Prays* means "to ask humbly" or "to implore." *(See Chapter V, Section D6c.)*

21. **C** The correct answer is *sense,* which is a noun meaning "intelligence." *Cense* is a verb that means "to perfume." *Cents* is the plural form of a *cent,* which is a coin or token. *Scents* is a noun that means "smells." *(See Chapter V, Section D6c.)*

22. **B** The word *english* should be capitalized because it is a proper noun. *(See Chapter V, Section D4.)*

23. **A** The word *south* should be capitalized because it refers to a specific region, the American South. When the word *south* is not used to describe a specific region, it should be lowercase. *(See Chapter V, Section D4.)*

24. **B** A semicolon should be used to separate the two independent clauses because the clauses have no conjunctions to connect them, and no commas are needed in the sentence. *(See Chapter V, Section D5.)*

25. **B** No colon is required in this sentence. A colon should never be used to separate a preposition from its objects. In the original sentence, the colon separated the preposition *of* from its objects, *billing, filing reports,* and *accounting. (See Chapter V, Section D5.)*

26. **A** *Iradiate* is spelled incorrectly. The correct spelling is *irradiate. (See Chapter V, Section E.)*

27. **C** *Couragous* is spelled incorrectly. The correct spelling is *courageous. (See Chapter V, Section E.)*

28. **A** *Defendent* is spelled incorrectly. The correct spelling is *defendant. (See Chapter V, Section E.)*

29. **D** *Resivoir* is spelled incorrectly. The correct spelling is *reservoir. (See Chapter V, Section E.)*

30. **C** *Maintainance* is spelled incorrectly. The correct spelling is *maintenance. (See Chapter V, Section E.)*

31. **A** *Camradarie* is spelled incorrectly. The correct spelling is *camaraderie. (See Chapter V, Section E.)*

32. **A** *Effagy* is spelled incorrectly. The correct spelling is *effigy. (See Chapter V, Section E.)*

33. **B** A *knife* could be described as *sharp,* just as a *club* could be described as *blunt.* This definition relationship is not supported by choices A, C, or D. *(See Chapter V, Section F.)*

34. C A *mare* is a female horse, and a *hen* is a female chicken. A *cow* is a female bovine and a *bull*, not a *steer*, is a male bovine, so choice A is incorrect. Choices B and D do not support the correct relationship. *(See Chapter V, Section F.)*

35. C *Timid* is a synonym of *shy*, and *volatile* is a synonym of *unstable*. Choices A, B and D are antonyms, so these choices are incorrect. *(See Chapter V, Section F.)*

36. A An *egg* is a component of *cake*, and *yeast* is a component of *bread*. *Cake* is not a component of *birthday*, *potatoes* are not a component of *steak*, and *milk* is not a component of *coffee*, so choices B, C, and D are incorrect. *(See Chapter V, Section F.)*

37. B A *hunter* is generally described as *stealthy*, and a *philosopher* is generally described as *wise*. The other choices do not support this type of relationship. *(See Chapter V, Section F.)*

38. D *Deluge*, which means flood, is the opposite of *drought*, which means dry, so the correct answer is *desert: rain forest*, because a desert is dry and a rain forest is the opposite of dry. The other choices do not support this relationship. *(See Chapter V, Section F.)*

39. C *Impurity* most nearly means "pollutant." It does not mean "error," "sentiment," or "catastrophe." *(See Chapter V, Section G.)*

40. D *Futile* most nearly means "useless." It does not mean "effective," "depressed," or "moveable." *(See Chapter V, Section G.)*

41. A *Benevolent* most nearly means "compassionate." It does not mean "gritty," "indifferent," or "desirable." *(See Chapter V, Section G.)*

42. C A *paragon* is a "model," not a "clown," "follower," or "wanderer." *(See Chapter V, Section G.)*

43. B *Recompense* most nearly means "compensation." It does not mean "knowledge," "jeopardy," or "condemnation." *(See Chapter V, Section G.)*

44. D *Censure* most nearly means "denounce." It does not mean "block," "feel," or "guarantee." *(See Chapter V, Section G.)*

45. A The word *everyone* is singular and requires the use of a singular possessive pronoun. Choice A corrects the error in the original sentence by using *his or her*. Choice B uses *them*, which does not agree with *everyone*. Choice C uses awkward construction. *(See Chapter V, Section H.)*

46. C The phrase *must be sent to the supervisor's secretary* is a nonrestrictive element. The word *that* should be used before restrictive elements, and the word *which* should be used before all other elements. Choice A confuses the intended meaning of the original sentence. Choice B does not correctly offset the nonrestrictive element. Choice C uses the correct word before the nonrestrictive element. *(See Chapter V, Section H.)*

47. B The original sentence sets off the phrase *that work at the courthouse* by commas. However, this is a restrictive element, which means that the commas are unnecessary. Choices A and C do not correct this error. Also, when you're talking about people, you should use *who* or *whom*, rather than *which* or *that*. Choice B corrects the problems in the original sentence. *(See Chapter V, Section H.)*

48. C *Myself* is a reflexive pronoun. In this sentence, the pronoun *me* should be used instead of *myself*. If Mr. Woodhouse were not a part of the sentence, then you wouldn't say, "All concerns about the new vacation policy should be directed to myself." You also wouldn't use the word *I*. This makes choices A and B incorrect. Choice C is correct because it replaces *myself* with *me*. *(See Chapter V, Section H.)*

49. D The original sentence is correct. Choice A is wrong because there is no need to change the construction of the sentence. Choice B is incorrect because *his or her* does not agree with *all employees*. Choice C is also incorrect because the phrase *their personal identification numbers* is a restrictive phrase that should not be surrounded by commas. *(See Chapter V, Section H.)*

50. C The original sentence contains an error in verb tense. Choice A fails to correct this error and uses the past tense of the verb *submit* when the present tense is needed. Choice B fails to correct the error in verb tense and creates a new agreement error by replacing the word *their* with *his or her*. Choice C is the only response that corrects the error in verb tense. *(See Chapter V, Section H.)*

Section 2: Mathematical Ability

1. C To convert $\frac{216}{16}$, an improper fraction, into a mixed number, you have to divide 216 by 16. So, $216 \div 16 = 13.5$. Since the question asks you for a mixed number (a fraction), not a decimal, you have to convert 0.5 to a fraction: $0.5 = \frac{1}{2}$. So, the correct answer is $13\frac{1}{2}$. *(See Chapter VI, Section A1.)*

2. D To solve this problem, you have to first convert all your mixed numbers to improper fractions and decimals and then follow the order of operations. Your first step would be to multiply $\frac{16}{4} \cdot 5.485$. You know that $\frac{16}{4} = 4$, so $4 \cdot 5.485 = 21.94$. You then subtract $21.94 - 3\frac{2}{8}$. To convert $3\frac{2}{8}$ to a decimal, you know that $3\frac{2}{8} = 3\frac{1}{4}$, which is 3.25 in decimal form. So, $21.94 - 3.25 = 18.69$. Finally, subtract $18.69 - 0.875 = 17.815$. Rounded to the nearest hundredth, the correct answer is 17.82. You may have chosen choices A, B, or C if you didn't follow the order of operations. *(See Chapter VI, Section A2.)*

3. B The police cruiser traveled 12 miles in 9 minutes. To solve this problem, first convert the minutes into hours: 9 minutes $\div$ 60 minutes per hour = 0.15 hours. Next, use the information you know to complete the equation: Distance = Rate · Time $(d = rt)$. You know that the rate is 80 miles per hour and the time is 0.15 hours. So, $d = 80 \cdot 0.15 = 12$ miles. *(See Chapter VI, Section B2.)*

4. D To solve this problem, add together the number of words Josie, Frank, and Ellen can type in 1 minute: $60 + 45 + 52 = 157$. Then, multiply this sum by 30 minutes: 157 words per minute · 30 minutes = 4,710 words. *(See Chapter VI, Section B2.)*

5. C To solve the equation $12a - 6a = 67 + 4a + 5$ for a, first subtract and add like terms: $12a - 6a = 6a$ and $67 + 5 = 72$, so $6a = 72 + 4a$. Next, subtract $4a$ from each side: $6a - 4a = 72 + 4a - 4a$, and $2a = 72$. Then, divide each side by 2: $\frac{2a}{2} = \frac{72}{2}$. So, $a = 36$. *(See Chapter VI, Section D3.)*

6. C According to the bar chart, 7 million drivers travel over bridge 1 and 3 million drivers travel over bridge 2. To solve this problem, subtract the number of drivers who travel over bridge 2 from the number of drivers who travel over bridge 1: $7 - 3 = 4$. *(See Chapter VI, Section F1.)*

7. D To solve this problem, subtract the number of employees working for Auto Plus from the number of employees working for Martin's Groceries: $68 - 27 = 41$. *(See Chapter VI, Section F2.)*

8. A To find the answer, first multiply the percentage of men who drive black cars by the total number of men and then multiply the percentage of men who drive green cars by the total number of men: Black: 55% or $0.55 \cdot 500 = 275$; Green: 5% or $0.05 \cdot 500 = 25$. Then subtract the number of men who drive green cars from the number of men who drive black cars: $275 - 25 = 250$. *(See Chapter VI, Section F1.)*

9. **B** To solve this problem, you must first determine the increase in the price of the oven repairs by subtracting the updated price from the original price. $500 – $420 = $80. The price of oven repairs increased $80. To determine the percentage of this increase, cross-multiply:

$$\frac{80}{420} = \frac{x}{100}$$
$$420x = 80 \cdot 100$$
$$420x = 8{,}000$$
$$x = \frac{8{,}000}{420}$$
$$x = 19.05$$

Therefore, x = about 19%. *(See Chapter VI, Section B1.)*

10. **C** To solve this problem, multiply the number of electricians by the time it takes to wire ten rooms to determine the amount of time it would take one electrician to do the job: 4 electricians · 9 hours = 36 hours, so it would take one electrician 36 hours to wire ten rooms. Next, divide the number of hours it takes one electrician to wire ten rooms by the total number of electricians who will perform the job: 36 hours ÷ 3 electricians = 12 hours. *(See Chapter VI, Section C1.)*

11. **C** To solve this problem, first convert the time to reciprocals to determine how much work each person can do when working alone for one. To find this information, convert the time it take each person to complete the job into reciprocals: 9 hours = $\frac{1}{9}$, 12 hours = $\frac{1}{12}$, and 18 hours = $\frac{1}{18}$. (This means that Ernie, by himself can complete $\frac{1}{9}$ of the total job in one hour, Fiona can complete $\frac{1}{12}$ of the total job in one hour, and Michael can complete $\frac{1}{18}$ of the total job in one hour.) Then, add these fractions together to find how much work the team can complete in one day: $\frac{1}{9} + \frac{1}{12} + \frac{1}{18}$. Before you can add the fractions together, find a common denominator for all three: $\frac{4}{36} + \frac{3}{36} + \frac{2}{36} = \frac{9}{36}$. Reduce the fraction to lowest terms to get $\frac{1}{4}$. Ernie, Fiona, and Michael can finish $\frac{1}{4}$ of the job in one hour, which means that to complete the entire job, they would need four hours. *(See Chapter VI, Section C1.)*

12. **A** To reduce the fraction $\frac{18}{81}$ to lowest terms, find a number that is divisible by both the numerator and the denominator. Although 3 is divisible by both 18 and 81, using this divisor leaves you with $\frac{6}{27}$. This fraction is a reduced version of the original, but it's not the lowest term. To attain the lowest term, divide the numerator and denominator by 9: $\frac{18}{81} = \frac{2}{9}$. *(See Chapter VI, Section A1.)*

13. **B** Since this question provides you with a fraction but asks you to answer using decimals, you should convert the fraction to a decimal. To do this, divide 3 by 5: 3 ÷ 5 = 0.60. You know that 0.60 = 60%. You now that 60% of Bill's jobs are not emergencies. Find the percentage of emergency calls by subtracting the percentage of nonemergencies (60%) from 100%: 100% – 60% = 40% are emergencies. To answer the question, multiply the total number of jobs Bill completes each week by the percent of jobs that are emergencies: 47 · 0.40 = 18.8. *(See Chapter VI, Section C1.)*

14. **C** To solve this problem, first find the total cost of the plumber's supplies: $15.62 + $80.45 + $55.03 = $151.10. The customer agreed to pay two-fifths of the price of the supplies. Because you're working with dollar signs and decimal points, convert the fraction to a decimal by dividing 2 by 5: $\frac{2}{5} = 0.40$. Now, multiply the total cost of the parts ($151.10) by the percentage the customer will pay: $151.10 · 0.40 = $60.44. Finally, subtract the price the customer will pay from the total price of the supplies to find the amount the plumber must pay: $151.10 − $60.44 = $90.66. *(See Chapter VI, Section A2.)*

15. **A** To solve this problem, convert the mixed number to an improper fraction. To find the numerator of the new, improper fraction, multiply the denominator (4) by the whole number (6) and then add that product to the numerator (3). The denominator of the improper fraction remains the same: $6\frac{3}{4} = \frac{27}{4}$. Now, following the order of operations, multiply $\frac{27}{4}$ by $\frac{2}{6}$. To do this, simply multiply across the numerators and denominators: $\frac{27}{4} \cdot \frac{2}{6} = \frac{54}{24}$. Next, find the common denominator between $\frac{54}{24}$ and $\frac{8}{3}$. Since 3 is a multiple of 24, the common denominator is 24, and 24 ÷ 3 = 8. Simply multiply the denominator and the numerator of $\frac{8}{3}$ by 8 to get $\frac{64}{24}$. Now that your denominators are equal, you can add across: $\frac{54}{24} + \frac{64}{24} = \frac{118}{24}$. To finish solving this problem, find the common denominator between $\frac{118}{24}$ and $\frac{1}{6}$, and then subtract. Again, 6 is a multiple of 24, and 24 ÷ 6 = 4, so multiply the numerator and denominator of $\frac{1}{6}$ by 4 to get $\frac{4}{24}$. Then, subtract: $\frac{118}{24} - \frac{4}{24} = \frac{114}{24}$. Since your answer options are all mixed numbers, convert your improper fraction: $\frac{114}{24} = 4\frac{3}{4}$. *(See Chapter VI, Section A1.)*

16. **C** To solve this problem, multiply 65% by 40. First, convert the percentage to a decimal (65% = 0.65) and then multiply: 0.65 · 40 = 26. *(See Chapter VI, Section B1.)*

17. **A** To solve this problem, write the ratio as a fraction and then reduce: $\frac{48}{72} = \frac{2}{3}$, which, written as a ratio, is 2:3. *(See Chapter VI, Section B2.)*

18. **B** To find the original price of the sweater, convert the percentage to a decimal (85% = 0.85) and divide the sale price ($42) by the percentage paid (0.85) for the sweater: $42 ÷ 0.85 = $49.41. *(See Chapter VI, Section B1.)*

19. **B** To solve this problem, first divide the total cash by the number of parts: 900 ÷ (2 + 3 + 4) = 900 ÷ 9 = 100. Next, multiply the answer ($100) by the number of parts each person will receive: 100 · 2 = 200, 100 · 3 = 300, and 100 · 4 = 400. So, three students will receive $200, $300, and $400. *(See Chapter VI, Section B2.)*

20. **D** To solve this problem, create a proportion (an equation with ratios on both sides). One side of the proportion should include the cost of 4 paper towels ($5) over the cost of 64 paper towels (unknown = x): $\frac{\$5.00}{x}$. The other ratio should be 4 (the number of paper towels that costs $5) over 64 (the number of paper towels that costs x): $\frac{4}{64}$. To solve this equation for x, cross-multiply the ratios:

$$\frac{\$5.00}{x} = \frac{4}{64}$$
$$4x = \$5.00 \cdot 64$$
$$4x = \$320$$
$$x = \$80$$

(See Chapter VI, Section B3.)

21. **B** To solve this problem, multiply the number of bakers by the time it takes to bake 300 loaves of bread: $5 \cdot 8 = 40$. So, one baker can bake 300 loaves of bread in 40 hours. Next, divide the number of hours it takes one baker to bake 300 loaves of bread by the total number of available bakers: $40 \div 4 = 10$. So, it would take four bakers ten hours to bake 300 loaves of bread. *(See Chapter VI, Section C1.)*

22. **A** To solve this problem, first subtract the difference between the expected cost and the original amount: $400 – $350 = $50. Next, divide the difference by the original amount: $50 \div $400 = 0.125. Next, convert the decimal into a percent: $0.125 = 12.5\%$. *(See Chapter VI, Section B1.)*

23. **D** To solve this problem, set 45:15 as a fraction and then reduce: $\frac{45}{15} = \frac{3}{1}$. *(See Chapter VI, Sections B2–B3.)*

24. **C** To solve this problem, multiply 42% by 120. First, convert the percentage to a decimal and then multiply: $0.42 \cdot 120 = 50.4$. *(See Chapter VI, Section B1.)*

25. **B** To solve this problem, convert 70% to a decimal and multiply by the number of questions on the exam: $0.70 \cdot 50 = 35$. *(See Chapter VI, Section B1.)*

26. **A** To find the answer, multiply the percentage of children who chose Halloween as their favorite holiday by the total number of students: 15% or $0.15 \cdot 200 = 30$. *(See Chapter VI, Section F1.)*

27. **D** According to the diagram, each truck represents 280 trucks and Interstate 95 is represented by $1\frac{1}{2}$ trucks. To solve this problem, first divide 280 by 2 to get the value for the half truck: $280 \div 2 = 140$. Then add the value of one truck to this number: $140 + 280 = 420$. *(See Chapter VI, Section F1.)*

28. **B** To solve this problem, multiply the number of machines (9) by the number of days (6) it takes to print 50,000 telephone books: $9 \cdot 6 = 54$. So, one printing-press machine can print 50,000 telephone books in 54 days. Next, divide the number of days it takes one printing-press machine to print 50,000 telephone books (54) by the total number of working machines (6): $54 \div 6 = 9$. It will take six printing-press machines nine days to print 50,000 telephone books. *(See Chapter VI, Section C1.)*

29. **A** It would take $1\frac{1}{3}$ days for Anna, Jorge, and Miles to complete the job working together. To solve this problem, you must first find out how much how work each person can do alone in one day. To find this information, convert the time it take each person to complete the job into reciprocals: 3 days $= \frac{1}{3}$, 4 days $= \frac{1}{4}$, and 6 days $= \frac{1}{6}$. (This means that, working alone, Anna can complete $\frac{1}{3}$ of the job in one day, Jorge can complete $\frac{1}{4}$ of the job in one day, and Miles can complete $\frac{1}{6}$ of the job in one day.) The next step in solving the problem is adding the reciprocals together to find the total amount of the job the trio can complete together in one day: $\frac{1}{3} + \frac{1}{4} + \frac{1}{6}$. Since you can't add these fractions together without a common denominator, change the fractions so they all have the same denominator: $\frac{4}{12} + \frac{3}{12} + \frac{2}{12} = \frac{9}{12} = \frac{3}{4}$. Anna, Jorge, and Miles can finish $\frac{3}{4}$ of the job in one day. To find out how long it would take the trio to complete the entire job, find the reciprocal of that number: $\frac{3}{4} = \frac{4}{3} = 1\frac{1}{3}$. *(See Chapter VI, Section C1.)*

30. **D** To solve this problem, you must first determine how many square feet the construction team paved within one hour. To do this, divide the area of the driveway by the time it took to complete the paving: 252 square feet $\div$ 6 hours = 42 square feet per hour. Now that you know how much work the group can finish within one hour, you can use that information to determine how many hours it will take them to pave the parking lot. To do this, divide the size of the parking lot by the amount of work they can complete in an hour: 714 square feet $\div$ 42 square feet per hour = 17 hours. *(See Chapter VI, Section C1.)*

31. A Solve the equation $9x + 6 = 50 - 2x$ for x:

$$9x + 6 - 6 = 50 - 2x - 6$$
$$9x = 44 - 2x$$
$$11x = 44$$
$$x = 4$$

(See Chapter VI, Section D3.)

32. C If t stands for the number of trees Phillip chopped down, and Martin chopped down nine more than two times the number Phillip chopped down, you should multiply the number of trees Phillip chopped down and add 9 to the product. So, Martin chopped down $2t + 9$ trees. Next, add the number of trees Phillip chopped down to the number of trees Martin chopped down: $2t + 9 + t = 3t + 9$. *(See Chapter VI, Section D1.)*

33. A To find the value of s, solve using proportions. Because the triangles are similar, they have equal angles and proportional sides. Use the proportion $\frac{ab}{ab} = \frac{bc}{bc}$ and solve:

$$\frac{ab}{ab} = \frac{bc}{bc}$$
$$\frac{6}{8} = \frac{11}{s}$$
$$6s = 11 \cdot 8$$
$$6s = 88$$
$$s = \frac{88}{6}$$
$$s = 14\frac{4}{6}$$
$$s = 14\frac{2}{3}$$

So, rounded to the nearest tenth, s is 14.7. *(See Chapter VI, Section E2.)*

34. C The coordinates of the point in the figure are $(-5, 7)$. Because the point is in Quadrant II, the x-coordinate is negative and the y-coordinate is positive. *(See Chapter VI, Section E5.)*

35. B A point with coordinates of $(-17, 4)$ would appear in Quadrant II. To plot this point, you would count negative 17 units on the x-axis and positive 4 units on the y-axis. *(See Chapter VI, Section E5.)*

36. D To solve this problem, replace the letter x with the numeric vale 15, and replace the letter y with the numeric value 25. The new equation will be: $5(15) \cdot (2(15) + 4(25))$. Follow the order of operations to complete the rest of the problem: $(75)(30 + 100) = 75(130) = 9,750$. *(See Chapter VI, Section D4.)*

37. C To solve this problem, plug the numbers into the distance formula: Distance = Rate · Time. So, $d = 35 \cdot 6 = 210$ miles. *(See Chapter VI, Section D6.)*

38. A If m stands for the number of miles Stanley ran, and Virginia ran 2 miles less than 3 times the number of miles Stanley ran, you should multiply the number of miles Stanley ran by 3 and subtract 2 from the sum. So, Virginia ran $3m - 2$ miles. Next, add the number of miles Stanley ran to the number of miles Virginia ran: $3m - 2 + m = 4m - 2$. *(See Chapter VI, Section D1.)*

39. **B** The correct answer is 1,242. To solve this problem, plug in 9 for x and 7 for y: $3x(9x - 5y) =$ $3(9)(9[9] - 5[7]) = (27)(81 - 35) = (27)(46) = 1,242$. *(See Chapter VI, Section D4.)*

40. **B** A triangle's angles will always equal 180° when combined, so add the values of the two sides given and subtract from 180°: $75° + 45° = 120°$ and $180° - 120° = 60°$. *(See Chapter VI, Section E2.)*

41. **A** To find the hypotenuse of the right triangle in the figure, use the Pythagorean theorem: $a^2 + b^2 = c^2$. The hypotenuse is c, so insert the values for a and b to solve:

$$3^2 + 9^2 = c^2$$
$$9 + 81 = c^2$$
$$\sqrt{90} = c^2$$

(See Chapter VI, Section E2.)

42. **D** To find the circumference of the circle, use the formula $C = \pi d$. First, find the diameter of the circle, which is two times the radius. Since AO is the radius, multiply the value for AO (6) times 2 to get 12. Then, insert the values into the equation: $C = 3.14 \cdot 12 = 37.68$. *(See Chapter VI, Section E4.)*

43. **C** To find this answer, you simply have to add the cost of the packages that the customer wants to ship: $5.65 + $3.82 + $7.14 = $16.61. You may have chosen D if you added all the packages' shipping costs together instead of only the packages the customer asked to ship. *(See Chapter VI, Section A2.)*

44. **B** To answer this question, divide the package's weight by its price to ship: $10.95 ÷ 2.5 pounds. To divide by decimals, you must move the decimal in the divisor (2.5) one place to the right to make 2.5 a whole number (so, 25). Then, because you moved the divisor's decimal one place to the right, you must also move the decimal in the dividend (10.95) one place to the right (so, 109.5). Your work should look like this:

$$2.5\overline{)\$10.95} \to 25\overline{)\$109.5} \to 25\overline{)\$109.50}^{\$4.38}$$

The shipping cost at the post office is $4.38 per pound. *(See Chapter VI, Section A2.)*

45. **B** According to the table, the average temperature for the month of September in Jonesville is 68°. *(See Chapter VI, Section F2.)*

46. **C** According to the line graph, the Cougars won 15 games and the Lions won 10 games in 2009, so $15 - 10 = 5$. *(See Chapter VI, Section F1.)*

47. **B** Since the bar chart shows the greatest surge in males choosing nursing professions from 1950 to 1960, the year 1960 is the correct answer. *(See Chapter VI, Section F1.)*

48. **B** To find the answer, multiply the shape's base by its height using the formula: $A = bh$. Insert the values for the base (15) and height (7): $A = 15 \cdot 7 = 105$. *(See Chapter VI, Section E3.)*

49. **C** The value of y is 120°. To solve the problem, remember that an exterior angle of a triangle is equal to the sum of its remote interior angles. The remote interior angles in this figure equal 75° and 45°, so add these together to find y: $75° + 45° = 120°$. *(See Chapter VI, Sections E1–E2.)*

50. **B** To find the answer, solve for x. To find the perimeter of a quadrilateral, add all the sides together: $60 = 14 + 12 + 10 + x$. To solve for x, add the three values together and then subtract that value from the total:

$$60 = 36 + x$$
$$60 - 36 = x$$
$$24 = x$$

(See Chapter VI, Section E3.)

Section 3: Clerical Ability

1. **B** Two of the names are written as "Steven E. Kelley." The other two are written as "Steven E. Kelly" and "Steven F. Kelley." *(See Chapter VII, Section D.)*

2. **D** All four are the same. *(See Chapter VII, Section D.)*

3. **C** Three of the names are written as "Nicholas R. Davis," and the other is written as "Nicholas R. Davies." *(See Chapter VII, Section D.)*

4. **A** None of the choices is the same. *(See Chapter VII, Section D.)*

5. **B** The correct answer is choice B, vital. *(See Chapter VII, Section A2.)*

6. **C** The correct answer is choice C, core. *(See Chapter VII, Section A2.)*

7. **D** The correct answer is choice D, exchange. *(See Chapter VII, Section A2.)*

8. **A** The correct answer is choice A, employee. *(See Chapter VII, Section A2.)*

9. **D** The correct answer is choice D, principles. *(See Chapter VII, Section A2.)*

10. **D** The correct answer is choice D, sending. *(See Chapter VII, Section A2.)*

11. **C** The correct answer is choice C, messages. *(See Chapter VII, Section A2.)*

12. **A** The correct answer is choice A, interpersonal. *(See Chapter VII, Section A2.)*

13. **B** The correct answer is choice B, communicate. *(See Chapter VII, Section A2.)*

14. **A** The correct answer is choice A, projects. *(See Chapter VII, Section A2.)*

15. **C** The correct answer is choice C, confidence. *(See Chapter VII, Section A2.)*

16. **D** *Corridor* would follow the word *correlate* in alphabetical order. *(See Chapter VII, Section B2.)*

17. **C** *Factual* would follow the word *facsimile* in alphabetical order. *(See Chapter VII, Section B2.)*

18. **A** *Prevalent* would follow the word *presentation* in alphabetical order. *(See Chapter VII, Section B2.)*

19. **C** The address 225 Charleston Road is part of route C. *(See Chapter VII, Section C1.)*

20. **A** The address 462 Grange Street is a part of route A. *(See Chapter VII, Section C1.)*

21. **B** The address 42 Manchester Drive is a part of route B. *(See Chapter VII, Section C1.)*

22. **D** The address 475 Washington Avenue is not included in the assigned delivery routes and would be classified as route D. *(See Chapter VII, Section C1.)*

23. **B** Two of the numbers are written as "29583740." The other two are written as "29583748" and "29583140." *(See Chapter VII, Section D.)*

24. **C** Three of the names are written as "Gregory M. Marshall," and the other is written as "Gregory N. Marshall." *(See Chapter VII, Section D.)*

25. **B** Two of the names are written as "Fredrick J. Meyer." The other two are written as "Fredrick I. Meyer" and "Fredric J. Meyer." *(See Chapter VII, Section D.)*

26. **C** Three of the names are written as "Rodger P. Clarke," and the other is written as "Roger P. Clarke." *(See Chapter VII, Section D.)*

27. **D** *Fredrick, Nathaniel* would be placed between *Francis, Simon* and *Fullerton, Peter. (See Chapter VII, Section B2.)*

28. **B** *Lancaster, Maxwell J.* would be placed between *La Bell, Marisa A.* and *Lasher, Thomas F. (See Chapter VII, Section B2.)*

29. **C** *Roberts, J. S.* would be placed between *Richards, M.* and *Rodd, R. P. (See Chapter VII, Section B2.)*

30. **A** The correct code for this document is HFACD. *(See Chapter VII, Section C2.)*

31. **C** The correct code for this document is EEBAB. *(See Chapter VII, Section C2.)*

32. **B** The correct code for this document is KCAEC. *(See Chapter VII, Section C2.)*

33. **D** The correct code for this document is CACDA. *(See Chapter VII, Section C2.)*

34. **B** Michael Francis would be second in an alphabetical list. *(See Chapter VII, Section B2.)*

35. **B** Fr. Peter O' Daniels would be second in an alphabetical list. *(See Chapter VII, Section B2.)*

36. **C** Connolly, Adeline would be third in an alphabetical list. *(See Chapter VII, Section B2.)*

37. The minimum speed for the typing test will vary from state to state. The number of errors allowed will also vary. Contact your local testing facility for more information on the requirements for the typing test. *(See Chapter VII, Section A1.)*

38. **D** The correct code for this file is AB3AC. *(See Chapter VII, Section C2.)*

39. **B** The correct code for this file is BB2MK. *(See Chapter VII, Section C2.)*

40. **A** The correct code for this file is AA4MA. *(See Chapter VII, Section C2.)*

41. **B** The correct code for this file is BB3HR. *(See Chapter VII, Section C2.)*

42. **D** *Harold Lee* would be third in an alphabetical list. *(See Chapter VII, Section B2.)*

43. **B** *Kevin Thomson* would be third in an alphabetical list. *(See Chapter VII, Section B2.)*

44. **A** *Atherton & Morris, Inc.,* would be third in an alphabetical list. *(See Chapter VII, Section B2.)*

45. **C** *Dr. Samuel Carter* would be third in an alphabetical list. *(See Chapter VII, Section B2.)*

46. **A** None of the choices is the same. *(See Chapter VII, Section D.)*

47. **B** Two of the numbers are written as "3161138." The other two are written as "3161130" and "3191138." *(See Chapter VII, Section D.)*

48. C Three of the names are written as "Gerald S. Daly," and the other is written as "Gerard S. Daly." *(See Chapter VII, Section D.)*

49. D All four are the same. *(See Chapter VII, Section D.)*

50. A None of the choices is the same. *(See Chapter VII, Section D.)*

Section 4: Other Abilities

1. B The text on the awning in the left side of the photograph reads Fish & Chips. *(See Chapter VIII, Section A1.)*

2. B Two men are standing in front of the ordering window. *(See Chapter VIII, Section A1.)*

3. C The man on the left is wearing sneakers. *(See Chapter VIII, Section A1.)*

4. A A fish net is propped next to the door on the right side of the photograph. *(See Chapter VIII, Section A1.)*

5. B The man on the right is wearing shorts. He is not wearing a hat, a scarf, or boots. *(See Chapter VIII, Section A1.)*

6. D The best method for putting out this type of grease fire is to put on the pan's lid. This will immediately smother the flames. Water should never be used because it will only worsen a grease fire. A fire extinguisher may spread the flames. Baking soda can put out a grease fire, but the amount of baking soda needed and the time required to find and apply it make this a less efficient option. *(See Chapter VIII, Section C.)*

7. C A miter saw is used to make an accurate crosscut. A jigsaw is used to cut an irregular shape. An abrasive saw is used to cut a very hard material. A scroll saw is used to make an intricate, curved cut. *(See Chapter VIII, Section C.)*

8. A The pliers in the picture are channel-lock pliers. Needle-nose pliers have long, pointed tips. Stripper pliers have special tips designed to remove insulation from wires. Pincer pliers have two long handles and a sharp-edged head. *(See Chapter VIII, Section C.)*

9. D Federal worker Michael Leonard Perry's initials are *M. L. P.* *(See Chapter VIII, Section A2.)*

10. D It can be assumed that the officer's nightshift patrol would begin during nighttime hours, so 11:15 p.m. is the correct answer. Since the officer works at night, the times of 10 a.m., 12:15 p.m., and 3:30 p.m. are incorrect. *(See Chapter VIII, Section A2.)*

11. A The correct answer is 64 because postal worker Kelly can deliver 64 letters per day, and postal workers in the United States deliver mail to residences on Saturdays, but not on Sundays. Therefore, she will deliver mail only one day over the weekend. *(See Chapter VIII, Section A2.)*

12. C The ideal choice for Bill would be to report his discovery to their supervisor. He may not want to get Maria in trouble, but the errors should be reported. Choices A and D are incorrect because if Bill corrects the errors himself or simply ignores them, he may be encouraging more poor work from Maria. Choice B is incorrect because Bill is not a supervisor and is not responsible for reprimanding others. *(See Chapter VIII, Section B2.)*

13. A Because the grocery store clerk is bleeding from a puncture wound and the cash register is open and empty, you can infer that the clerk was stabbed in the course of an armed robbery at the store. It might be possible that the clerk somehow injured himself, but the open, empty register makes it more likely that the injury occurred as a result of an armed robbery at the store. *(See Chapter VIII, Section B1.)*

14. **D** The report in choice D is the clearest and most accurate. This report clearly states the time and location of the incident, provides a description of the assailants, includes exact details of the attack, mentions the make and model of the car, and states the directions in which the assailants fled. Choice A leaves out the time of the incident and make and model of the car. Choice B leaves out the description of the assailants. Choice C leaves out the location of the incident and some details of the attack. *(See Chapter VIII, Section B1.)*

15. **B** A probation officer would be responsible for investigating an inmate attack on a prison guard. *(See Chapter VIII, Section A2.)*

16. **A** A correctional officer would be responsible for monitoring inmates during their meal times. *(See Chapter VIII, Section A2.)*

17. **D** A correctional treatment specialist can administer questionnaires and tests to evaluate inmates' progress. *(See Chapter VIII, Section A2.)*

18. This personality question has no correct or incorrect answer. This type of question is designed to test your ability to be on time. *(See Chapter VIII, Section D.)*

19. This personality question has no correct or incorrect answer. This type of question is designed to test your ability to multitask. *(See Chapter VIII, Section D.)*

20. This personality question has no correct or incorrect answer. This type of question is designed to determine your work preferences. *(See Chapter VIII, Section D.)*

21. This personality question has no correct or incorrect answer. This type of question is designed to test your ability to get along with others. *(See Chapter VIII, Section D.)*

22. **C** The full-charge voltage of an AA-size dry-cell alkaline battery is 1.5 volts. The standard voltage of all AA-, AAA-, C-, and D-size dry-cell alkaline batteries when fully charged is 1.5 volts. *(See Chapter VIII, Section C.)*

23. **B** The crankshaft converts the linear motion of the piston into rotational motion. The connecting rod connects the piston and the crankshaft. The camshaft operates the intake and exhaust valves. The cylinder is the encasement in which combustion takes place. *(See Chapter VIII, Section C.)*

24. **B** The pictured tool, which is a hand planer, is used for shaping a piece of wood. A scraper or sander is used to scrape paint from a surface. A sharpening stone or a similar device is used to sharpen a knife. Sandpaper is used to sand a surface. *(See Chapter VIII, Section C.)*

25. **C** When drilling a hole for a dowel you would most likely use a spur-point drill bit. This type of drill bit is considered ideal for this job. A twist drill bit is the most common type of bit and is used for drill a normal hole. An auger drill bit would be used to drill a deep, wide-diameter hole in a piece of wood. A countersink drill bit would be used to for a conical recess for the head of a countersunk screw. *(See Chapter VIII, Section C.)*

26. **C** The minimum required certification level for an EMT to administer the proper medication to a patient suffering from heart arrhythmia is EMT-Intermediate. *(See Chapter VIII, Section A2.)*

27. **B** The minimum required certification level for an EMT to use an automated external defibrillator on a patient in cardiac arrest is EMT-Basic. *(See Chapter VIII, Section A2.)*

28. **D** The minimum required certification level for an EMT to provide artificial respiration through endotracheal intubation is EMT-Paramedic. *(See Chapter VIII, Section A2.)*

29. **B** The report in choice B is the clearest and most accurate. It provides a precise description of the suspect and his vehicle, states the location of the incident, and outlines the entire sequence of events. *(See Chapter VIII, Section B1.)*

30. **C** The best thing for Carol to do is to talk to Norma and calmly discuss the situation. Since the situation is clearly upsetting her so much, it would be appropriate for her to try to talk to Norma about it in a calm, civil manner. She should attempt to take this step before taking any more serious actions, so choices A and B would be incorrect. Choice D would also be incorrect because it would clearly be inappropriate to engage in harassment under any circumstances. *(See Chapter VIII, Section B2.)*

31. **D** The best course of action for Steve would be to tell his friend that he can't help because he could be fired. It obviously would be wrong for Steve to dispense free stamps to anyone, and doing so could certainly be grounds for dismissal. Choices B and C are incorrect because Steve should not give his friend free stamps under any circumstances. Choice A is incorrect because there is no need to involve anyone else at this point, and doing so might only escalate the situation. *(See Chapter VIII, Section B2.)*

32. **B** Because last week's deposit was $200 short and the secretary was responsible for making it, the manager can infer that the secretary kept some of the money. It is extremely unlikely that the secretary went to the wrong bank or that she was charged a $200 processing fee, so choices A and C are incorrect. Choice D is incorrect because it is less likely that the bank lost some of the money than it is that the secretary stole it. *(See Chapter VIII, Section B1.)*

33. This personality question has no correct or incorrect answer. This type of question is designed to test your ability to manage time. *(See Chapter VIII, Section D.)*

34. This personality question has no correct or incorrect answer. This type of question is designed to test your ability to work with others. *(See Chapter VIII, Section D.)*

35. **D** The correct name of the company in the memo is Paulson Sanitation. *(See Chapter VIII, Section A1.)*

36. **B** The maximum allowable speed for a garbage truck on its route is 15 miles per hour. *(See Chapter VIII, Section A1.)*

37. **A** The letter writer's title is General Manager. *(See Chapter VIII, Section A1.)*

38. **B** Samantha's best course of action would be to attempt to calm the caller and convince him to discuss his problem rationally. The man is obviously upset and not thinking clearly, so she should try talking the man into a more relaxed, reasonable state of mind. Choice A is incorrect because she should not indicate that she can fix the problem before she is sure she can. Choice C is incorrect because she should transfer the caller to her supervisor only if she can't control the caller by herself. Choice D is incorrect because threatening or chastising the caller would most likely make the situation worse. *(See Chapter VIII, Section B1.)*

39. **C** Due to the current state of the home and the presence of char marks and scattered debris, the firefighters can infer that an exploding gas tank ignited the fire. Based on the information provided, there is no evidence of the cause of the fire being related to an electrical short or arson, so choices A and B are both incorrect. Similarly, choice D is also incorrect because the paragraph does not mention anything about the homeowners. *(See Chapter VIII, Section B2.)*

40. **D** Since Phil's lock is broken and his wallet and other items are missing, you can infer that someone broke into the locker and stole Phil's things. Choice A is incorrect because it does not account for the broken lock or other missing items. Choice B is incorrect because a maintenance person breaking the lock does not account for the missing items. Choice C is unlikely to be correct because Phil knows which locker is his and recognizes his broken lock. *(See Chapter VIII, Section B1.)*

41. D Rubber safety gloves would be most appropriate for use when handling caustic chemicals. These gloves are chemical resistant and will protect your hands from the potentially serious injuries that caustic chemicals can cause. Leather and canvas safety gloves can protect your hands from cuts and burns. Fabric safety gloves can protect your hands from small debris, abrasions, and chafing. *(See Chapter VIII, Section C.)*

42. C A pulsating brake pedal usually indicates a warped brake rotor. A low brake pedal usually indicates a rusted or sticking shoe adjuster. A soft brake pedal usually indicates air in the braking system. A hard brake pedal usually indicates low engine vacuum. *(See Chapter VIII, Section C.)*

43. D Steel piping is most often used for cold water systems. This type of piping is best suited for aboveground cold-water systems. Cast-iron piping is normally used for soil piping. Copper piping is commonly used for hot-water systems and underground piping. Brass piping is primarily used for hot-water systems. *(See Chapter VIII, Section C.)*

44. C The destination of the train featured in the picture is Perth City. This information is displayed in the front window of the train. *(See Chapter VIII, Section A1.)*

45. D The daily departure times for the train are 9:30 a.m. to 5:55 p.m. These times are indicated by a sign hanging from the ceiling above the train. *(See Chapter VIII, Section A1.)*

46. B The three men in the far left of the photograph are all wearing hats. None of the men is wearing a necktie, a windbreaker, or glasses. *(See Chapter VIII, Section A1.)*

47. This personality question has no correct or incorrect answer. This type of question is designed to test your leadership abilities. *(See Chapter VIII, Section D.)*

48. This personality question has no correct or incorrect answer. This type of question is designed to determine your work experience. *(See Chapter VIII, Section D.)*

49. This personality question has no correct or incorrect answer. This type of question is designed to determine your work habits. *(See Chapter VIII, Section D.)*

50. This personality question has no correct or incorrect answer. This type of question is designed to determine your work preferences. *(See Chapter VIII, Section D.)*

Civil Service Employment Opportunities

Many civil service tests are targeted toward specific occupations or positions, so it's important to know what type of civil service job you're interested in before you sign up to take a test. If you're experienced or educated in a particular field, it's a good idea to look for a job in that field. You might also look for jobs in other fields that interest you.

After you decide on a field of employment, consider whether you want to apply for a federal, state, or local civil service job. The type of civil service job for which you apply will depend on the availability of jobs. For example, if you're an electrician looking for work, you should determine if the federal, state, or local government has open positions that require experience in electrical work. Also, the jobs you apply for will depend on where the job openings are located. Civil service jobs are spread across the United States, but Washington, D.C., has a larger concentration of federal civil service jobs than most areas. State and local civil service jobs are more likely to be located closer to where you live, but you should still have a clear understanding of the job location before applying.

Federal, state, and local civil service jobs involve many different professional fields and include millions of positions. Read the following sections to review the types of jobs available at all different levels of the government.

Federal Civil Service Jobs

The federal government employs approximately two million people and is the country's largest employer. The U.S. government offers countless positions for workers to fill. These positions are available in many different fields and many different locations throughout the country. The positions vary in pay and in education and work experience requirements.

In addition to the categories of jobs that follow, other categories of jobs in the federal government include communications, social work, law, administration, foreign affairs, education, computers and technology, engineering, science, and math. Today, the federal government employs people from almost every type of professional field. If you're interested in working for the federal government, start researching available job positions so you can apply and take the appropriate civil service exam.

Tip: The Internet is a great tool to use while you search for a federal civil service job. The Web site www. usajobs.gov lists all the federal civil service jobs for which people can currently apply. The site lists the qualifications and requirements for each position, as well as the location(s) in which the position is available. If you find a job you're interested in on the Web site, you can begin the application process online.

Clerical and Secretarial

Clerical and secretarial jobs are available in many different government departments and offices. These positions range in education and work experience requirements and in pay. The following are examples of federal clerical and secretarial civil service jobs:

- Coder
- Computer clerk
- Correspondence clerk
- Data transcriber
- Information receptionist
- Management assistant
- Messenger
- Sales representative
- Secretary
- Stenographer or reporter
- Telephone operator
- Typist

Law Enforcement

Law enforcement officers are important at all levels of the government because they help maintain peace and order. Although many people think of agents in the Federal Bureau of Investigation (FBI) when they think of federal law enforcement, many other types of federal law enforcement positions exist. For example, Border Patrol agents and Customs inspectors are important federal law enforcement employees. The following are examples of federal law enforcement civil service jobs:

- Alcohol, Tobacco, and Firearms inspector
- Border Patrol agent
- Consumer safety inspector
- Correctional institution administrator
- Correctional officer
- Criminal investigator
- Customs inspector
- Game law enforcement officer
- Investigative assistant
- Mine safety and health investigator
- Nuclear material courier
- Park ranger
- Security guard

Accounting and Finance

Another important field in the federal government is that of accounting and finance. Employees in these positions can work for the Treasury Department and similar agencies. Often, accounting and finance positions require education or experience in the field, but some entry-level positions do exist. The following are examples of federal accounting and finance civil service jobs:

- Accountant
- Accounting technician
- Auditor
- Budget analyst
- Budget clerk or assistant
- Cash processor
- Credit union examiner
- Financial analyst
- Financial clerk or assistant
- Financial institution examiner
- Financial manager
- Internal Revenue Service agent
- Loan specialist
- Tax technician

Health and Medicine

Although you might not think about a career in health and medicine when you think of working for the government, healthcare workers are a large part of the federal government's workforce. For example, Veterans Administration hospitals employ doctors, nurses, physician's assistants, laboratory technicians, and many other medical workers. The following are examples of federal health and medicine civil service jobs:

- Animal health technician
- Dental assistant
- Dental hygienist
- Dental laboratory aid and technician
- Health aid and technician
- Industrial hygienist
- Medical clerk
- Medical instrument technician
- Medical officer
- Medical records administrator
- Medical technologist
- Nurse
- Nursing assistant
- Occupational therapist
- Optometrist
- Pharmacist
- Pharmacy technician
- Physical therapist

- Physician's assistant
- Railroad safety specialist
- Safety and occupational health manager
- Speech pathologist and audiologist
- Veterinarian
- Veterinarian technician

Transportation

The federal government monitors different types of transportation in the United States, and it needs a staff of skilled workers to help all types of transportation run effectively and safely. Many workers involved in transportation work for the Transportation Department. The following are examples of federal transportation civil service jobs:

- Aerospace engineer
- Air safety investigator
- Air traffic controller
- Aircraft operator
- Aircrew technician
- Aviation safety inspector
- Highway safety inspector
- Transportation assistant
- Transportation clerk
- Transportation industry analyst
- Transportation specialist

Labor and Mechanical

The government employs many Americans in labor and mechanical positions. All parts of the government have a need for skilled labor and maintenance workers. The following are example of federal labor and mechanical civil service jobs:

- Blacksmith
- Building and repair worker
- Carpenter
- Cement worker
- Crane operator
- Custodial worker
- Drill rig operator
- Electrician
- Equipment operator

- Food service worker
- Forklift operator
- Freight loader
- Gas and radiation detector
- Laboratory support worker
- Lock and dam operator
- Locksmith
- Machinist
- Mechanic
- Mechanical parts repairer
- Metal worker
- Motor vehicle operator
- Painter
- Pipeline worker
- Warehousing and stock handler
- Welder
- Woodworker

State Civil Service Jobs

Just as the federal government employs people in many positions from different fields, state governments in the United States have thousands of employment opportunities for interested workers. Each state is unique, so not all states have the same positions or the same application processes. You need to find out about the jobs available in your state and the process you must follow to apply for those jobs.

All state governments in the United States have official Web sites, and many of these Web sites include information about civil service employment opportunities. Often, the Internet is the best place to begin your search for a civil service job. You also may get information by contacting your state government.

Often, state civil service jobs include positions in the following fields:

- Administration
- Clerical and secretarial work
- Communications
- Corrections
- Education
- Health and medicine
- Housing and urban renewal
- Labor and maintenance
- Law enforcement
- Natural resource management

- Public welfare
- Sanitation
- Science
- Sewage disposal
- Social work
- Technology

Tip: Many civil service jobs require you to fill out an application. These applications usually require general information such as your name, address, and telephone number. Civil service job applications sometimes include sections about your work history and education. You can make the application process easier by keeping a file that includes notes about the places you worked, when you worked there, for whom you worked, and so on. You also can keep information about your education in the file. When you fill out a civil service job application, you'll have most of the information you need right in front of you so you don't have to go searching for it.

Local Civil Service Jobs

Just as state civil service jobs vary in type, so do local civil service jobs. Often, local civil service jobs include jobs offered by cities, boroughs, and counties. A good place to begin searching for local civil service jobs is the Internet. The city or county's Web site may include a list of job vacancies. If you can't find a list of job vacancies online, contact your local government officials to determine where you can find such information.

Often, local civil service jobs include positions in the following fields:

- Administration
- Clerical and secretarial work
- Health and medicine
- Labor and maintenance
- Law enforcement
- Libraries
- Parks and recreation
- Social work
- Technology
- Utilities

Benefits and Veteran Information

Benefits

Civil service employees working for the federal government are offered a wide variety of benefits in addition to normal compensation. These benefits include the following:

- **Health insurance:** The U.S. government sponsors an optional healthcare program for all federal employees. This program provides members with a wide variety of health plans designed to fit their personal needs, including minimum coverage and major medial protection against serious illnesses. The government covers part of the premium, and the employees pay the remaining balance through deductions from their salaries.

- **Vacation and sick time:** All federal employees earn 13 days of sick time each year, regardless of how long they've been employed. The majority of federal employees earn vacation time and other time off based on how many years they've worked in the federal service. Most new full-time employees begin with 13 vacation days per year and earn more time over the course of their careers.

- **Injury and death compensation:** The federal government also offers compensation benefits for those employees who suffer debilitating injures while performing their official duties. In the event that a federal employee dies in the line of duty, his or her survivors are compensated accordingly.

- **Group life insurance:** Some federal employees may be entitled to low-cost term life insurance without having to submit to a physical examination. The federal government offers two types of life insurance: normal life insurance and accidental death and dismemberment insurance.

- **Retirement program:** The Federal Employees Retirement System (FERS) provides government employees with retirement coverage with a reliable retirement package that combines Social Security and a supplemental retirement program. In addition to the government's contribution, employees are free to contribute as much as they would like.

- **Paid holidays:** Federal employees regularly receive the following paid holidays:
  - New Year's Day (January 1)
  - Birthday of Martin Luther King, Jr. (third Monday in January)
  - Washington's Birthday (third Monday in February)
  - Memorial Day (last Monday in May)
  - Independence Day (July 4)
  - Labor Day (first Monday in September)
  - Columbus Day (second Monday in October)
  - Veterans Day (November 11)
  - Thanksgiving Day (fourth Thursday in November)
  - Christmas Day (December 25)

- **Additional benefits:** Some additional federal benefits include the following:
  - Flex time
  - Child care
  - Elder care
  - Employee assistance program
  - Medicare eligibility
  - Long-term care insurance

Certain jobs also may offer additional bonuses, such as a relocation bonus or a recruitment bonus. Other benefit programs that may be offered on a job-by-job basis include: employee development programs, incentive rewards, retention allowances, student loan repayment programs, and interagency transfers.

To learn more about federal benefits, visit www.usajobs.opm.gov.

Veteran Information

The hiring practices of the federal government include special preferences for military veterans. Anyone who has served in active duty in the U.S. military and has been separated under honorable conditions may be eligible for veterans' preference. Veterans who began their service after October 15, 1976, must have a Campaign Badge, an Expeditionary Medal, or a service-connected disability to be eligible for these preferences.

Veterans' preference does not apply to Senior Executive Service (SES) jobs or when competition for a position is limited to status candidates, such as present or former federal career or career-conditional employees.

Certain jobs in the competitive service are restricted by law to those candidates who are entitled to preference as a result of the veteran preference laws. Some of these types of jobs include custodian, messenger, elevator operator, and guard. In most cases, nonveteran employees cannot be transferred into such a position if there are any available veterans to fill the position first. This restriction does not apply in situations where such a position is filled by a nonveteran who is already serving in a federal agency in a similar position that is covered by the same generic title.

To learn more about veterans' preference, call the U.S. Office of Personnel Management at 912-757-3000 and select Federal Employment Topics, followed by Veterans. To reach an electronic bulletin board, call 912-757-3100.

Notes

Notes

Notes

Notes

Notes

Notes